DEADLINE
AT DAWN

By the same author

Decoding Advertisements
Ideology and Meaning in Advertising

Consuming Passions
The Dynamics of Popular Culture

JUDITH WILLIAMSON

DEADLINE
AT DAWN

Film Criticism 1980–1990

Marion Boyars
London · New York

First published in Great Britain and
in the United States in 1993
by Marion Boyars Publishers

24 Lacy Road, London SW15 1NL
237 East 39th Street, New York, NY 10016

British Library Cataloguing in Publication Data

Williamson, Judith, *1954–*
Deadline at dawn : film criticism 1980–1990.
I. Title
791.4375

Library of Congress Cataloging in Publication Data

Williamson, Judith, 1954–
Deadline at dawn : film criticism 1980–1990/Judith Williamson.
Includes bibliographical references.
1. Motion pictures.   I. Title.
PN1994.W463   1992
791.43'09--dc20   91–39021

ISBN 0–7145–2964–8 Hardcover
ISBN 0–7145–2925–7 Paperback

Printed and bound in Southampton
by Itchen Printers Limited

AUTHOR'S NOTE

Where the columns and reviews in this book first appeared in magazines,
their source is indicated by the following abbreviations:
N.S. (*New Statesman*), T.O. (*Time Out*) and C.L. (*City Limits*).

Contents

Foreword

Deadline at Dawn

This is a book not just about films, but about writing about films —
something I have done for my living over many years, under circumstances suggested by its title. The contents have been structured,
neither chronologically, which would make it a simple record of my
own career, nor through categories of films, which might have made it
appear more inclusive than it really is. Film criticism itself — types of
approach, modes of writing — has been the ordering concept of the
collection, and it is intended to raise questions about what film
criticism can be and how it can function within a wider culture. The
Introduction that follows goes further into this issue and offers a
general critique of the field in which I have been working.

But the book can also be read along other axes. One is as a resource:
I hope that the index, divided into a range of categories, will allow it to
be used for reference, to be dipped into as well as read straight
through. An index cuts through the text and allows specific threads to
be pulled out — genres, social topics, works of individual directors.

Other threads, however, are more personal. In introducing each
section below I have tried to give enough of its context to make sense of

the work, without becoming too anecdotal or describing my feelings about every enterprise. What is personal is the work itself. It is impossible to write regularly, week after week, under intense pressure, without feeling that you are squeezing a little bit of yourself into it all the time. Being personal doesn't have to mean being quirky. I live and work within the same culture that produces the films I write about; my feelings and reactions may be my own, but they are not necessarily *only* my own. I have never even tried to be impersonal in my writing, rather I have tried to make clear, as far as possible, where my personal reactions are coming from. The enormous response I have had from readers (whose letters would make an interesting collection on their own) suggests that, far from stressing one's individuality, this approach allows people to make connections and find how precisely *un*-alone they may be in their responses to films. During my *New Statesman* days, in particular, I received hundreds of letters from 'single working women' who swapped notes about many of the issues I was finding in those eighties films which became particularly preoccupied with that apparently neurotic figure.

Neurotic or not, that figure, or a version of her, was what I was during most of the time I turned out all this work. And since the foreword is the key to another axis of this book — my own life — I have chosen to outline briefly the sets of circumstances that were its backdrop over a decade.

At film school (The Royal College of Art) between 1977 and 1980, I had been working on a film about advertising funded by the Arts Council of Great Britain. By 1980 A SIGN IS A FINE INVESTMENT was shot, but only half put together, owing to a string of financial and production difficulties. On leaving college I had to get a job, both to pay my rent and to finish the film, and I applied for the post advertised as film critic and listings compiler on *Time Out* magazine. Starting work there in the September of 1980 was a revelation to me. I had been an avid movie-goer all my life, worked on films — and directed my own — at film school, but never really understood the complicated network of their distribution, publicity and exhibition which I discuss in the Introduction. Much of my time was spent on the phone to cinemas and distributors, and even more of it was spent typing out listings (I compiled the 'Independents' section) and slowly learning the ways of a magazine office.

The *Time Out* story will no doubt be written one day by someone else, but here is a short outline. In the spring of 1981 — when I had barely been on the magazine six months — we went out on strike in defense of our house agreement, an arrangement whereby every worker on the staff, from journalists through receptionists, typesetters, even the editor, earned the same salary. Obviously this was both fair, and made working relations far better than if we had all been on differentials, but the early eighties were a time of change in British business culture and the management wanted to drop the egalitarianism and introduce a pay hierarchy. At first the staff occupied the offices in protest — sleeping under your desk in a sleeping bag is a novel experience — and this in itself spoke of a commitment to the magazine: it was 'ours'. After being evicted from the building we set up strike headquarters in the basement of a nearby theatre, and besides picketing, raising money and campaigning, we brought out our own, broadsheet version of the magazine, *Not Time Out*. *Time Out* then sued us for using their name, and after one memorable day when, following the court hearing, the entire staff spray-painted the words 'Time' and 'Out' off thousands of broadsheets, we carried on producing it as *Not* throughout the summer of '81.

No matter what people may think to the contrary, being on strike is not an enjoyable experience. Financial difficulties and the disruption to one's usual working rhythm can be an almost intolerable strain, though the sense of solidarity counteracts it to some extent. What the strike did bring out, though, was the relation between the magazine and its readers, to whom we distributed *Not* free, while collecting voluntary contributions around central London and on the picket line. (My rent was paid from money thrown into plastic buckets, something I recalled vividly a few years later when the miners were out.) Writing for *Not*, I was constantly aware of no longer being an anonymous commentator on movies, but being in a situation known to every reader of the broadsheet, and I learned one of the first lessons of journalism — your readers are real. They are actually there. You are not writing to yourself. There was a sense of liberation and for me, perhaps a loosening up of style and tone, which lasted through the rest of my time as a critic.

When it became clear that we were not going to 'win' the strike, the majority of ex-*Time Out* staff decided to set up a new magazine, *City Limits*, and this began in October 1981, in a building rented from the GLC in Islington. It was an unusual journalistic enterprise in a variety of ways. The film section office was furnished with chairs and rugs collected off skips, we built our own desks — rough benches round the room — and my work lamp was something I'd concocted from an old Ovaltine jar as a child. We no longer had access to the resources of back-reviews, film credits and pictures that had been on file at *Time Out*, and still compiling 'Independents' I spent a day each week in the

British Film Institute library looking up dates and credits of obscure films. We also had to review not only new releases, but all the older films playing in the repertory cinemas. I found myself knocking out, in an afternoon, brief reviews from memory of early Soviet films, Hollywood classics, documentaries — a sample of which is found in the third section of this book.

Post-strike debts meant I had to find a source of income besides *City Limits*, where we earned a fraction of our old salaries, and so I also started teaching, in two different places, Maidstone College of Art and Middlesex Polytechnic. At Maidstone I became responsible for film studies, and found myself constructing courses which not only (I hope) educated my students in film genres and history but also educated myself. There may be no obvious trace of my years of film teaching in this book, except perhaps the occasional tendency to 'lecture', but it fed into my sense that explaining is a big part of criticism, that people should know a little more after reading a review, not just about the film in question but about film as a medium. I left Maidstone in 1986, after I was offered the job of film columnist on the *New Statesman* (and after finishing my own film in 1983), but I still feel an enormous debt to all my students there whose interest and enthusiasm helped to fire my own.

Starting at the *New Statesman* marked a big change in my position as a film critic. The arts editor, Harriett Gilbert, had previously been books editor on *City Limits* (as had Malcolm Imrie, the deputy arts editor) and claimed, when she offered me the post, that it was on the basis of a peculiarly short and irreverent review of a Chantal Ackerman film, JE, TU, IL, ELLE, which is included in the section Ways of Telling, below. Whether or not this was entirely true, I was now being given a space to do more or less as I liked, and I did my best to transform the weekly cinema column from a straightforward review into a place to debate and discuss issues of contemporary film-making. I also (and this was hard!) decided to sacrifice a bit of my writing space to include a publicity box, in which I flagged upcoming events or screenings of otherwise under-publicized films. At first on the *New Statesman* I was extremely nervous, but as letters from readers started to come in I again felt a sense of response and support which carried me like a wave through the most highly pressurized period of journalism I have ever known (or hope to know).

By this time I had left *City Limits* but was teaching half the week at Middlesex Polytechnic (in Film and Contemporary Cultural Studies), spending every evening in preview screenings and writing on the weekend to meet my Monday deadline. I cannot imagine having survived this without the phenomenal support of three people in particular. Two of these were Harriett Gilbert and Malcolm Imrie at the *New Statesman*, who bought me snacks and kept their tempers even when I was changing punctuation with a bike waiting to go to the typesetters, and from whom I learned something invaluable — how to edit my own copy. The first version you write *isn't* necessarily the best, it *can* be improved, sentences *can* be reorganized; they taught me all this at the same time as encouraging me to use my own voice, a double lesson which has stayed with me ever since. I left the *New Statesman* in 1988 when Harriett and Malcolm lost their jobs because I could not imagine working there without them.

The other person I cannot imagine that whole period without is Barry Curtis, with whom I taught — and still teach — film at Middlesex Poly. If he would ever have rather *not* been phoned up on a Sunday night to hear the final draft of a column, he never let it show; he accompanied me to endless previews, helped me relate the concepts we were teaching to my writing, and was indescribably generous with suggestions and comments.

That leads me to the main point of this foreword. Film is a shared medium; sometimes an audience response has been the basis for a review (cf. WISH YOU WERE HERE) and ideas about film are also shared, not owned. The work in this collection owes so much to discussions with, and the support of, other people, that I could often have footnoted the particular collaborations that fed into my arguments and conclusions. I have learned a lot about film editing from Brand Thumim and my brother, Trevor Williamson. I have benefitted enormously from my constant film-going companions: Chris Hale, with whom I have been going to movies for nearly twenty years; Mark Finch, with whom I also worked on the programme discussed in Ways of Showing; and many others, including Jane Root and Paul Kerr, who gave me air time on *The Media Show*, Jenny Turner, who often encouraged me to hold on to an unfashionable line, Geoff Andrew, who let me hang around the Electric Cinema at the peak of its rep days, Liz Wren and Peter Howden for allowing me the same state of grace at the Hampstead Everyman and Penny Ashbrook, at the Brixton Ritzy; Don Macpherson, my colleague and flat-mate during the strike and with whom I did the Scorsese interview in Ways of Speaking, my sister Janet, who came with me to the BBC for the filming of Fatal Attractions . . . I could go on and on.

And the compiling of this book, like every enterprise, would not have been possible without my friends. Christine Muirhead has given me constant support through every problem; Nigel Fountain has encouraged and commiserated through the ups and downs of production; and Petra Fried has immersed herself in the project for months, proof-reading, editing, researching, and helping to compile the index without which it would be a very different volume.

To all these people, I would like to say thank you, for helping me through countless deadlines at dawn.

London, 1992

Introduction

Film Criticism

When people find out you're a film critic, the first thing they usually say is, 'You get *paid* to watch films?' Obviously, critics do more than just watch, and what this question (usually asked with varying degrees of incredulity and envy) really means is, 'You get *paid* to say which films you like and don't like?'

It's a perceptive response because it concurs pretty accurately with most reviewers' own conception of their jobs, though for 'like' and 'don't like' they would probably substitute, 'saying which films are good or not so good'. In this jump exists the greatest, gaping flaw in Western film criticism: its assumption of some scale of artistic merit which is too ineffable ever to be outlined or even discussed, except in relation to individual films, in which context good and bad do seem uncannily close to the 'like' or 'don't like' of the particular reviewer. Popular ideas about almost any phenomenon are revealing because they often make explicit, assumptions that are *implicitly* held by more elite groups; and over the years that I have tried to bite back my irritation at being asked, 'you get *paid*. . .?' it has become vivid to me that certain 'common sense' ideas about film criticism are held by critics and their readers alike.

Film criticism seems self-evidently to be about films. But it is also about ideologies, taken-for-granted attitudes towards our society and its cultural forms. Further, it is linked into a very specific network of distributors, exhibitors and publications within which context a relatively small number of writers may be disproportionately influential on matters like which films get to be seen in a country at all. (Distributors have been known to seek critics' approval *before* buying films.) But both the ideologies underlying film criticism, and the *realpolitik* of critical practice ('if you plug our film then we'll place an ad in your paper') are hidden by the single, sweeping assumption that criticism is about individuals interacting with a particular 'artistic' work and then pronouncing on its merit. To discuss the criteria that determine such 'merit' would be impossible for most reviewers; a fact which then seems a measure of the profundity of their judgements, as though the less one were able to explain a choice, the more true, deep down, it must be.

The notions of individual taste and choice that underpin this critical perspective are deeply embedded in our society across a range of enterprises. You only have to examine the rhetoric surrounding the recent changes in Eastern Europe to realize that choice and taste are seen as the greatest guarantees of freedom Western capitalism has to offer. Taste, in the sphere of Art, is seen as something unspeakably profound.[1] But it is also the ideological concept most at play when we celebrate the Market being thrown open behind the Iron Curtain, so that all those deprived people can choose other cars besides the Trabant. Choosing as consumers between products is supposed to be our primary means of expression as individuals, and so it is important that taste be seen as an entirely personal affair, not linked with class, education or other social factors. Any attempt to understand taste as *more* than an effect of 'identity' is dismissed as an attempt to *reduce* identity — alongside such grim limitations as only letting people buy Ladas.[2]

This may seem a very wide context in which to place film criticism, but it is the emphasis on individualism, choice and taste in the broader social arena which renders their ideological effects invisible in the narrower world of the critic. It is obviously irrational that taste should

---

1   I discuss this further in 'But I Know What I Like' in *Consuming Passions*.
2   The Lada was the Soviet state-manufactured car, the Trabant its equivalent in East Germany.

be seen as at once highly individual, and yet significant of deep value, but this is where the peculiar position of the critic comes in: someone whose 'personal' judgements represent something supposedly inherent in the objects of judgement (the films) themselves. Because the premises of traditional criticism are fraught with contradictions, it is a hard task to outline them simply; but to summarize, one could say that critics' judgements are seen as at once totally personal, and yet — paradoxically — profoundly objective. I have tried to suggest that the 'personal', supposedly random nature of taste effectively depoliticizes it, takes it away from the realm of class. But the other side of this contradiction, the idea of inherent value, plays a key role in *maintaining* what amount to class divisions in the realm of Culture, where some products are seen as infinitely more 'value-ful' than others.

The dominant feeling about culture in our society is still that there is a 'High' and a 'Low' culture and these are still seen as roughly dividing into 'Art' and 'Mass Media'. Most 'serious' film critics in our national press still have a vague notion of artistic worth that fixes more happily onto, for example, a Bergman film than a Hollywood block-buster. It is interesting that the one piece of film theory absorbed into general critical use is the *auteur* theory, which views directors as 'authors' of films, thereby admitting them to the approved rank of artists, alongside the 'high cultural' figures of the past.

The same division works in reverse with a more populist approach, which will ridicule anything supposed to be 'arty' or pretentious, and thereby rules out taking seriously any more experimental or unconventional attempts at film-making. Anti-intellectualism is one of the strongest strands in British cultural life, and it takes a great many forms, from the snobs who disdain to discuss or explain an 'artistic' judgement, to the rabble-rousers who dismiss anything remotely 'difficult' or demanding on an audience. To side with one or other of these positions is to miss their complicity in denying people — audiences and readers — access to intellectual structures whereby they (the audiences and readers) might make their *own* critical judgements and decisions.

This enabling function of ideas and theories, which transcend individual examples, has been all but forgotten in a period which has seen the 'theoretical world' (mainly academia) move into an ever more baroque parody of itself, producing books, essays and journals that are almost incomprehensible even to those who *want* to read them. Theorists who set out, in the seventies, to change the world, have found themselves for the most part increasingly distant from a mainstream culture which, in the eighties, has been more in tune with

popular anxieties and concerns than either left or right in the more
overtly political arena. A whole edifice of ideas and theories about
films grew up in the seventies around magazines like *Screen* and
Afterimage, at a time when the Edinburgh Festival and the British Film
Institute provided institutional foundations for important debates and
developments of theory. Yet these have had, it now seems, little lasting
impact on the broader critical scene, and it is important to ask why.
Maybe the theorists were a little too 'pure', maybe a little *too*
antagonistic to the mainstream, a little too unwilling to get their feet
wet. Maybe the conventional critics — who have changed little, even
in terms of personnel, over decades — were a little too threatened, a
little too complacent, a little too lazy to re-examine their assumptions.
But none of these factors can be as crucial as the way that, again, the
two 'opposites' merely confirmed and strengthened one another's
positions, forming a complementary whole. If you want to put people
off ideas, there is no better way to do it than by making them appear
difficult, obscure, accessible only to a few dedicated brains. Some
people are afraid of encountering ideas and theories, and some people
are afraid of sharing them: the two go together. Thus a great many
useful perceptions about film are unavailable to the film-going public,
who continue to rely on the consumer advice broadcast by those few,
and largely unchanging, arbiters of 'taste'.

I have so far discussed the social, cultural and intellectual assumptions affecting film criticism today — but what of films? Are they 'Art'
or 'Entertainment' — are they tools of the 'dominant ideology' or
channels of subversion? Most criticism takes up one side or the other
in each of these paired questions, thereby again pre-empting an
examination of the polarities themselves. Usually up-market critics go
with the 'Art' idea, but the form of 'Art' that film is most frequently
treated as is *literature*. You could take the cinema columns of most daily
papers and read the reviews in them as if they referred to novels: very
often it is the 'story' that is being judged, not its visual rendering. Ours
is a strongly literary culture and the number of British films based on
novels is itself an index of our fear of 'pure' film. It is striking at the
moment that novelists are seen as 'natural' choices for film reviewing,
or even directing: as if all art or media forms were immediately
interchangeable. Writers have suddenly become film 'experts' and are
granted fellowships at the British Film Institute, or canvassed for their
opinions on CITIZEN KANE in national newspapers. All this increases
the sense that film is merely an adjunct of writing, and not a medium
with its own, quite specific, modes of meaning. Those of us engaged in
teaching film studies face an uphill task, as we teach our students to

see film as *film*, only to have them go home and read or hear some novelist of the moment expounding their — usually non-visual — impression of cinema today.

The view of film as Entertainment perhaps comes closest to an acknowledgement of the place of cinema in social and cultural life: it engages with the notion of an audience's enjoyment of, or at least 'kick' from, films, and also gets closest to linking consumption and production, which are — since film-making is an industry — intimately connected. Yet the 'entertainment' brigade usually use the prefix 'just' or 'only' as their particular device for avoiding closer examination of a film's meanings. 'Oh, it's just entertainment' someone will say, when you venture to suggest that some popular film is racist, or a Disney extravaganza reinforces gender roles. This attitude incorporates the phrase, *'You're reading too much into it'* — an accusation which constantly crosses the path of any serious writer about popular culture. The fact that film as video is now a major part of home entertainment has remained largely unaddressed critically owing to a combination of the 'just entertainment' position on the one hand, and on the other, a dislike of the big screen reduced to the small which has prevented many of us from getting to grips with its ideological and commercial importance. (Sony bought up Columbia Pictures not to become film producers, but to control the software — film-as-video — that belongs with its own hardware — VCRs.) Entertainment as popular pleasure, and entertainment as commercial enterprise, are aspects of cinema, and now the film-video industry, that few critics have systematically investigated or engaged with.

Perhaps this is partly because critics' own contribution to the commercial enterprise is often a source of hard-to-give-up glamour. How exciting to be flown out to Los Angeles to interview a big star! How impressive to be able to use directors' first names casually in conversation! How clear that those intoxicating privileges would be withdrawn if they were to result in truly critical copy! Most of the critics on daily papers and TV film programmes work in close collaboration with film producers and distributors, a collaboration that works well for both sides. Critics provide punchy copy that can be used on posters — *'A masterpiece'*, *'Best film of the year'* — while their names on the posters enhance their fame and reputations. The sycophantic attitude of most critics towards 'big name' actors and directors guarantees that in exchange for hobnobbing with these figures, critics will produce, if not wholly favourable, at least greatly softened critical appraisal. Anyone starting out as a critic — as I did on *Time Out* in 1980 — is usually amazed at the close circle formed by film producers, makers, distributors, exhibitors and critics. (I remember being shocked when crates of wine and whiskey turned up in the film department at Christmas, 'gifts' from 'independent' distribution and exhibition groups; and I vividly recall being told off by my editor after a distributor claimed I had not said hello to her at a party.) If you decide to operate outside that circle, many doors will be closed to you, many film clips unavailable, many interviews denied. But most critics are critics precisely because they like to feel the glamour of the movie world rub off on them — a pathetic exchange of independence for vicarious fame.

But what of the 'independent' scene itself, the field of low-budget, non-commercial film-making, the experimental, self-consciously political arena? Here, perhaps in defense against a more powerful mainstream, the collaboration between film-maker and critic is equally tight and fraught with anxiety. The 'alternative' film culture that grew up (again in the seventies) around the Independent Film-Makers' Association and the film workshops, has, on the whole, shown a depressing unwillingness to accept lively criticism, and many would-be left-wing critics are so frightened of seeming not to be right-on that they cannot bring themselves to point out serious problems with, not just individual films, but the atmosphere in this field overall. A discussion in the last section of this book touches more specifically on this area, one in which I have been engaged not only as a critic but as a practitioner. The great contribution of independent film-making has been to propose the notion of a film culture that goes beyond mainstream production and criticism; its shortcoming has been its inability, for a variety of reasons, to produce it. Important as this oppositional scene has been, it is even more important to ask what we can learn from its failures.

If I were to make one general, indeed rather 'cosmic', point about all this, it would be that the greatest enemy of thought is *fear*. Fear of being judged; fear of being rejected; fear of appearing stupid; fear of seeming reactionary; fear of losing connections; fear of being misunderstood; fear of ridicule; fear of not being glamorous; and so on. But the privilege of writing in the public arena should demand a certain kind of courage. Ours is in some respects a peculiarly 'critical' culture, partly because it takes less courage to imply something obliquely in terms of hidden criteria than it does to reveal what one actually thinks. The problem with almost all criticism today is that it does not reveal its premises, it projects a certain kind of view while giving readers and viewers no critical access to what that view is. Film writing could be a way of producing and distributing knowledge — to borrow terms from film-making itself — but it tends at present to obscure knowledge, to refuse access to ideas which people could use *for themselves*. In this sense it reproduces precisely the political ideology we have habituated ourselves to in the so-called Western democracies whereby, as Marx once said, it is the *arbitrary*, inexplicable quality of events that guarantees, in our eyes, their unquestionable naturalness.

I have sketched rapidly across areas about which there is much more to say: to examine them fully would demand an entire book about film criticism, while this is, at its simplest, a collection *of* film criticism. Yet I hope it *will* function in some respects as a book about film writing, or, still more broadly, about the potential for a film culture, an arena consisting not just of films and critics but of informed audiences and public debate: an arena of development and change rather than assessment and critique.

I have organized the book very much with this aim in mind. All the original material — reviews, programme notes, transcribed debates — is passionately concerned with films themselves. But I have selected and structured the material not so much in terms of films — their content or genre, directors or themes — as in terms of formats and approaches: ways of discussing films. I hope that these ways go against the grain of the patterns I've described here, and that the formats show the range of contexts in which such discussions can take place.

I finish this introduction with two columns from the *New Statesman*, a 'manifesto' written when I was a few months into the job, and a 'farewell' written when I was about to leave. Between them they summarize my own project in film criticism, and they mark out the ground for the next section of this book, Ways of Looking.

Viewfinder

During the recent London Film Festival I took part in a symposium on
'The Function of Film Criticism'. Since the people most affected by my
views on that subject are the readers of this column, it seems a good
place to outline some of them.

The LFF debate was not as productive as it might have been
because a dichotomy was set up from the start between 'Artist' and
'Critic'. This polarized concept is never a very useful one, but in the
case of cinema it is particularly unhelpful because planning, raising
the money for and making a film is a very different process from, for
example, writing a poem. The idea of an audience is built in from the
outset, otherwise most films would not be funded: which means that
films, perhaps more than any other medium, not only carry the
particular obsessions of a single 'artist' but usually indicate some of
the preoccupations of the society they're made in, the audience they're
made for.

This is also true of film criticism itself. The criticism found in almost
all the daily and weekly national press sees its role as *assessing* the latest
releases: fitting seamlessly into the familiar structures of consumer
choice by letting us know whether films are good, quite good, not very
good, bad, and so on — in other words, whether they're worth
spending our money on. But what this liberal humanist criticism never
asks is, good for what? Bad for whom? This form of criticism assumes a
consensus which fails to distinguish different interests of different
groups and the different functions of different films.

Perhaps the most pointless of all criticism is found in the *Time
Out/City Limits* sloganizing — 'unmissable', 'avoid', 'a must-see film'

(what precisely *is* a must-see film?) — pointless because the variety of reasons for which people go to see a film is completely ignored. Where the 'miss/don't miss' formula coincides with a simplistic 'right-on' politics, it also obscures the ideological complexities of a film like, say, TOP GUN — the most popular film of the year in the USA, yet dismissed in one line by *City Limits*.

At the other end of the spectrum from the Hit or Miss ('I'll give it five') brigade there is the enormous body of film theory, developed through the seventies in journals like *Screen* and *Framework*, which has drawn on semiotics and psychoanalysis in an attempt to analyze films as 'texts', to understand the position of the viewer ('reader') of the text, and focusing on the ways that meaning is produced in the relation between the two, rather than simply being 'put in the film' by the director. These theories offer a completely different approach to cinema; given the similarities in the form of films and dreams, psychoanalytic theory in particular is very helpful in offering a perspective on mainstream movies like E.T. or RAMBO and their widespread appeal.

However, the biggest problem about most academic film theory is that it is often very hard to understand, partly because of the terminology used but also because most of its debates have remained sealed off in the academic world and there seems to have been little will to communicate theoretical ideas to a wider audience. It is true that the notoriously incomprehensible *Screen* has been turned into a more accessible journal under the current editorship. Yet there is still an enormous gulf between film theory and most film criticism.

I believe that this gulf is neither necessary nor inevitable. Film theory offers not so much comments on particular films, but ways of looking at films which can be used more than once, as it were, going against the grain of the consumer ethic. I would like to use this space to suggest ways of *thinking* about different kinds of film (as with the role of women in horror films, which arose recently with SMOOTH TALK[1]). Unlike many academic theorists I strongly believe that all really useful ideas can and should be expressed clearly. On the other hand there is a strongly anti-intellectual streak in our mainstream press; but the fear of ideas is only the other side of the coin from obscuring them.

One aspect of putting ideas forward is that you can no longer be the invisible arbiter but have to declare your position. It should be clear to anyone who has read this column over the last few months that I am

---

1   See p. 39.

writing with a feminist and a Marxist politics: though as a film school graduate and having worked as a film-maker before coming to this job I see no reason why a political criticism should preclude an *enjoyment* of cinema. But just as film theories can provide ways into the structure of films, so can a political view of cinema provide ways of questioning assumptions about the structure of society, of challenging what we take for granted.

I have already tried to move away from the old system of reviewing all the week's new releases. While I do intend mainly to focus on current films, I will also, in future, discuss other films, not necessarily new — or *kinds* of films (as with the recent column on animation[1]).

In trying to provide a background to the film workshop movement, in last week's column,[2] I also became aware of the dearth of information in the press about the really thriving film culture in Britain — the infrastructure created by the workshops. Here is another gulf, between a whole area of activity and its near-invisibility in the mainstream press; one which I will also try to bridge in this space.

N.S. 12 December 1986

The Short Good-bye

Film is a unique medium. Writing about a film is different — or should be different — from writing about a book, or writing about a record. Yet our traditional film criticism, the kind familiar in the mainstream press, has always tended to treat films like novels: plot and characterization are assessed, themes drawn out and, by the more socially minded, some sort of Leavisite analysis of cultural and moral worth attempted.

Around the time I started this column in 1986 I wrote a 'manifesto' which was both a critique of what I call mainstream criticism and a laying out of guidelines for myself. I attacked the notion of films as

---

1   See p. 102.
2   See p. 116.

discrete art objects that it is critics' job to evaluate according to some supposedly objective criteria. The idea of the art critic responding in isolation to the individual painting and pronouncing its intrinsic worth, the film critic sitting in the dark and deciding which films are 'good' and which 'bad', ignores the extent to which meanings are determined by social context and also assumes that the critic herself has no position but is somehow 'neutral'.

Against the backdrop of this evaluative criticism it has been an important project to place cinema in a social context and examine its meanings as part of a wider cultural currency. As I have frequently pointed out, to 'work' successfully (make money) mainstream films have to deal in some way, however oblique, with the concerns of their audience and thus function to some extent as a barometer of the social climate. It is possible to read films 'symptomatically' and such a criticism can be politically valuable for its diagnosis of ideological conditions.

Yet there is one phenomenon which worries me more now than it did in '86 and that is the tendency to use this kind of 'cultural criticism' perspective to treat all media as interchangeable, all simply as channels for ideological messages or fashionable concerns — an approach which shares precisely the same premise as the more traditional criticism. Whatever the difference between treating films as pure art objects or as mere ideological symptoms, both approaches fundamentally ignore film as *film*.

A concern for the specific physical properties of film has always been a characteristic of the avant-garde — to the extent that some experimental film-makers have created works without even filming but by scratching the surface of the film stock — but it should not be a concern which is *confined* to the avant-garde. A materialist criticism which seeks to understand the real world (an unfashionable concept these days) must get to grips with the medium as something concrete, not just as a vehicle for ideas or meanings which can be extracted and then critiqued. What are the particular qualities of film? What can it do that other media can't? How does film work, spatially, aurally, graphically? These are questions that film-makers must ask (not that they always do) — and so should critics.

However, they are not questions that are easily answered except through a lot of watching. There is no short cut to the experience of films, actually seeing them, seeing how they work, seeing how they work in different ways. And this is the other thing about both the traditional and, even more, the new postmodern approach: specific knowledge of film forms and of their history appears redundant.

Each film exists temporally on two axes: socially, culturally, politically, it is a part of the present in which it is made — but it is also a part of the history of cinema, belonging perhaps to a particular genre whose framework has developed over time, drawing perhaps on technical innovations that have produced specific visual effects, drawing, perhaps consciously, perhaps unconsciously, on the styles of films that are already a part of that history. This is not to suggest that cinema 'progresses': it doesn't necessarily get better, but it does *have* a history (the two notions have been so mixed up in recent theoretical writings that history is rapidly becoming another outdated concept). And it does help, in understanding film, to know something of that history, to have seen films.

But knowledge, too, is becoming a dated category. It has never been all that easy to produce serious, informed journalism in a profession dominated by short deadlines and short memories. This is the last cinema column which I'll be writing in this magazine; I hope that in the last two years I have done more or less what I'm talking about here.

N.S. 3 June 1988

Ways of Looking

Even before ways of writing, speaking, informing about films, one needs ways of looking at them. How to see films both in relation to society and to the cinema itself, how to approach them both as works in their own right and as part of our wider history, how to enjoy them and at the same time to interpret or understand them — all these questions demand, not one single answer, but a sense of the different perspectives from which a film can be viewed. At the same time, there may seem to be so many of these that it can be hard to get an *over*view on the varied approaches, theories and positions available.

Very roughly and crudely, all these ways of looking at films could be seen as falling into two categories. These are not necessarily separate in practice, since a single film is always doing many things at once, and the tools for understanding what it's doing may be drawn from a wide repertoire of conceptual frameworks — even if some of these are declared, by their most avid proponents, to be incompatible. There is not space here to discuss in detail Marxism, feminism, psychoanalytic theory, or semiotics, all of which offer useful tools for understanding cultural phenomena, and all of which I use to some degree in almost every piece of criticism. But in structuring this section I have, at the risk of oversimplifying, taken a wide sweep and outlined two broad and complementary approaches to film: you can see it as *symptomatic*, expressing, reflecting, *de*flecting — not necessarily deliberately — key experiences and concerns of the society that produces and consumes it; and you can see it as *strategic*, involving a deliberate use of, and engagement with, the cinematic medium, for some specific aesthetic and/or political purpose. The two approaches are obviously not alternatives; in looking carefully at any film one would expect to employ *both*. It is worth noting that one corresponds, very roughly, to a sort of 'unconscious' of film-making/popular culture: films may be barometers of moods and events whether or not their producers and makers intend this to be so. On the other hand, film-making is a process loaded with choices at every stage, and most films do have a definite project, even if it is simply to 'be entertaining' or 'look good'. Examining people's uses of the medium helps us to understand its specific properties and potential; while, interestingly, examining how films work as symptoms of issues beyond themselves also brings us round to these same properties and potential, by a different route.

Understanding how films work must be the primary aim of both film-makers and critics, and would liberate film *audiences* from being at the mercy of either.

This section consists almost entirely (there is one exception) of columns written for the *New Statesman* between 1986 and 1988. Having a regular space allowed me, over those years, to develop approaches to film which I intended to be useful beyond the instance of any one movie: which could, in effect, be recycled. Because I wanted to suggest *ways of looking*, rather than simply review new releases, the selection of films to write about each week was made on the basis of the issues they raised, as much as what I thought about a particular film itself. Similarly, the division of this section into two parts has been on the basis of the critical approach used in each column, rather than type of film, director, or theme.

Symptoms

Big budget films are expected to return money to their producers. To do this, they have to draw in large audiences, and to do *that*, they must appeal to those audiences, 'strike the right chord'. Popular films always address — however indirectly — wishes, fears and anxieties current in society at any given moment. This is not to say that films can be designed to do this on purpose, otherwise producers would never make a loss; rather, that those which 'hit' (as GHOST did recently, breaking box-office records) must be touching on a nerve. Sometimes a spate of films, all on one theme, suggests a general concern: GHOST, to pursue this example, is one of about a dozen films (FLATLINERS, ALMOST AN ANGEL, etc.) concerned with an afterlife and with defying death. One could link this with a general interest in 'New Age' and spiritual matters at the moment and one could, more revealingly, see it as a deflected or re-worked concern about death just when the Aids epidemic is spreading to the so-called general (i.e. straight, white) population in Western countries. Anyone interested in the fantasies and fears of our culture should pay close attention to successful films, for their success means precisely that they have touched on the fantasies and fears of a great many people.

However, being a film critic and not a sociologist, I have to ask not only how films function symptomatically in relation to social concerns, but how they do this *as films*. The nature of the film medium makes it particularly apt for the articulation of wishes and anxieties, and the way the history of the medium has developed to produce highly formalized, repetitive patterns known as *genres* allows for the handling of often very difficult or disturbing themes within reliably familiar formulae. It is only by understanding *how* films produce meanings that it is possible to 'read' them symptomatically, to find out *what* they mean.

All films work on two axes, the temporal and the spatial. A film takes place in time: a plot unfolds, a story is told. But inseparable from the film's constant narration of its story is the image, which is the means of narration, and which nevertheless has an existence, a capacity for meaning, not entirely harnessed to its narrative function. Usually it is what films picture, not what they *tell* us about what they picture, that stays in the mind. The way things are visually presented in a film is known as *mise-en-scène*: and this is a key element in producing meaning, 'setting the scene'. We are all familiar with the kind of process where a movie will set up, for example, an image of glamorous underworld life where gangsters are sexy and get whatever they want — until they are killed or arrested in the last five minutes: early US gangster films were required to produce such endings to avoid illegal 'incitement to crime', but nevertheless the ending cannot remove the *imagery* that functions throughout the rest of the film. Equally, movies have traditionally brought us images of sexually desirable women while insisting — through the plot — how bad and *un*desirable they are.

The tension between plot and image is what gives film an enormous capacity for containing contradictions — a sort of having your cake and eating it process which is ideologically very effective. Films are, of all media forms, the closest to dreams, and Freud suggests that dreams function to re-work conflicts and anxieties which might otherwise disturb an individual's sleep. Popular films re-work conflicts and contradictions within a wider cultural field; like other commercial media (e.g. advertising) they must be quick to address new experiences in their audiences (markets) while at the same time, no matter how frightening or disturbing those experiences, they must deal with them in a way that is bearable, even enjoyable (in other words, marketable). Just as Freud describes 'overdetermination' — the converging of several factors in determining an element of a dream, which will then serve several purposes at once — so films usually perform a variety of (sometimes contradictory) functions or address several apparently conflicting issues at once. Large as their budgets may be, mainstream films are, on the level of meaning, nothing if not economical.

None of this can be understood by thinking of films as if they were

merely animated novels. Images have a visual grammar of t.
language which is utterly different from verbal language. But o.
above the visual language it shares with photography and painu
film has its own very specific ways of producing meanings anu
pleasures. In particular, music, movement and montage are three
dimensions of film-making which can transform a written script. I
have written at length about the visual and *physical* undercutting of a
verbal script in an essay on '10' in an earlier book, *Consuming Passions*.
In this book, an example where the physical dimension enhances,
rather than counteracts, a film's project is the movie TOP GUN: its
flying sequences produce an actual sensation of movement which,
allied with a powerful music track, work to create an extraordinary
level of excitement. This film, however, is not without its contradictions; ostensibly a love story between the young flying recruit (Tom
Cruise) and his instructor (Kelly McGillis) it functions *visually* as a
romance between Cruise and his male opponent/alter ego (Val
Kilmer). Their eyelines are constantly matched as the film cuts
between glances from one to the other; tensions are created and
connections made through editing, which function against the more
obvious grain of the boy-woman romance. This level of meaning could
not be found in the film 'on paper' and cannot be 'seen' in its dialogue:
it is entirely visual.

Equally specific to film is the pattern of audience expectations
constructed around *genres*. Genre is a means through which an
audience *brings knowledge* to a film: thrillers, westerns, horror films,
comedies etc., provide frameworks in which the audience's capacity to
recognize certain stock elements of plot, theme and image creates the
potential for great subtlety of meaning where these conventions may
be stretched, played with or subverted. In the horror film, for example,
it is a convention that a shaky camera roaming through woods or
round a house represents the viewpoint of the monster — so expectations and suspense can be built up, exploited or exploded. Conventions from one genre can be used in a film that doesn't initially appear
to be within the category: I argue in this section, for instance, that
FATAL ATTRACTION can be seen as a version of the horror film, and it
employs the mechanism just described. Through use of genre conventions an apparently run-of-the-mill horror movie may speak eloquently about sexuality and the body, or a 'second-rate' thriller
articulate widespread fears about knowledge and secrecy. Much has
been written about genre — both general and specific — within film
studies, yet it is striking how regularly genre films are ignored by most
'highbrow' critics. Many writers block off almost all popular genre

productions from their critical interest by dismissing them as silly or nonsensical. I have repeatedly read critics on national newspapers dismiss out of hand some runaway success like PRETTY WOMAN or DIE HARD 2 without a glimmer of interest in *why* the film has been successful, what it has appealed to in so many millions of people. That position may be all right for self-confessed elitists, but not for those who think of ourselves as socialists. We have to take seriously the complexities of film language and not assume that things we don't like or understand don't make sense. The term 'symptom' itself is borrowed from psychoanalysis and it is worth remembering how radical was Freud's perception, at the beginning of this century, that 'symptoms *have a sense* and are related to [the patient's] experience.'[1] (My italics.) Films also have a sense, and are related to *someone's* experience: the critic's job is to find out what that sense is, and if possible whose experience it relates to.

The columns in this part of the section all, in various ways, look at films symptomatically, and certain concerns crop up again and again. Obviously issues of class, race and gender have been dealt with throughout film history, but I think it is possible to trace some new ways of experiencing them, new *categories* of experience, in these movies of the late 1980s, which tell us a lot about our own time. A key example is the Single Working Woman — the 'SWW' — a repeated and developing figure found in very many of the mainstream movies I viewed week after week. Eighties movies also articulated anxieties *about* the New Woman in a variety of ways, bringing us the nervous, sensitively goofy 'New Man' on the one hand, the iron-clad, baby-faced RoboCop and Rambo on the other. A fascination with femininity as dangerous, and with the mutability of the body, was linked to a voyeuristic fascination with the 'other side of town' — other for 'yuppies', that is: the side where working-class and black people live. An extraordinary number of films hinged round a trip of this kind made by white, middle-class men. Class is a political issue that has been grossly neglected by those in left-wing politics during this era, yet popular films have spoken vividly of class anxieties and the fantasy of permeable class barriers. The wish to escape class has been linked, in these movies, to an obsession with 'lifestyles', and more generally with social surfaces: clothes, furnishings, the trappings of social existence

---

1   'The Sense of Symptoms', *Introductory Lectures on Psychoanalysis*

which, *because* they are trappings, can be easily bought, changed or exchanged (and are particularly vividly portrayed through mise-en-scène). Perhaps a certain class resentment and social outrage could also be read in the number of upwardly mobile interiors that got smashed up in the films of the 1980s. Popular films have also — at a time when left-wing theorists have been obsessed with the 'personal' — explored de-industrialization, the breakdown of city life, new financial markets, the growth of corporate power, corruption within big business and the collapse of law and order, in a series of dystopian scenarios that have used genre formulae of the thriller or PREDATOR-type horror pic to full-blown effect. Urban decay, deep racial anxieties, the aftermath of colonization, a search for the 'exotic', a love-hate romance with colonized cultures — all this can be found in the mass-market films of the eighties, more clearly than in any political analysis I have yet read.

Ordering these columns was difficult, as themes appear right across the films, not neatly demarcated but often in complex overlays; however, I have organized them so that a read straight through should both illustrate the more general ideas I have outlined here, and trace the specific concerns that the movies of this period in Western culture have explored.

In Dreams

A Nightmare on Elm Street 3: Dream Warriors

At a party last Saturday a complete stranger asked why I don't use this column to say which films are worth going to. To me, that seems as inappropriate as asking a geographer or geologist why they don't tell you where to go for your holiday: my job — as I see it — isn't to provide a brochure of favourite beauty spots but to map out the ground and try to understand its construction. Different things are 'worth seeing' to different people for different reasons; the mainly middle-class, leftish professionals who most often ask me that question usually have in mind a meaningful art movie which will address what they see as 'relevant' issues at the same time as giving them pleasure.

But this is exactly what all cinema does, for someone. In particular the highly structured formats of genre films — the western, the thriller, the melodrama — offer ways of speaking about the concerns of a society while producing pleasure, in part through recognition and repetition of these structures, for precisely the audience to whom those concerns are most pressing.

Horror films are a particularly interesting genre, because they deal by definition with the unacceptable, the horrifying or 'unimaginable', and are thus able to speak in variously coded and structured ways about taboo issues that merely lurk off-screen in other genres. Since disgust is written into their very form, they provide an expression of feelings about what is seen as disgusting: sex, the workings of the body, physical decay and death. Inasmuch as disgust and fear are linked with transgression — and anthropologist Mary Douglas has suggested that dirt can be defined as that which is out of place — this also provides a way of speaking about boundaries, frequently those of class or race. In horror films, what can't be held in or kept down erupts like guts from the body or bones from the ground. This inability of things to stay buried in the horror genre has been characterized by Robin Wood's phrase 'The Return of the Repressed': a reference to Freud's theory that nothing repressed disappears, but resurfaces as symptoms. If this is true of what is buried in the individual psyche, it is also true socially: the past is felt in the present and the inhabitants of horror films are haunted by their repressed history.

A NIGHTMARE ON ELM STREET 3: DREAM WARRIORS is the latest in a series which speaks about both sex and class — about what has been buried by a suburban American community. Along with films like HALLOWEEN it is both about and addressed to (despite its 18 certificate) adolescent kids, functioning as a B-side to the BREAKFAST CLUB or PRETTY IN PINK teen-problem movies. Adolescence is, of course, the time when sexuality almost literally erupts and in all the Elm Street movies this provides a hinge for the horrific events. The first starts when a girl invites her boyfriend to stay the night and is clawed to death in her sleep by a monster; the second turns to homophobic anxieties; but Part Three is perhaps the most interesting so far, involving not so much sexual fantasies as fantasies of bodily power, which ultimately enable some of the kids to overcome the monster.

He is the by now familiar figure of Freddy Krueger: the ex-janitor and child killer burned alive by Elm Street parents in a past act of gruesome vigilante-ism. With his battered hat and stripy jersey, Krueger is a kind of lumpen-proletarian figure — certainly the only 'worker' on Elm Street — whose 'place' is a boiler room underground. In social terms it is possible to read Krueger as the unsavoury working classness suppressed and fought off by the aspiring, middle-American parents who are presented as at best inadequate — alcoholic mothers and dictatorial fathers abound. Freddy is *their* victim even as their children, in a vicious cycle of effects, are his.

The territory of Freddy's revenge is dreams, and the horror device which is these films' hallmark is the seamless welding of sleeping and waking reality, so that nightmare events turn out to be true. The atmosphere is permanently like that gluey moment when you try to tear youself awake during a bad dream. Interestingly, this sensation is perfectly illustrated in the Samaritans ad playing with the film, which shows a head and hands trying to break through a sheet of some opaque plasticky substance with the caption: 'Is there anyone out there?'

It is not a coincidence that this ad plays with NIGHTMARE 3. On its release the Samaritans and other organizations tried to blame it for teenage suicides; Alexander Walker attacked it in the *Evening Standard*, linking its depiction of violence to kids with the incidence of child abuse and claiming that it increased the 'horrendous stock of contemporary fears by victimizing the family.'

The idea that films *add to* the 'stock' of fears in society is completely antithetical to my notion that films are required not only to express but in some way to deal with contemporary fears which already exist. NIGHTMARE 3 does indeed speak to the issue of child abuse, but in a very different way from that which Alexander Walker suggests. The Elm Street kids all experience something that no one else will acknowledge: this becomes the central issue in DREAM WARRIORS, which brings back Nancy, a survivor of Part One, as the understanding 'dream therapist' who alone, in a modern psychiatric hospital, believes them because she has had the same experience herself. The kids are in hospital because Freddy's attacks on them in their sleep are *interpreted* by adults as suicide attempts: but this is hardly an invitation to suicide since the whole point is that they are fighting off Freddy, only nobody believes them. The strongest drive of the film is towards validation of the kids' experience, in explicit defiance of the head psychiatrist who claims they are perpetrating the violence on themselves and — in what is almost a re-run of the seduction-theory debate — blames the 'bad dreams' on 'guilt and moral conflicts'. She, like the unbelieving mother of one 'patient', is held accountable for the real deaths which follow. Freddy himself twice appears in the role of a bad father; the sense of abuse is underlined by the irresponsible behaviour of other adult characters, like the hospital attendant who tries to push drugs on a young junkie. Thus the teenagers have to look to each other and to Nancy for support; and DREAM WARRIORS introduces to the series a more organized resistance.

Who can say which films are 'worth seeing' in the abstract? This is a film which deals in its generic fashion with a tangle of 'relevant issues' to its predominantly young audience, at the same time as providing the pleasure which brings them to the cinema in the first place. What is particularly striking is the way it unwaveringly takes their side against a repressive and unbelieving world of adult hypocrisy.

N.S. 11 December 1987

Hearts of Men

The Good Father

Men are back in vogue. Not that they were ever exactly out of it; but in the limelight of seventies feminism women's feelings and concerns occupied the screen for a while in a spate of films (GIRLFRIENDS, ALICE DOESN'T LIVE HERE ANY MORE, etc.) that attempted to explore a woman's-eye view of patriarchal relations. Whether or not these films succeeded, it was their project itself which marked the era. But since the women's movement put the politics of emotional life on the screen, men have been wanting one too: and films like KRAMER VS KRAMER and TOOTSIE have paved the way for a general preoccupation with the 'new' man. So all at once men are centre stage again — but this time with feelings.

If that seems like a vast generalization, many films opening later this season (e.g. TWICE IN A LIFETIME and one actually called MEN) will bear it out. In France, a comedy about three men and a baby by a little-known director has been the surprise blockbuster of the year — so charming and novel is it to see men changing nappies etc. Or compare the Bob Hoskins character in THE LONG GOOD FRIDAY and MONA LISA, thrillers which share a brutal underworld setting: between '81 and '86 the man has softened practically to butter. He feels, he cares, he has learned to cry!

THE GOOD FATHER is both a symptom of this phenomenon and, in its better moments, an investigation of it. Set in South London's down-home professional belt, the film follows the difficulties of two fathers separated from their children (conveniently, an only child in each case) and on bad terms with their ex-wives. Its scenario is similar to that of the recent TV drama *What If It's Raining?* and, besides a preoccupation with middle-class lifestyles, they share a penchant for rather whiney visual ploys like showing father and child in empty playgrounds (straining credibility to the limit when Clapham Common is deserted *every* time they go there).

However it is unfair to take the comparison beyond the symptomatic level because in other ways THE GOOD FATHER is infinitely more interesting than the flimsy TV drama. The complexity of the script and the rounded performances of Anthony Hopkins and Jim Broadbent (the fathers) prevent it becoming a simple sob story, and the cleverest aspect of its structure is the way the men's legitimate anger merges into revenge and culminates in a court action so grotesque as to shock even themselves. Two topical concerns cross over here in a way that enriches the film but foils anyone trying to claim it as a campaigning tract. It is, indeed, being used as a platform by Families Need Fathers, because part of the plot involves the Broadbent character's wife trying to remove their child to Australia. However, it could equally be used by a lesbian mothers' campaign, as it is her lesbianism that is used to prevent her taking the child.

Having raised so many bitter and important issues, it is slightly unconvincing, if emotionally pleasing, to find that both couples arrive at satisfactory resolutions to their problems. But the film is really about men: men cutting up carrots, men falling off their motorbikes, men sitting in garages reading their ex-wives' pamphlets from the 1969 Crouch End Women's Collective. This last image has a symbolic resonance throughout the whole film: whose task is precisely to chart the reactions, changes and upheavals arising from — so to speak — the days of the Crouch End Women's Collective.

In this sense the film is about a particular generation — and a particular class. One of the joys of THE GOOD FATHER is that in it director Mike Newell does for London in the eighties what his DANCE WITH A STRANGER did for the London of the fifties (the return of London to the screen has been one of the immense pleasures of recent British films). But it does it for the London of the 'poor' middle class, the bourgeoisie of Battersea and Crouch End. In one of the films' most revealing lines, father Hopkins, who has moved from his Battersea flat to a room overlooking a flyover, says of his new place, 'I can't take my son there', and the film presents this statement as self-evident. But why? Millions of families live in rooms overlooking flyovers (including many erstwhile inhabitants of Battersea). Ultimately, though THE GOOD FATHER's emotional perceptions might speak to a wider audience, its practical concerns are those of that newly-important consumer class, the well-meaning, hard-done-by professionals. One of the great flaws of seventies feminism was its failure to represent the problems of working-class women; now it seems that public focus has already moved on to middle-class men. For a completely different kind of movie about the male psyche see TOP GUN, reviewed next week.

N.S. 3 October 1986

Above the World

Top Gun

TOP GUN isn't just *like* an ad for the US forces. It *is* one: made with full cooperation from the Pentagon, it places military personnel (real, not fictional) higher than film technicians on the credits. It is hardly necessary in this magazine to spell out the implications of such a project in relation to Reaganite policy and US military involvements. However, TOP GUN's sweeping popular success in the USA (grossing a thousand million dollars) must depend on something more than simple army propaganda.

For decades the image of the US army has been dominated by Vietnam, and the image of a US soldier most in the American public's eye has been that of a war-vet. Instead of John Wayne figures the movies offered Jon Voigt as the disabled hero of COMING HOME; even THE DEER HUNTER, despised by the left, attempted to confront this aftermath. And years after the war ended there would still be a wheelchaired, often paraplegic, veteran in every class on every course on every US campus: those same campuses that had appeared on the world's screens torn apart by the anti-war movement. One way or another Vietnam had dominated both the experience of a generation and the image of the nation.

But out of this confusion of demonstrating hippies, long-haired vets in wheelchairs, *M*A*S*H*, dope-smoking and — a more recent addition to the list — the half-crazed Rambo, there now emerges an absolutely pristine, unsullied image of strength and purity, riding on a generation to whom hippies are geriatric. On paper, TOP GUN's story of a young fighter pilot (overcomes loss of both father and best friend, finally carries out heroic deeds in a 'war') may reveal the same old Western values cranked round yet again. But in TOP GUN the *film* you can see the phoenix-like rebirth of those values, cleansed, laundered, completely renewed, brought to us fresh and steaming with the gorgeous young bodies presented in shower-rooms for so much of the screen-time: the well-worn ideology of heroic nationalism resurfaces as smooth and unmarked as young skin. For, however old its macho theme, it is the new imagery of male narcissism that makes TOP GUN so modern, so appealing, and — in a way — so sensuous.

Sensuous experience is the heart of the film: something critics overlooked in pointing to the weakness of its plot and dialogue (much of which goes 'Zero zero mustang roger negative vector' etc.). These just aren't the main point; after all, you can get plot and dialogue any time in a novel. Only film can bring you the full physical experience of *flying* — by halfway through I sincerely wished I'd taken travel-sickness pills, so powerful is the capacity of film to reproduce the experience of movement. The title sequence is an exquisite hymn to the mobility of men and machines, whether or not you like what they stand for. The beauty of action and speed becomes more powerful than their political point, and thereby absorbs it, almost in passing.

The other dimension of sensuality takes us back to the shower-room (whose imagery is generally current at the moment: e.g. the Under-ground ad for a department store showing a naked young man with just a towel draped round his loins). TOP GUN's underlying romance is between the hero and his rival: their embrace is the climax of the film, and their eye-contact produces the most *frissons*. It is no coincidence that the overt romance in the movie is between the young hero and his instructor, an *older* woman, allowing the physical focus of the film to remain on the young male bodies, presented as desirable as much as desiring.

This is all part of the mood of the moment: but it's no simple reversal of the days when men provided action and women bodies to look at. Today, men can have the action *and* the sensuality. It is interesting to compare TOP GUN with an earlier men-and-flying film, Howard Hawks' ONLY ANGELS HAVE WINGS. The difference is partly that TOP GUN is really about *boys*, whose sexuality is more dispersed and polymorphous than the enclosed male personae of ONLY ANGELS. A more contemporary comparison could be made with AN OFFICER AND A GENTLEMAN, which stars Richard Gere, another new male sex symbol. But where OFFICER only *promised* to 'take you up where you belong' (the title song) TOP GUN actually *does* it. And anyone who doesn't understand what a turn-on this is will never get to the heart of its political power.

N.S. 10 October 1986

Fear and Loathing

Smooth Talk
Extremities

Women's function as a register of terror in movies is nothing new. Being frightening means, almost by definition, frightening a woman: the poster for THE SHINING summed up this classic mechanism in the economical montage of Jack Nicholson with an axe/Shelley Duval screaming. Without the image of the terrified female, the grammar is incomplete: power is a two-way relationship and Jack Nicholson rolling his eyeballs on his own just looks plain dumb. The power of the man is written in the fear of the woman.

In the traditional horror genre, woman screaming or woman fainting acts as a barometer to the horror of whatever the film deals in: ghosts, zombies, monsters, werewolves. However, in the early eighties a form emerged which used women not just as vehicles for the frighteningness of other situations, but as the focus of fear in precisely 'their own' situations (e.g. babysitting, in HALLOWEEN). Most of these films wore their message in their titles — DON'T ANSWER THE PHONE, HE KNOWS YOU'RE ALONE — and their particular trademark was posing women under threat in domestic space so that danger results not merely from venturing out of a 'woman's place', but by being in it.

It is perhaps a measure of our supposedly 'post-feminist' times that both SMOOTH TALK and EXTREMITIES can simultaneously reproduce these structures while purporting either to interrogate or to overturn them. SMOOTH TALK starts off as an adolescent-awakening movie, following three high-school girls through their rituals of shopping-mall games, chasing after boys, being misunderstood by their parents. Through this small-town Californian teenage limbo drifts the central figure of Connie (Laura Dern) whose 'awakening sexuality' is characterized by an aimlessness and lack of affect which give her the appearance of sleepwalking much of the time. This is hardly contradictory since one of the essential qualities of the 'feminine sexuality' she is acquiring is not being fully aware of it (she is 'awakening' to a slumber, as it were) and therefore not being in control.

This lack of awareness and control is presented at once as Connie's downfall, and as an inevitable part of her new identity. At the height of her restlessness and sexual ventures, she annoys her parents by

choosing to stay home from a family outing. Once alone, she wanders
through the house, turning on radios in every room, dancing, trying on
make-up — filling the space both in a narcissistic enjoyment of herself,
and in waiting for a hypothetical man. Her activity in this sequence is
brutally violated by what comes next, and yet, on the film's more
insidious level, can be read as a kind of preparation for it.

For what happens next is that an indescribably slimy older man,
Arnold Friend (Treat Williams) drives up (he knows she's alone) and
smooth talks (terrorizes) her in a very long sequence into getting into
his car — presumably to be raped. 'Presumably', because the act itself
is never shown, leaving an ambiguity perversely — and irresponsibly
— heightened in the US ad which shows Treat Williams and Laura
Dern together (an image not found in the movie itself) as if on a date,
with the (bizarrely un-fictional) caption 'Laura Dern is in for a treat'.

If this treat is to be raped, it nevertheless is presented as a form of
seduction. Nothing really adds up. Connie doesn't go inside immediately, lock the door, and phone her parents or the police. She appears
almost hypnotized. The creepily-named Mr Friend knows all about
her. Her home is no longer a protection but becomes suddenly flimsy;
rickety doors and open windows are sadistically lingered over by the
increasingly claustrophobic camera. Arnold Friend is master of external space: Connie, indoors, has none left. In the face of her persecutor
she is presented as completely without will of her own. One of the
effects of showing such lack of resistance is that it suggests, in
contradiction to the film's social realist opening, a sort of psychodrama
where Arnold Friend appears as the living projection of Connie's own
fears and desires. She appears in these sequences as so drained of
meaning except as an index of Friend's power, it is as if all her
strength, such as it was, has been given over to him as personification
of the sexuality she was supposedly discovering. On one level this is a
very moral tale about what happens when young girls are left alone.
But on another, the fact that Friend represents what Connie both
desires and fears (sex) and that she both gets it and is frightened by it
(rape) suggests that what women really have to fear is ourselves — it is
our own sexuality which appears as a state of perpetual danger.

EXTREMITIES is, on the face of it, a reversal of SMOOTH TALK
because its heroine (Farrah Fawcett) manages to turn the tables on
her attacker and ends up tormenting him. However, both films are
structured in two very distinct parts, and the first half of EXTREMITIES
bears a striking resemblance to the second half of SMOOTH TALK. The
Farrah Fawcett figure is assaulted in a car park by a man who then
comes to her house when she's alone. As in SMOOTH TALK, the setting

is daylight domesticity and the attacker saunters in with ease. As in SMOOTH TALK, he knows 'all about' her, startling her with the names of her flat-mates and family. (This insistence on the knowledge of the attacker makes it particularly clear that the absence of anywhere to hide is a psychic as much as a literal component of this scenario — in case the point isn't clear enough, birdcages and goldfish bowls abound in the domestic interior.) And as in SMOOTH TALK, she seems (at first) incapable of disobeying him: for perhaps an hour Farrah Fawcett runs through every possible combination of terror and tears as she does everything the man tells her.

Halfway through the film, however, she grabs a flyspray, gets her attacker in the eyes, and from this point takes her revenge, finally forcing him to confess to the attempted rape. Yet this sudden reversal cannot undo what has gone before: instead it allows the film to have its cake and eat it, affording the audience both the sadistic terror of the first half and the righteous revenge of the second as its justification.

The real point about both these films is that they employ a mechanism based on the assumption of male power and female vulnerability. Yes, Farrah Fawcett nails the guy in the end, but how did he get in there in the first place? If the home can be seen as the site of traditional femininity, then its representation as inherently penetrable sets up femininity as a space permanently available and assailable, without boundaries, while at the same time presenting it as the only possible place for women. Fortunately, however, it is not a real space. So, frightening as it may seem, we need waste no time imagining that we inhabit it.

N.S. 21 November 1986

Male Order

Men
Parting Glances
Gone to Earth
Mala Noche

Just in case anyone still doubts that men are the most marketable
subject of the year, here is a startling fact: MEN, Doris Dörrie's zany
but soft-centred comedy about — you've got it — men, has been the
most popular film in Germany since the war, attracting 4.2 million
admissions in just 22 weeks, and also breaking house records during its
run in New York. Coupled with the runaway success of THREE MEN
AND A CRADLE (outgrossing RAMBO in France) this must say something about the audience for 'post-feminist' man. I say 'post-feminist'
not because they are *past* feminism, far from it; but feminism has had
an effect on the way men are represented — one expects to see them in
legwarmers any minute now.

Clothes play an important part in Dörrie's film; for like all good
social comedies it is about lifestyles as much as characters. Its plot is
simple: Julius, a successful designer, discovers that his wife is having
an affair and moves in (incognito) as her lover's flat-mate to find out
what she sees in him. The lover, Stefan, is a semi-unemployed hippy,
and part of the attraction is obviously that he represents an alternative
to the couple's heavily bourgeois existence. Its social comment is the
sharpest aspect of the film, whose zappy narrative makes no pretence
to realism: gradually the two men swap roles, a change charted by the
descent into tee-shirt and unshavenness on the one hand, and the
acquisition of suit and haircut on the other.

The men's comic relationship is, in plot terms, competitive: Julius
deliberately turns his rival into a better bourgeois than himself so as to
win back his wife. Yet the film's *imagery* shows us men together without
women for most of the screentime, and this is really its soft heart: men
jogging together, men cooking together, men having pillow-fights
together, etc. At the same time, the fact that the *plot* hinges on a
woman keeps everything safely heterosexual; the film has its cake and
eats it in this respect, which is perhaps why it is so devastatingly
popular. The whole scenario is a brilliant device for having men
romping around on beds without a moment's anxiety: they are rivals,

not lovers. The atmosphere of the movie is rather like that of a conversation between heterosexual feminists about their boyfriends: full of snappy observations about sexism (Men. . .!) but no questioning of heterosexual identity itself.

PARTING GLANCES, on the other hand, sets out deliberately to show gay life as totally normal — director Bill Sherwood's aim is to make a film about 'people, not homosexuals'. Its 'people' are nevertheless very clearly located in class terms by their Manhattan yuppie interiors and high levels of consumer-durability. The extremely moving story of a couple whose relationship is faltering while the friend and ex-lover of one of them is dying of Aids is set against a backdrop of rubber plants and ansa-phones, publishers' dinners and arty parties. The one film ingredient as popular as men at the moment is the middle-class consumer lifestyle; aimed, presumably, at the same audience as the Habitat catalogue. Or perhaps it is a sign of hard times that we can all peek into the world of parquet and Perrier for the price of a cinema ticket.

Either way, it is the taking-for-granted not of homosexuality, but of this setting, that marks the film's weakness. And in its eagerness not to be 'about' homosexuality it is slightly blind to certain stereotypes within its own repertoire: for, within this milieu where you feel you could safely bring your grandmother for tea, it is the rock star, the way-out crazy musician friend of one of the partners, who has Aids. It's as if HIV could only be caught on an excursion away from the world of rubber plants — although for a film which claims to be so straightforward it is surprising that there is no dialogue at all about the other kind of rubbers or indeed any form of safe sex, now such a crucial part of gay life. But Aids appears only on the dangerous fringes of this too-safe world. PARTING GLANCES could do with some of MEN's alertness to social stereotypes: the wacky ease with which its protagonists exchange roles loosens the sense that identity is fixed in characters and alerts us to its social nature. Why couldn't one of the yuppies have Aids — the publisher instead of the musician? Having said all this, PARTING GLANCES is, on the 'human' level it sets up for itself, both a funny and a deeply moving evocation of a man's love for two people, one within an established day-to-day relationship, one dangerously outside that.

GONE TO EARTH, Powell and Pressburger's re-released 1950 classic, is worth noting in this context for, with its heroine torn between a 'safe, domestic' love (the parson) and a 'dangerous, sexual' one (the squire), it poses a similar dichotomy and also, in a way, one between men. In the very different setting of the Shropshire landscape, some of the same lines are drawn, between social acceptability and rejection, between a tame and a wild sexuality. Far from being the underlay to a realist drama, as in PARTING GLANCES, in Powell's film these themes are like the bare branches of one of his turbulent trees: stark, gothic and frightening. No matter how over-the-top it seems today, or how bizarre Jennifer Jones' 'rural' accent, GONE TO EARTH is powerful because it portrays a real and impossible dilemma which is at the heart of desire itself.

On this note, I recommend MALA NOCHE (Bad Night), a raw, roughly stylish film from Oregon which reminds you how exciting independent film-making can be, let alone desire. For this is what charges the film's aesthetic; it has a story, of sorts, but what it is *about* and catches so well in its black and white shadows is sexual longing across an imbalance of power — and how the extremity of that longing reweights the balance in some ways, without touching it in others. Fired by the electricity of crossed needs, it shows how the social inequality between a gay white kid and the streetwise Mexican kids he befriends both feeds his desire while making it impossible to reciprocate freely. In its own way this film lays more on the line than any of the others, and has a sure feel for the more awkward corners of sexual exchange which we might prefer to forget.

N.S. 31 October 1986

Kookies Crumble

Jumpin' Jack Flash
Hour of the Star

In the last year or so the US media have been obsessed with the Single Working Woman. When a now-famous Harvard study was published supposedly proving that the chances of a woman over thirty getting married were practically nil, the press and TV news leapt into a frenzy of concerned interviews with SWWs and, after the initial shock horror, the next step was a series of interviews in every major magazine in which SWWs testified to their happiness with their state and the joys of being able to eat junk food in the middle of the night, go to bed with face cream on, etc.

This preoccupation surfaces in a number of contemporary mainstream US movies; in LEGAL EAGLES, for example, Debra Winger plays a stereotypical SWW, the kind who compensates for being good at her profession by wearing slightly off-beat clothes, eating all night until she's sick, being a back-seat driver, and getting nearly run over by a cab after refusing a male offer to put her in it.

JUMPIN' JACK FLASH offers Whoopi Goldberg the playpen of just such an SWW role. She plays Terry Doolittle, a bright, funny SWW who, like the Winger character, tends to wear clothes in layers, braces, skirts with socks, legwarmer-type garb. This signification extends to the SWW's apartment, which is as wacky as her clothes and may contain such things as Mickey Mouse pillows and giant toothbrushes, expressive of the SWW's slightly un-grown-up personality. All these women form friendships with male colleagues and are almost one of the boys, but it is a *sine qua non* of their roles that they should be single — at least until the end of the film. JUMPIN' JACK FLASH neatly combines the two key elements of the SWW genre. Terry is presented as especially good at her job, a computer operator: she has a way with electronics, she's the one colleagues turn to when their computers don't work. And her whole persona hangs on her singleness, underlined by the fact that, for almost the entire film, her relationship to the male 'lead' is in fact a relationship to the computer screen on which they exchange messages. There is no room for an actual boyfriend within this representation of modern SWW autonomy.

The departure from traditional femininity is highlighted in one memorable scene where Terry crashes an embassy party dressed as a Diana Ross figure in a straightened wig, tight dress and high heels — an image of the 'feminine', 'whitened' black woman which is clearly not 'herself'. A similar scene occurs in the forthcoming BLACK WIDOW, where Debra Winger also has to appear at a party in a borrowed dress and a hairdo which turn her temporarily into a 'feminine' as opposed to SW woman.

JUMPIN' JACK FLASH is on the cusp of several other contemporary film genres, one of which is the zany black performer's comedy (the Richard Pryor-type movie). Another is the NINE TO FIVE genre — the office worker's revenge. Terry Doolittle, though good at her job, is not in the professional bracket of the Winger characters and lightens the tedium of her post in a banking emporium by swapping recipes and personal advice. Her break comes when an urgent plea for help appears on her screen, signed Jumpin' Jack Flash, and she is suddenly precipitated into a spy adventure, helping a British agent to escape the Iron Curtain. The movie emphasizes the fantasy life of the woman stuck in a boring office job: her passion for old movies, romantic novels. In true Hollywood fashion, JUMPIN' JACK FLASH makes the desire for excitement come true, dramatizing the fantasy of being suddenly lifted into a thrilling role culminating in romance and escape from insignificance.

The extraordinary HOUR OF THE STAR (winner of the Best Film award at the Latin American Festival in Havana) by Brazilian film-maker Suzana Amaral deals in a similar situation but one where the dreams and desires of a young, lonely woman living at breadline level in a Brazilian city are felt through their denial rather than their filmic fulfilment. This brilliant and moving film shows at every turn what real poverty and loneliness are, as its heroine Macabea (Marcelia Cartaxo — winner of the Best Actress Lion at Berlin), at the very bottom of the job market, the housing market and the love market, finds intellectual stimulus from information given with time-checks, physical excitement in dance music from the radio; where four women sharing a slum lodging watch silent soap opera through their landlady's window. Like a bizarre parody of the North American SWW, Macabea wakes in the night to eat a piece of chicken from a foil container; she too is sexually unfulfilled and, as with her US counterpart, she too has her moment of traditional 'feminine' beauty when she dresses glamorously in contrast with her usual style.

HOUR OF THE STAR shows not only hardship but, more importantly, that even those in the most extreme hardship need passion and beauty in their lives. Macabea's tentative search for these is constantly undermined, yet the spirit which repeatedly surfaces gives an even greater sense of poignancy than these downfalls. When the film was previewed, many critics were heard to say that it was humorous; I can only say that I found it heartbreaking as only the relentless crushing of someone's hopes can be. The film's bleak irony is that the dreamy Macabea does indeed have her hour as a star; her split second of fantasy comes true but in a way that only confirms how, for the bottom of society's heap, dreams really don't. And the relation of Hollywood to such lives of extreme loneliness and oppression is, the ending bitterly suggests, one of destructive irrelevance.

N.S. 8 May 1987

The Male of the Species

The Morning After

No cultural product works in isolation, but films are particularly interdependent in their meanings; partly because our reading of them relies on our knowledge and memory of generic conventions, and partly because the star system creates a complex pattern of links which also depends on our filmic memory and expectations. We remember the names of stars in mainstream films long after we have forgotten their fictional names, and meanings produced in one film will be carried over into another by the very presence of a particular actor or actress around whom certain connotations have accrued.

Sidney Lumet's latest thriller THE MORNING AFTER is an interesting example of this phenomenon. Even its visual style is full of references: Lumet's flat, painterly use of urban surfaces is reminiscent of Edward Hopper, and his tongue-in-cheek use of generic clichés — for example, an overhead shot of a toilet just after a bloody body has been found — plays heavily on our knowledge of other films. The story is relatively simple: a failing, alcoholic actress, Alex Sternbergen (Jane Fonda), wakes up in bed with a dead man unable to remember how she got there — presumably through a sexual encounter. The question to be solved is, initially, whether or not she has murdered him. However, when she meets Turner Kendall (Jeff Bridges), an ex-cop turned repair man, the question shifts to whether he is a trustworthy ally in uncovering the real murderer or whether it is in fact he who has set her up. (If you don't want to know, don't read this to the end.)

Fonda brings a powerful complex of meanings to any film, not least through her trajectory from sixties sex-doll to liberated woman of the seventies. And the film most strongly evoked in THE MORNING AFTER is KLUTE (1971) where, as Bree Daniels, Fonda is also elaborately framed by someone who has exploited the 'weakness' (in that case prostitution, not drink) which makes her 'untrustworthy', and where, interestingly, she is also befriended by an ex-cop, Klute. Like Turner Kendall, Klute is an old-fashioned moralist from outside the city (there NY, here LA) where the corrupt events take place. Kendall and Klute are slow, silent men given to doing paternal things like tidying up other people's apartments, and Fonda in both films plays a woman at once alone — quasi-independent — and yet needy in a way that is

twisted from sexual to child-like. In both cases what she '*really*' needs'
isn't sex, but looking after.

Of course, Fonda's most recent off-screen image is her work-out
trip, and the opening sequence of THE MORNING AFTER makes oblique
reference to it in the form of a TV show which is playing as Alex
wakes. The programme is about the dead man, a photographer, and
asks whether his images of women's bodies doing work-out and
pumping iron are pornographic: 'Is he glorifying the new female form
or is he the king of sleaze?' We are then treated to the film's only
glimpse of *that* body, the famous Fonda thigh; the rest of the film
denies us such images, but here it coincides with the moment where
her integrity is most in doubt.

But, most importantly, the opening TV show raises questions about
her apparent date from the night before. And this kicks off the real
drive of the film, which, unlike earlier *films noirs*, hinges on whether or
not a desired *man* is to be trusted. Much has been written about the
role of the *femme fatale* in movies — that figure of both sexuality and
treachery who represents the contradictory desires and fears of the
male protagonist. I would contend that there is a relatively new '*homme
fatale*' figure in contemporary films (though since both figures function
within an ultimately patriarchal framework this is not a simple
reversal) and this is precisely where the 'carried over' connotations of
Jeff Bridges come into play.

The publicity image for THE MORNING AFTER is a split square with
Fonda's face on one side, Bridges' on the other. Fonda's face suggests
fear, though also possibly desire. But the most striking thing about
Bridges is that the cool, threatening face in the poster resembles not so
much the solid, red-necked persona of Turner Kendall as the sexy and
treacherous Jack Forrester — Bridges' previous incarnation in JAGGED
EDGE.

And it is on this that the film relies, heavily, for its central frisson: is
the man Alex comes to desire the real killer? Because in JAGGED EDGE
it was desire which prevented the lawyer making this perception about
her client. Unlike the old films noirs where the plot unravelled through
the eyes of the male protagonist, this new type of post-COMA thriller
takes us through events mainly via the subjectivity of the woman. And
just as the old films noirs offered the hero a choice of good and bad
women without initially making clear which was which, here the
heroine is offered a gradually unfolded and equally murky choice
between good and bad men.

For Kendall's opposite is Alex's ex-husband. Played by Raul Julia
(the straight revolutionary in prison with William Hurt in KISS OF

THE SPIDERWOMAN) he is initially Alex's closest friend and adviser. He is also a hairdresser, sexually 'ambiguous' and non-white. His foreignness is emphasized by his name — Joaquin Manero — and his sexual ambivalence in his nickname, Jacky ('all hairdressers are called Jacky' says the superstraight Kendall). An outsider, Jacky's aspirations to enter upper-class WASP circles are ultimately his downfall, so that he is both villain and victim. In one central exchange Alex says to him, 'You've been on the outside long enough, now you want in . . . all that breeding, all that early American stuff.' The fact that the whole film takes place over Thanksgiving underlines this theme; but the plot ultimately shows how corrupt the 'top' All-Americans are.

So who really represents 'all that early American stuff' in the movie? The red-neck ex-cop with the heart of gold, who talks about spics and spades, who assumes that a hairdresser must be gay, who doesn't believe in divorce and who *repairs things*. Kendall's handiness in the workshop is strongly reminiscent of Ally Fox in MOSQUITO COAST. He is the real raw material of Americanness. But the most unpleasant thing about the film is that his 'jokey' racism is finally justified in the plot by Jacky's treachery. Meanwhile Kendall himself is remarkably reclaimed from his jokeyness, stops making racist comments and starts wearing tasteful check shirts instead of his tacky brown tee-shirt. I will return to *hommes fatales* next week.

N.S. 12 June 1987

Fatal Strategies

White of the Eye
Nobody's Fool

Since last week I have found not only that *homme fatal* doesn't have an 'e' but also plenty of fresh fodder for my new theory. Donald Cammell's WHITE OF THE EYE is a chic thriller whose structure is remarkably similar to THE MORNING AFTER's in that solving the plot involves choosing between two men who might be the killer. In both films one of these is the ex- and one the current lover/husband of a

woman who provides the subjective pivot through which we experience the choice. This is also the framework for the much less macabre
NOBODY'S FOOL, in which Rosanna Arquette has to choose between
her old lover and a newcomer, Eric Roberts.

This switch to a female subjective base, in which *men* are the
unknown factor, is increasingly common in films; and if the old *femme
fatale* can be seen as a projection of *male* sexuality, it would make sense
to examine the new *homme fatal* not as a screen expression of anything
about men, but rather as indicative of an attitude towards women and
our desires — part of a general interest in 'female sexuality' at the
moment.

The *homme fatal* menace in JAGGED EDGE is activated by the
woman's 'unprofessional' sexual relationship. In THE MORNING
AFTER, it is only after Jane Fonda sleeps with him that the film taunts
us with Jeff Bridges' potential treachery. And WHITE OF THE EYE,
though its central couple (the 'Whites') are married, draws particular
attention to Joan White's *desire* for her husband: indeed their decade-
long relationship is measured in the span between their first fuck on
the floor with him on top and their most recent, with her on top —
scenes which the film cuts back to repeatedly. The first time we see
husband and wife together, after we have already been shown the first
horrific murder, she takes him to bed; and at the very end, after she
knows he *is* the murderer, there is another hot sex scene. The film is
punctuated with shots of Paul White's crotch and, in a rage of jealousy
at his infidelities, Joan starts yelling about his big dick. As in film noir,
where the unfaithful wife would also be capable of murder, so sexual
treachery is here made to coincide with much worse crimes.

Skipping over the film's clever visual and conceptual structure,
which is all about eyes/seeing/hearing (Paul White has uncanny audio
powers; his counterpart, Joan's ex-boyfriend, has video-memory
vision) we are left with a plot which, like THE MORNING AFTER's, sets
up *both* men as potentially dangerous even though ultimately only one
is. In both scenarios there is a non-WASP 'ex' set against a chunky
handyman type — for Paul White is another of these tinkerers-in-
workshop men, a technical wizard, another backyard inventor with
the slightly Neanderthal morality that goes with it in all these films.
He justifies his murders of middle-class women by the fact that they
lead lives of vacant yuppiedom, and part of the film's imagery, as in
the opening murder sequence, is that of despoiled yuppie decor: a
mêlée of wine, meat and tulips, overturned designer chairs, smashed
cuisinarts and broken glass tables — like mayhem in Heals, a Class
War daydream. I'll come back to yuppie-destruct imagery in future

weeks; it certainly seems to be deeply associated with eruptions of sex and violence in current US films.

The use of yuppie kitchen accoutrements as an iconography of danger is reminiscent of the scene in 9½ WEEKS where Mickey Rourke slices vegetables with a vicious and expensive assortment of knives and gadgets before getting into yet more funky sex. He too can be seen as a *homme fatal*: sexy, gorgeous, but with a fatal flaw. In his case, it is merely kinkiness; but the way 9½ WEEKS works is by keeping you on the edge of your seat in case he does do something more violent, and it is this *sense* of danger, even if ultimately unrealized, that characterizes the type. Even in the basically harmless NOBODY'S FOOL, the dishy New Guy is presented as potentially dangerous: he looks at Rosanna Arquette with a strange intensity, accosts her when she's walking alone in deserted places, and finally takes her for a drive, in a sequence that's — momentarily — very like SMOOTH TALK. He starts to confide in her about his past acts of violence and, just when he starts to seem wild, an accident ahead forces him to drive right off the road, making him appear really unstable.

Today's *homme fatal* does have some antecedents; Cary Grant in SUSPICION and Joseph Cotten in SHADOW OF A DOUBT play apparently trustworthy men who cannot be trusted — but part of their impact has been that these were the exception rather than the rule. Only in horror films have men never been trustworthy; in terms of the gender of sexual threat, this genre could be seen as the opposite of film noir.

But what's striking about the present spate of *hommes fatals* in movies is that almost *any* man who's presented as desirable seems slightly spooky. A sexy husband; a wonderful new boyfriend; a gorgeous lover who adores you — these are all men who are *too good to be true*. And the two-men new/old formula (in 9½ WEEKS there's a nice but boring ex-husband too) gives an added frisson along the lines of 'just when you thought it was safe to go back in the water'. No matter which side the film comes down on — old lover good, new lover bad/new lover good, *old* lover bad — the very fact of sexual choice for a woman is problematized in these movies. Perhaps *this* is what they mean by post-sex cinema.[1]

N.S. 19 June 1987

---

1   See p. 139.

Under the Volcano

Black Widow

Bob Rafelson's FIVE EASY PIECES was one of the few American films to speak explicitly about class. That this is a displaced issue in most US movies and much of its culture can be seen in a film like RAISING ARIZONA, which, if its comic accents and 'horrid' decor were located in Britain, would be revealed as the piece of simplistic snobbery it really is. And the current spate of yuppie role-reversal movies deals in class difference less as a social reality than a set of style options which is fundamentally as wide as your wardrobe.

Rafelson's films have all involved characters moving across a social landscape which is presented not as a manifestation of psychic life but a frustrating limitation on it. In FIVE EASY PIECES the Jack Nicholson character tries to escape his middle-class musical background but is equally dissatisfied working on an oil rig and going out with a woman who sings along to Tammy Wynette. In STAY HUNGRY the Jeff Bridges character leaves his wealthy milieu for that of the gym, where he meets people from a different class and a different world. While Rafelson's restless heroes have so far been men, it is women who represent the social positions they experience their angst in. This is particularly clear in FIVE EASY PIECES, with Karen Black as the vulgar Tammy Wynette player who asks for ketchup at a middle-class dinner set against the cultured woman from the hero's more classy family past; but it can also be seen in STAY HUNGRY, where Sally Field as the gym's receptionist represents the other life Bridges falls in love with, in KING OF MARVIN GARDENS, where neither of Bruce Dern's women turn out to be what they seem, or even in THE POSTMAN remake, where Jessica Lange and Angelica Huston represent different possibilities for Jack Nicholson.

If these films have a common theme, it is dissatisfaction — as in 'Can't get no': an existential frustration with social roles and the impossibility of escaping them. What is interesting about BLACK WIDOW, Rafelson's first film for five years, is that these themes reappear but the protagonists this time are women, which reinflects the basis of the frustration from the social to the sexual: we are back on psychic territory once more.

I have written already in this column about the Single Working

Woman in US imagery; that figure played by Whoopi Goldberg in
JUMPIN' JACK FLASH or Debra Winger in LEGAL EAGLES. Here, as
Alex (a suitably androgynous name), Winger reappears as exactly the
same character. A federal agent in the Department of Justice, her
dedication to her work is seen by her boss — and by the film — as a
sign of sexual deficiency. She wears baggy clothes which the NFT
programme notes describe as 'dowdy' (I rather like them), eats
boil-in-the-bag food (another key characteristic of the SWW is that she
can't cook) and plays cards with the boys in the office (being friends
with men at work is — in this genre — a sure sign of sexual
inadequacy). She is, however, extremely good at her job, and picks up
on the slender connection between two cases of rare poisoning in
wealthy men who both died shortly after marrying a younger woman.

What she guesses, through examining photographs, is that these
apparently different women are the same: the deceptive appearances
of make-up, dress, hair colour and style are not enough to fool another
woman who knows, in a sense, how manipulable such surfaces are.
However, Alex's boss tries to put her off the case — he says what she
really needs is a boyfriend — and she actually has to leave her job to
follow it up.

Here are the typical Rafelson elements of dissatisfaction and escape:
the Department of Justice is vividly dreary (if that's possible) with
endless corridors, institutional furniture and, most significant of all,
green-painted windows shutting out the sun. And yet — Alex likes her
job: in plot terms she isn't trying to escape it but to do it. What the
film's *imagery* presents, however — behind her back as it were — is an
escape from the drabness of SWW-dom, from the cave of the sexless
office to the sunshine of sexuality. This is found in Hawaii and in her
alter ego, the seductress/murderess Catherine (Theresa Russell).

If Catherine stands for Alex's repressed sexuality, they have one
thing in common: diligence in their careers. For Catherine takes her
work (marrying men) very seriously, à la Helen Gurley Brown —
'Research his life totally . . . read anything written about him. . . get
involved in all his projects' — and does her homework well, becoming
a sexy southern girl for Dennis Hopper's toy manufacturer, a cultured
archaeologist for Nicol Williamson's museum board chairman. Both
women are preoccupied with supporting themselves: one in the
'feminine' way of working on a man, one in the 'masculine' way of
working at a job.

But when they meet in Hawaii the social dimension gives way to the
psychosexual. Rafelson claims that 'Catherine brings out Alex's
femininity, teaches her more about the feminine qualities in herself';

and the supposedly natural nature of these qualities is suggested by the backdrops of jungle and erupting volcano against which both women play out their affairs with the same man. Yet when Catherine invites her to a party and Alex has to get a concrete hairdo and high heels, 'femininity' is seen as constructed through a simple change of appearance (just as the yuppie/bohemian exchanges suits for tee-shirts). And despite the man they are supposedly competing for, there is a strong, physical relation between the women: in a diving class they do mouth-to-mouth resuscitation — the line 'you're not taking this personally are you' ensures that we are — and in the closing sequence of the film Catherine kisses Alex on the mouth again. However, in plot terms this hint of a different sexuality is just left in a void.

The whole Hawaiian excursion into femininity is deeply confused. On one level, the film has far too many endings and becomes impossible to follow. But its contortions are the result of an impossible project — to show, as Rafelson claims, the repressed femininity of an SWW when both this femininity and the SWW are merely stereotypes that the film itself employs. If indeed they were handled more consciously it could have been interesting: with Russell as the film noir femme fatale and Winger as the comedy-romance lead, it's like the meeting of two movie genres. But Rafelson, so powerful at depicting the frustrations of his male heroes in their social roles, seems unable to create the sense that femininity, too, offers a set of social positions that are as hard for women to occupy comfortably as it is for Jack Nicholson in FIVE EASY PIECES to feel at home with either his oil rig or his grand piano.

N.S. 24 July 1987

Under the Hood

Blind Date
Tin Men

It was way back in 1963 that Betty Friedan diagnosed the emptiness felt by many apparently well-off, middle-class American women as 'the problem that has no name'. This emptiness was middle-class femininity itself; since then we have had men with no name, indeed horses with no name, but the phrase came back into my mind while trying to think about a consistent theme in recent US movies without using the word 'yuppie'.

For 'yuppie' merely cloaks in a lifestyle that familiar, problematic and yet dominant figure, the white middle-class male. If there is any deep-lying connection between this week's movies it is this new problem that has no name: the emptiness of middle-class male's success, and the equal emptiness of would-be middle-class male's failure.

This may seem a strangely serious way to kick into discussing two of the funniest movies in town; yet comedy and unease have always gone together, and their perfect marriage is found in that most potentially anarchic of film and theatrical devices, the gag. BLIND DATE is directed by veteran (PINK PANTHER) gag-master Blake Edwards; which gives a peculiarly physical dimension to its topical theme of Successful Executive discovering Other Life through Wacky Woman. There has been so much of this recently that it hardly needs reanalyzing: sweet, straight, slightly goofy guy (Bruce Willis) in suit meets gorgeous woman (Kim Basinger) who goes berserk if she drinks; while — as in BLUE VELVET and SOMETHING WILD — the oedipal structure of Another Man (previous boyfriend) turns the plot from its initial downhill slide of female-invoked craziness into a drawn-out battle between the two men for the woman. By the end of the film our hero has swapped suit for sweatshirt and, having lost his job, turned back to his 'real' love, music; its naturalness as an occupation is shown by his having a black musician friend, who performs in a studio near the start of the film.

This is all sub-SOMETHING WILD, and yet there is a unique way in which the film almost physically produces the upheavals it's about. Gags are quite different from jokes; they seem to sidestep the conceptual circuit of verbal humour and function through the body, both in their enactment and their reception, where you're jerked into gut-laughter like going over a hump-backed bridge. There is something pleasurably infantile about that delight in destruction and chaos — it seems to correspond to a kind of polymorphous disorder, where custard pies defy cleanliness and motor co-ordination disappears.

In BLIND DATE this disorder is unleashed in a string of social eruptions, escalating from the important company dinner which Basinger turns into chaos to the posh party where Willis goes wild and throws food at people. In the meantime the ex-boyfriend is made to smash his car into a variety of shop fronts. And this is the anarchic quality of gags: things fall apart. The shop-window smashing is only the visual form of a well-known riot activity: we love the sound of breaking glass. But it's not just the external world which cannot hold: an increasing number of gags suggest bodily disintegration as well. Anyone who's ever had the smallest crash knows the meaning of what I think of as My Car, My Self: and the moment when Willis' car is actually taken to pieces is a kind of ultimate stripping, echoed in the following bed-falling-apart scene and finally one where bits actually fall off a house.

Yet the exhilarating sense of social chaos is ultimately contained: films like this shake up a social order only to let it re-settle more securely. In the wilder parts of the film even the characters have a kind of plasticity, like animation figures who can fall out of windows and spring up undamaged. But right at the end things snap back into place, as the subversion of a society wedding turns with ease into a love scene applauded by the entire wedding audience who were, a few minutes earlier, being rebelled against. Order is finally re-established on an apparently truer level as Willis, in his sweatshirt, strums his guitar by the sea, and the two lovers forsake alcohol for Coke: '*It's the real thing*'.

What makes TIN MEN — also hysterically funny — a more serious and depressing film is that there is no such easy location for the real thing, the missing meaning and inner self. Like much of BLIND DATE, TIN MEN could easily be titled 'Car Wars': its two salesmen anti-heroes (Richard Dreyfuss and Danny DeVito) meet by crashing into each other and there is much smashing of windscreens and denting of bumpers during the course of their antagonistic relationship. But the repeated knocks to this shell of male identity (a notion implicit in the film's very title) are more difficult to take as the social constraints that mould it are felt powerfully and painfully in Levinson's acute portrayal of economic and peer-group pressures. The sense of surfaces, which BLIND DATE so joyously smashes through in the certainty of something real beneath, is here more fragile as so much of male identity is located, not behind, but precisely *in* those surfaces — and this is what most of the film is about, from its opening, chrome-caressing close-ups of Dreyfuss' new Cadillac to its closing, overhead shot of the same car with the rivals driving together in it among the traffic of other men. In BLIND DATE breaking up someone's new car is just fun; here, a sense of the desperation that conflates importance and cars makes it just a little more edgy.

Femininity, too, is felt through *things*: Dreyfuss' memorable description of being with a woman (his rival's wife) is 'You go into the bathroom and see things you never saw before.' And DeVito exorcizes her from *his* life by throwing all her belongings out of the window in one of the film's most fast-cut, breathtakingly gaggy scenes, muttering what sound like department-store categories — 'Gloves and Scarves', 'Toiletries' — as he empties the paraphernalia of femininity on to the sidewalk. As he does it, he yells, 'I'm a free man': the fact that he isn't is evident as the Inland Revenue come to confiscate his house and car.

That the gags are not simply boundless acts of freedom in this film is shown vividly when DeVito knocks Dreyfuss on the head and then carefully goes to the fridge to collect eggs and tomatoes, comes back, and throws them at him one by one, 'to humiliate you'. He ends up in the police station for this: social order is, as Durkheim says, as much a *thing* as any other, and a subtle form of slapstick is when you walk right into it. In a more cathartic film like BLIND DATE, gags draw the audience safely into the joy of being out of control; you can do what you like, it feels, and nothing's really damaged. But in TIN MEN, revealingly, Dreyfuss says, 'I hate the fact that I'm not in control': in this film, as in social reality, excess is punished.

Set in 1963, TIN MEN says as much about the present as BLIND DATE does. Its salesmen protagonists both lose their licences; the hero of BLIND DATE loses his job. In both cases this is presented as progressive for the individuals concerned. Of the two films, TIN MEN is more interesting socially, and more honest sexually; yet in their comic, anxious ways both express the wish for, and fear of, something different. To rephrase Freud's famous question: what is it that white middle-class men *want*?

N.S. 14 August 1987

Diabolical Liberties

The Witches of Eastwick

A wide, aerial shot of a small New England town; the camera moves slowly down over the rooftops of white wooden buildings, into that perfect picture of orderliness familiar from countless films.

But which films? This could be the Sirkian suburbia of ALL THAT HEAVEN ALLOWS, where 'all hell breaks loose' (metaphorically) when a middle-aged woman rediscovers her sexuality. It could be the creepily harmonious Stepford, whose Wives wear compulsory frilly aprons and discuss nothing but recipes. It could be the small, enclosed community of THE BIRDS, where old residents tut-tut over newcomers and the sky holds unknown fears.

THE WITCHES OF EASTWICK is all of these: the extraordinary thing about this film (whose director, George Miller, made the MAD MAX series) is its generic lawlessness. Rather than falling into any one category — melodrama, with its stress on 'women's problems'; sci-fi, the 'body snatchers' genre of personality change; horror, with all the powers of the supernatural at its disposal — it incorporates aspects of them all. And it does this not simply as a bricolage, a tacking together of generic trademarks, but through very self-conscious reference: for example, a little old woman who owns a shop remarkably like the one in THE BIRDS is shown talking about the town's new resident — Daryl Van Horne — with a bizarrely-angled model of a seagull in the corner of the shot.

So here is a strange phenomenon: a horror film that isn't frightening, a melodrama that isn't heart-wrenching, sci-fi that isn't spooky. The film is, however, funny. With a horror plot which resembles THE EXORCIST or ROSEMARY'S BABY, its scripting and playing resemble rather the NINE TO FIVE comedy genre of wacky women sticking up for their rights — in this case against the Devil.

The film offers no single framework by which to interpret its events. Its meanings are products less of a consistently coded narrative (as in most films) than of constantly shifting *references*, both to the language of other films and to social discourses, specifically those of Women's Liberation and the New Man.

For the 'witches' are women without men: one widowed, one deserted, one divorced. A feminist angle on their situation is established at the start of the film as the objectionable headmaster uses the opportunity of Jane's (Susan Sarandon's) divorce to fondle her bottom. As he drones on at speech day, the three friends simultaneously wish for something to happen: immediately a thunderstorm halts the proceedings. When they wish for the perfect man to arrive, Daryl Van Horne — Jack Nicholson in a completely mad ponytail — moves into a disused Gothic mansion and seduces them in turn.

He does this by offering each exactly what she wants: and this is where New Man-dom comes in. While the women's specifications include old-fashioned things like size of penis, Daryl himself has a quite remarkable capacity for anti-patriarchal analysis. To the creative, restless Alexandra (Cher) he bemoans her energies wasted on repetitive housework. With Jane, a cellist, he brings out her musical depths and repressed passion; with Sukie (Michelle Pfeiffer), mother of six, he wheels out his admiration and envy of 'what you can do with your bodies . . . make babies . . . make milk. . .' The three women end up a cosy threesome as Daryl's harem, eating, drinking, flying (!) and fucking.

The spoken language of the seductions is taken from real-life feminism; but the visual forms are a series of exaggerated film clichés. Jane's cello 'burning with passion' actually catches fire; the measure of the women 'letting their hair down' is to have it stick out in a frizzy perm (obviously sex makes your hair curl). The harem itself is like a special effects fun-palace; meanwhile, the demonology element is carried by the respectable townswoman Felicia who 'knows' evil is present and is punished by Daryl's speciality, remote-control vomiting.

It appears to be Felicia's death and Eastwick's general disapproval that finally stop the women seeing Daryl (though it could also be seen as boredom, or the return of the superego). After attempting to woo them back with phonecalls and flowers, Daryl switches to using his supernatural powers to punish them with their worst nightmares. Yet when we next see him he is doing his ironing in front of a portable TV balanced on a marble staircase — the very image of hard-pressed bachelorhood, beer can and all, in the incongruous setting of the Gothic mansion.

This scene epitomizes the film's technique. In demonic-horror-film terms, the devil has absolutely no need to iron his own shirts. But here we are presented with a moment of bedsit Play-for-Today drama, and treated to a speech that could be described as New Man's Complaint: 'I was everything you wanted . . . did you ever care about my needs? I want a little attention . . . trust. . .' and so on. And when the women return, pregnant, Daryl rushes out in a *pink dufflecoat* — surely the sartorial apex of New Man-dom — to meet their cravings for icecream. It is precisely at this point that the women turn the tables and start to torture him.

What makes this daft film fascinating is that, while its mêlée of genres refuses us any one 'filmic reality', its thematic concerns are very real indeed. In dealing with a shifting balance of power between the New Man/Devil and the three Liberated Sisters/Witches it allows multiple points of entry to the viewer, none of which is privileged by the film itself. Its inconsistent narrative fits perfectly the confusion about roles and desires that characterizes these issues. For the bizarre series of natural and supernatural events is no less perplexing than the mysterious fact that Modern Woman conjures into being New Man but doesn't like him when she gets him.

N.S. 30 October 1987

Having Your Baby and Eating It

Broadcast News
Baby Boom
Three Men and a Baby

The SWW is back; or rather, unlike her chronicler (who's been having a break), she never went away. Her latest incarnation seems to be Holly Hunter, as dynamic producer Jane Craig in BROADCAST NEWS, James L. Brooks' first feature since TERMS OF ENDEARMENT.

BROADCAST NEWS centres on three characters: Jane and her work-mates Aaron (Albert Brooks) — a tough, 'old-school' reporter who lacks on-screen charisma — and Tom (William Hurt) — the dishy but supposedly dumb blond anchor-man who provides the acceptable face of the news for viewers. Besides the emotional ins and outs of this trio, the film is 'about' the changes taking place in TV news and the shift of values from content to presentation.

Yet despite the film's preoccupation with TV's fine moral points, overall its newsroom setting offers something else which is very much a part of 1980s movies: the *drama* of work, suggested through all the paraphernalia of charts, pagers, people running through offices, yelling orders, talking on several phones at once. All this is, of course, the essential backdrop for the SWW (excuse me please while I answer two phones, meet my deadline, have an emotional trauma — and meanwhile, hold the cover!) and one of the truly enjoyable features of BROADCAST NEWS is seeing Holly Hunter do all these dashing things so well.

But she pays for it. The film constantly shows her weeping into her wordprocessor and ends years later with both men happily married, Aaron's cute child playing with still-SWW 'Aunty Jane'; *she* is allowed a token ski-instructor — mentioned verbally as someone she's sort of interested in — but clearly her dynamism and high standards have taken their toll. What's clever about the film is that, like TERMS OF ENDEARMENT, its lack of narrative resolution (the emotional triangle is never really played out) masquerades as authenticity. On one level this is what reviewers are calling 'adult' drama precisely because it doesn't end neatly. But on another it is just more classic SWW stuff; typically, we must be shown both the glamour of her working life, and the failure of her emotional life. Now BROADCAST NEWS is apparently highly sensitive in showing the SWW's loneliness and tears and difficulty with men. But while the film purports to sympathize with her predicament, who is it that has put her in it in the first place? The film! The brilliant producer doesn't become Aunty Jane by an act of fate, but an act of script. And it is because such scripting *is* near the bone in terms of Real Life that it is hard to see *as* script.

If the construction of BROADCAST NEWS suggests that the SWW certainly can't have it all, BABY BOOM, dealing with the same problems, provides a fantasy resolution in which she can. Here again we have all the drama of eighties 'working life' as J.C. Wiatt (Diane Keaton) — management consultant at a big New York corporation — strides through offices, dishes out orders and answers multiple phones in a maze of wall-charts, maps, sales figures etc. When she becomes the guardian of a distant relative's orphaned baby, she at first resists parenting, then tries unsuccessfully to combine it with her Top Executive role, then moves upstate (as in FATAL ATTRACTION, the country is a key signifier of home and wholesomeness) where, ultimately, she finds love with a vet and business success with her home-made apple-sauce baby food.

In the early part of the film, when she is Ms Ambitious, Keaton appears sexless, or at least, unsensual, and this links with some very specific role reversals also found in BROADCAST NEWS. There, Tom is cast as the 'bimbo' in an archetypally 'feminine' role: in a fascinating piece of dialogue, after Jane has fed him his lines over headphones, he says, 'It felt wonderful having you inside me' — a sort of reversed penetration image. Both films, despite their 'working woman' politics, suggest that deviation from traditional male/female *sexual* roles brings frustration and unhappiness. J.C.'s initial boyfriend wears a cucumber face-pack, deliberately 'feminized', and their relationship is shown as deeply lacking; it is a crucial part of her renovation that the vet, Sam Shephard, is a 'real' man (i.e. he kisses her forcibly even when she says 'leave me alone' — because he *knows* she's neurotic and doesn't mean it).

BABY BOOM is very clear about the issues it's addressing: in the key scene where J.C. is invited onto the board, her boss says, 'A man can be a success and still have a personal life. I'm lucky — I can have it all.' J.C. quickly replies, 'I don't want it all.' But of course she does, and the film — which, like Sam Shephard, knows what she 'really wants' — gratifies this wish by giving her, in the end, a beautiful house, a darling baby, acres of apple orchards, a dishy lover, a multi-million-dollar business and the chance to get back at the creeps who fired her.

Yet whether or not the film lets (as in BABY BOOM) or doesn't let (as in BROADCAST NEWS) the SWW 'have it all', this question — of what, exactly, the SWW *can* have apart from a job — is the theme on which a whole new wave of sex comedies is riding. Generically, there are strong links with the Hollywood sex comedies of the thirties and forties, which also dealt with spirited women (Katharine Hepburn, Claudette Colbert) and with role reversals. The particularly new ingredients in this 1980s version of the genre are (1) the *psychologizing* of the SWW (what I call her neuroticization) and (2) babies.

The power of this theme is becoming evident as THREE MEN AND A BABY has already outgrossed FATAL ATTRACTION at the US box office (outgrossed being the *mot juste* where these films are concerned). In this movie three SWM have a baby dumped on them by the girlfriend of one while he is away (here, it seems, it is okay to have men and a baby in a 'pretended family relation' — Mary lives with Peter and Michael[1]). Into their yupped-out-to-the-max apartment tumbles all the novelty cuteness of nappies, gurgling smiles, shit, toy giraffes, sterilized nipples etc. But, *vice versa*, doesn't the *baby* look newly cute in

---

1   At the time there was a public 'scandal' over a children's book, *Jenny Lives with Eric and Martin*: see footnote on p. 68.

its little up-market lifestyle — the perfect consumer object?

Both baby films have the obligatory supermarket scenes: the dilemmas of caring for a child become the dilemmas of what to buy for it (indeed baby and product become merged in the memorable image of J.C. weighing her infant on the supermarket scales). BABY BOOM, by far the more complex film, richly exploits this theme by making the Secret of J.C.'s Success her tapping of the market for 'gourmet baby food' (early on she and her boyfriend try to feed the baby yup foods like fresh pasta and Perrier, just as in THREE MEN the actor father plays waiter for his baby's dinner: 'for your delectation tonight the chef has squeezed the juice of one cow. . .').

Also important in both films is the cuteness produced by juxtaposition of baby and job. In THREE MEN the baby goes to work with architect Tom Selleck in a tiny hard hat — adorable! BABY BOOM creates comedy with cuddly toys in the executive suite and milk from the baby's bottle spilling all over a client. The mode of both films' dealing with baby/work, baby/consumerism is slapstick. But the content of the comedy — baby throwing food over Corb chairs, shit on designer jackets — what is all this about?

There is a yuppie fascination with the limits of yuppiedom; and babies, while on the one hand providing endless opportunities for consumer cuteness, also represent those uncolonized areas (whether sublime or abject is a case in point) where the meaning of money stops. (Keaton, to coat-check attendant in restaurant: 'I'll give you my Visa card if you'll take her [the baby]'; Man, to baby, in THREE MEN: 'I'll give you ten bucks if you'll stop crying'; neither appeal works.) Bourgeois ideology always feeds off what it *can't* colonize, and the heart of the humour in these films is the play between babies as natural and cultural objects. Inasmuch as they are, patently, 'natural', they are available — as its opposite — to carry the 'natural' delights of yuppiedom. Now that woman has become the tough and neurotic SWW, she can no longer provide the soft centres in Hollywood's emotional chocolate-box (only the nut cluster, perhaps?). So babies take over where women left off: it is no coincidence that baby films tend to make use of pop songs where the word baby originally meant lover (this only works with baby girls, which, of course, the babies in these films are). Babies become the signifiers of emotional life, in representation, now that women are no longer available for that task (though what babies and SWWs have in common is that they both do a lot of crying).

Of course, ultimately the issues surrounding parenthood/work/ emotional life are very real ones. Mainstream films can only be successful if they *do* hit on deep-felt problems. But while bravely presenting 'realistic' tears at the office, smelly-nappy changing and so on, these films' ideological success lies in the psychic drives that underpin their narratives. BROADCAST NEWS, despite its supposed sympathy with the SWW, in fact punishes her: it locates a real issue but still leaves us with two married men and SWW aunty, knuckle-rapped for her pickiness. The two baby films equally address the real issues of childcare and work: here, the psychic drive is not punishment (though THREE MEN certainly involves womb-envy) but, rather, the wish for perfection, to avoid conflict and choice through imaginary resolutions — indeed to 'have it all'.

But in the discussions about whether or not we can 'have it all' no one has thought to challenge the very terms of the question. For the concept is a totally consumer one in the first place. Why not consider whether one can *be* all those things (a worker, a mother, a lover etc.) — which one obviously *can* — or whether one can *do* all the things one wants, which does involve choice, being mainly a question of time. Why is the whole issue of job, partner, child characterized as one of what you can *have*? It is extremely revealing that in both BABY BOOM and THREE MEN the babies, if not actually bought, like Baby M, are *got*: J.C. is left hers in a will, the Three Men find theirs delivered — like a bottle of milk — on their doorstep. While in one way this dropping of a biological bond might seem quite progressive, in another the lack of process (no fat tummy! no visits to the hospital! no morning sickness!) does make 'having' a baby more of a consumer affair.

In these terms, Holly Hunter (like Glenn Close) is punished by having her ration book docked. BABY BOOM and THREE MEN, by contrast, represent the emotional equivalent of sale time in Bloomingdales. Martin Jacques, in the *Guardian*, recently suggested that the left should relate more strongly to consumer culture. I, however, would rather cry into my typewriter than check off my desires as items on life's shopping list.

N.S. 15 April 1988

Nightmare on Madison Avenue

Fatal Attraction

Last year I thought I had identified a new stereotype in American movies — the Single Working Woman. Frequently played by Debra Winger, this character is noted for being good at her job, neurotic about men, and having a bizarre assortment of food in her refrigerator (to which she often repairs at night).

She also tends to have that kind of permed-crinkly hair, a style that makes hair occupy a good deal of space, traditionally a sign of power. This is not an insignificant detail; when Debra Winger played the dying wife and mother in TERMS OF ENDEARMENT her hair hung right down flat like nature intended. Think about it.

Glenn Close, last seen with demurely swept-up hair in JAGGED EDGE, now reappears as an SWW much closer to the archetype, with snaky locks that give her the appearance of a Medusa. However, FATAL ATTRACTION doesn't just feature Glenn Close as the classically screwed-up SWW. On a second level of signification — which relies, in a sort of domino effect, on the first — it features the SWW as the HIV virus. And if on the first level the movie is a kind of 9½ WEEKS-style sex drama (both are directed by Adrian Lyne) fitting into that genre of films about yuppie sex lives in Manhattan, on the second level it is quite clearly a horror film, with both structural and thematic links to the whole genre of 'Body Horror', explored most interestingly in a film like THE FLY. Yet while Cronenberg uses the conventions of Horror in order to push our sympathies beyond their usual bounds — something I would argue is progressive — FATAL ATTRACTION employs Horror in order to rein them back sharply within the tight corral of the nuclear family. These two films probably represent the most diametrically opposed responses to Aids we have yet seen in the cinema.

The generic link between them is far from spurious: in locating FATAL ATTRACTION as a horror film I am not simply talking about its being frightening or its being 'about Aids'. Genre films usually have quite specific structures which vary very little no matter how different, superficially, the stories they hold together. There are also particular conventions regarding the way films within a particular genre are shot and edited. The *setting* for a film may belie the genre of its structure and shooting: for example, most critics identified the film OUTLAND

(1981) as a Western set in space, a sort of re-make of HIGH NOON in sci-fi-land with Gary Cooper replaced by Sean Connery. FATAL ATTRACTION is fundamentally a horror film in yuppie-melodrama-land; its whole structure becomes blindingly clear once you realize that the part usually played by the Thing/the Blob/the Bug is played by the SWW.

It is impossible to pursue this analysis further without revealing parts of the plot, so people who like surprises should stop here and come back after seeing the film. Yet it has been so widely hyped that most people must know its story by now. Michael Douglas plays a 'happily married' attorney, Dan Gallagher, who meets SWW publishing executive Alex Forrest (Close) over the sushi at a book launch and again at a business meeting on a weekend when his too-good-to-be-true wife Beth and cutesie-pie daughter Ellen are out of town. According to the publicity synopsis, Alex 'seduces' Dan — in other words, they go out for dinner and end up in her bed, a 'mistake' on his part which the film weakly psychologizes by showing his impulse to make love with his wife in the previous scene thwarted by having to take the family dog for its nightly shit on Manhattan's pavements.

Alex and Dan's sex sequence, true to form within the upwardly mobile city drama which I will from now on call *genre 1*, takes place in the kitchen and follows a tradition of cinematic fucking — the only appropriate word — launched by LAST TANGO IN PARIS. A closer analogy is with 9½ WEEKS which also links sex very strongly with both food and non-white ethnicity (after all, the white urban middle class' main taste of 'otherness' is through cuisine). Whereas there the couple meet in a Chinese grocery and pursue their affair through increasingly funky 'ethnic' venues of the city, here the lovers progress from sushi to a fashionable Latin disco in their quest for kicks. FATAL ATTRACTION deals with its need to locate the Other in the heart of the city by placing the entrance to Alex's apartment on a street corner where funkiness takes the form of a Jarmanesque brazier and people carrying meat carcasses to and fro. This kind of stuff has already become part of an eighties iconography of urban decadence and taboo sexuality; meanwhile the Gallaghers move wholesomely upstate to the country and keep pet rabbits. (The fact that Alex virtually lives in an abattoir ought to have alerted us to what she might do with these).

This city/country, Bad/Good dichotomy is kept up relentlessly even in the names: Alex gets a man's name while nobody could have a more long-suffering name than Beth (cf. *Little Women*). This very relentless-ness should be a clue to its social importance: clearly, the SWW poses a major threat if the film must resort to making her *cook bunnies*. In story terms, the outcome of Alex and Dan's encounter is that she becomes pregnant, and pursues him with increasing obsessiveness to make him take some responsibility. Since on paper everything she says makes perfect sense, the film must carry its Good/Bad message by other means.

Within *genre 1* this works as a series of ads. Lyne came to movies from commercials and not only is the whole film a continuous ad for family life (or condoms, whichever way you look at it), its component scenes are actually identifiable as specific ad types. There is the underwear ad where we see how much Dan really fancies his wife. There is the 'people like you' ad where the Gallaghers and their buddies go out bowling. There are the after-dinner coffee ads where their friends chat delightfully round the polished table. There is the 'listening bank' ad where they paint their new home wearing dungarees and perched cutely on step-ladders. The only blight in this adland packed with more *things* than I want to see in a lifetime (perhaps it is a play on Goods) is the phone, Alex's initial means of infiltration, which the film places ominously in the corner of shots. Alex herself is allowed no friends, no parties, no bowling, no knick-knacks — visually humiliated by her consumer barrenness which, even in terms of *genre 1*, does not explain but rather confirms her weirdness.

Indeed, pyschologically nothing adds up. Quite early on in Alex's 'pursuit' Dan says, 'If you tell my wife I'll kill you.' But if he has such a good marriage, why not just tell Beth himself? This key flaw in terms of *genre 1* is, however, essential to the functioning of *genre 2* because, if the underlying threat is infection, Dan's fear must simply be Alex/the virus reaching his wife and child. In a central scene, Dan comes home to find Alex *in his living room* talking to Beth, having answered the ad for their house. The shock effect of this scene is only explicable in terms of *genre 2*'s theme of contamination, for Alex does nothing to reveal her identity. She does, however, shake hands with the Gallaghers rather too lingeringly, exactly as if she were infecting them with some contagious disease.

The threat of invasion which Alex represents is conveyed cinematically by a classic Horror convention: the hand-held camera circling the family house, giving us the point of view of the monster roaming menacingly outside. While the image of the single woman pressing her nose against the window of family life might evoke poignancy at her exclusion — as in the famous ending of STELLA DALLAS — the use of the horror film's point-of-view convention evokes something far more monstrous than the mere sight of a distraught woman with frizzy hair. In fact, it evokes no person or character at all, but rather the lurking-ness of threat itself, structured, conversely, as an intrusion.

The horror film can eschew the logic whereby a sexual encounter may *result* in disease. Images, as Freud said, can collapse linear reasoning — the person sexually encountered *becomes* the disease. And Horror, as a popular genre structure, functions as a discourse way beyond the world of film.

FATAL ATTRACTION's opening here has been preceded by a phenomenal success in the USA, where box-office takings have been at record level. Such an unprecedented hit suggests that the fears mobilized by the film are widespread and deep, which makes the loathing it unleashes even more pernicious. This fear and loathing are part of the wider climate in which, for example, our government's 'promotion of homosexuality' bill is being passed[1]: and FATAL ATTRACTION represents a milestone of intolerance on the rightward path down which we seem to race faster every day.

N.S. 15 January 1988

Cutest Little Baby Face

RoboCop

Set in a dystopian 'near future' of high tech and dereliction, ROBOCOP looks set to follow BLADE RUNNER in its blend of glamour, violence and social commentary as the thinking person's version of a popular movie genre. Any vision of the future speaks, of course, about the present: and these films are seen by many as products of 'postmodernity', with their replicants and simulacra, global power systems and sealed image circuitry in which the world is as real as the latest broadcast.

Yet in their supposedly affect-less universes these films pursue

---

1   Clause 28 of this bill prohibited local authorities from 'promoting' homosexuality in any way. In particular, they were not to finance the representation (e.g. in public arts events, school teaching, library books) of gay and lesbian relations as 'pretended family relationships'. This became law as the Local Government (Amendment) Act 1988, the infamous Clause becoming Section 28 of it.

almost blindingly romantic aims: blinding because their simplicity and sentimentality are rendered invisible by the clever conceptual backdrops which explain their cult status (functioning alongside their appeal to a wider audience, shared with movies like PREDATOR and TERMINATOR).

I have to say that I found ROBOCOP a very enjoyable film. Its pace is zappy, its script is witty and the political satire is acute: we are whisked through a wryly topical future in which the Detroit Police Dept. has been privatized and is run by a business conglomerate, OmniConsumer Products (OCP). One current conception of future-ness seems to be embodied in the very construction of these words, OmniConsumer and RoboCop: a construction identical to that signal of newness found in the title of the new *TheGuardian* (or, come to that, the newest of soap operas, *EastEnders*). What does this obsessive semantic suture mean? What do RoboCop and *ReviewGuardian* have in common? The craze for welding adjectives and prepositions onto the nouns they qualify seems to me interesting in itself, but with RoboCop it assumes a literal form: the cybernetic amalgam of robot and cop which constitutes the key 'character' and, in a looser sense, the generic compound which explains the film's success — postmodern ideas and TERMINATOR-esque fantasies.

The film starts with a hilarious news broadcast in which inanely smiling announcers reveal that South Africa has the bomb but that crime is the most serious threat to US society, before ads offer up privatized medicine at the Family Heart Centre ('you pick the heart — we do the rest') and NUK'EM ('Another quality home game from Buffalo'). This kind of snappy critique of contemporary politics and media makes the film instantly appealing to people like myself and no doubt many *New Statesman* (not yet *NewStatesman*, thank God) readers; and is wound into the plot so that it is little surprise that the chief Baddy in OCP turns out to be the paymaster of the chief Baddy in the drugs-crime-ring — the cold-blooded, bespectacled villain who kills the cute, blond policeman Murphy in a scene of extraordinary sadism which provides, simultaneously, the organic fodder for the RoboCop creation, and the narrative rationale for RoboCop/Murphy's surfacing emotion of revenge.

The linking of business powers with organized crime is hardly a new theme — it provides the backdrop to, for example, THE BIG HEAT — and it is convenient to know that the real nasties are all, ultimately, in the pay of the capitalist pigs (abandoning any politicized notion of criminality). ROBOCOP is a brilliant thriller within this format, but what is really specific to its appeal is the grafting of certain infantile body-fantasies onto a satisfyingly political framework.

For within the social realm RoboCop is the ultimate right-on hero, saving a little old couple from being robbed in their sweetshop, protecting a woman who is about to be raped (even phoning a rape crisis centre) and generally doing good and useful deeds in accordance with his directives, which are to serve the public trust, uphold the law, and protect the innocent. The fourth (classified) directive prevents him from attacking any employee of OCP.

This is because an earlier model, the purely robotic 'enforcement droid' ED 209, has gone berserk in an exhilarating scene near the start of the film which leaves an OCP employee splatted all over the table at a board meeting. The comic-strip nature of this violence (straight from the Judge Dredd school) is characteristic of the whole film, whose explosions and eruptions are so extreme as to have an almost amoral, purely physical quality. But nothing better illustrates the film's strong bond with animation than the very existence of RoboCop — revived, in a kind of fantasy denial of death, after Murphy has been turned virtually into a sieve with bullets: 'he' doesn't die any more than Tweetie-Pie does when flattened by a steamroller. Despite its symbolic political language, this film actually functions in the prelinguistic realm of the Imaginary.

This centres on the *figure* of RoboCop. He embodies an infantile, ungendered (oral) vulnerability — suggested by his mouth, significantly the one part of his body visible under the helmet — combined with a fantasy *in*vulnerability, the machine part of him which has the power to carry out incredibly satisfying acts of violence in the name of Good (which fortunately coincides with his own revenge motive). This blond, baby-mouthed (he *eats baby food*) do-good machine touchingly combines Golem-like stirrings of human feeling with his super-human armoured physique. As an icon this figure is close to that of Rambo — who is equally baby-faced and practically the same shape: i.e. that of an American Footballer.

It hardly needs saying that this image of masculinity which, like Andrex, is soft/strong and very very long, is extraordinarily phallic. But it is also *Romantic*: in the classic sense of a split between inner self and outer shell. RoboCop physically embodies the notion of a child within, a sensitive core to be reached only by the most searching. In conjunction with a rigid masculinity this inner fragility suggests an innocence and lack of culpability that are linked with notions of being 'driven' and which can make acts of aggression seem almost poignant (as with sulky-puss Rambo). The fantasy of the metallic body covers a disgust at the frighteningly assailable flesh 'beneath' — while at the same time a sentimental attachment to the needs thus contained compensates for their suppression.

What ROBOCOP does, very well, is what many 'exploitation movies' do: take a popular, psychoanalytically resonant schlock genre (horror, sex, violence etc.) and 'fill' its structure with a political slant. What is interesting about ROBOCOP is that in bringing this format to a mainstream production it has become a 'phenomenon' in that apparently meaningful but totally unexamined way that many things are in journalism today. It is, as I said, highly enjoyable: but why? Partly, of course, because it is an almost dazzlingly speedy film, whose camera dives in and out of scenes like a big dipper and never leaves us in one place for a second longer than necessary.

But also because it allows us to let loose a very simple, self-dramatizing fantasy in the language of a sophisticated knowingness; a double gratification not unfamiliar to followers of various postmodernist theories. In this ROBOCOP couldn't be more of the moment: it provides the left-wing brain with just enough activity to make it feel busy and mask the fact that emotionally and morally it isn't taxed in the slightest.

N.S. 19 February 1988

Exorcism of a Nation's Guilt

Platoon

It isn't often that a movie draws editorial comment from the *New York Times*, but last month its op.ed. page carried the serious suggestion that all young boys should be taken to see PLATOON. Winner of four Oscars, topping the box office here for weeks,[1] PLATOON is the movie Americans love to love about the war they have learned to love to hate. Director Oliver Stone has become a national hero; a Vietnam vet, the fact that he raised the money for the film and produced it outside the

---

1   This column was written from the USA.

studios on a budget somewhat lower than the millions required by Hollywood is seen as proof that it represents some imperative drive to expression of the Vietnam experience.

For the idea common to both the American public's and publications' response to PLATOON is that this is the film that really tells it like it is (was). 'I think what you're saying is that for the first time you really understand what happened over there', Stone told the Academy of Motion Picture Arts as he accepted his awards last month. The national dailies unanimously concurred, and even the left press seems to share the popular view. The film makes its own aspiration to tell it like it is very clear at the outset, with bodies in bags leaving Saigon and the much remarked close-up of flies crawling over our hero's skin as he toils through the jungle. But, although PLATOON continues to wear its nitty-gritty naturalistic pretensions on its sleeve for perhaps the first half hour, it is fundamentally an entirely formulaic war movie, more 'artistic' than many in its genre but true to conventions in both characters and narrative.

We join the platoon with Chris Taylor (Charlie Sheen) who, having volunteered from college, conveniently provides us with a literate, white, middle-class sensibility through which to observe the war. With the structure of identification typical of the genre, his 'greenness' channels our entry into army life; as he becomes absorbed in it, so do we. Like all its genre the film places a high value on good soldiery and we rapidly become engaged in the mechanics of combat. Other generic clichés abound: The Bad Sgt Barnes (Tom Berenger) is covered in ugly scars while the Good Sgt Elias (Willem Dafoe) is a hippy hero endowed with almost supernatural insights about the outcome of the war — and with an almost supernatural capacity to absorb lead. The most gut-wrenching moment of the film is when he staggers out of the jungle raising his arms to the US helicopter as Barnes flies on, deliberately leaving him to die.

This Christ-like image is the one chosen to advertise PLATOON, with the caption 'The first casualty of war is innocence'. This now ubiquitous slogan contains the key to the real issue at stake not only in the film but in the wider discourse surrounding it. PLATOON's whole narrative is a journey from innocence to experience, as the clean-cut boy finally becomes a man, covered in mud and blood. The film's opening quotation from Ecclesiasticus, 'Rejoice O Young Man in thy Youth', the elegiac use of Samuel Barber's Adagio for Strings and the nostalgic use of 1960s pop music all suggest a mourning for not merely an individually but a nationally lost innocence and youth. Yet, even at the very end, its hero still has that shell-shocked baby look reminiscent of Rambo.

Rambo's Look — an icon of our time — is central to the way US macho values are coping in representation with the frustrating failures of US imperialism. Rambo may be a maniac but his expression resembles nothing so much as that of a hurt, sulky child. Within that enormous, muscular body, it suggests, lurks a lost, innocent little boy, dumb with righteous pain. Nothing could more nearly express a certain strand of sentiment within the USA in relation to 'Nam. TOP GUN has already shown us that US marines are really cute, mixed-up kids. In PLATOON, innocence is set up as a key value through the very emphasis on its destruction by experience.

But most revealing of all is the way the innocence/experience dichotomy displaces another, more telling, dichotomy hinged on the same word but more threatening to the American public. For the other quality which is the obvious opposite of innocence is guilt. This is the emotion conspicuous by its absence from the whole PLATOON discourse. The film manages to displace a moral focus from what the US army did to the Vietnamese onto a fundamentally macho conflict within its own ranks: the massacre of an entire village — clearly standing in some way for My Lai — serves PLATOON's narrative only to detonate its more central antagonism, the almost familial feud between the two US sergeants, whom Taylor refers to at the end as fathers. Whatever problematic feelings might be engendered by this terrible act are thus neatly dealt with through the simple device of splitting: the human face of the US army is embodied in the biblically-named martyr Elias, while all its evil is loaded onto the scarred face of Barnes, whom Taylor eventually kills in a final act of expiation.

So why is this need for absolution surfacing now? There have been many generic films about Vietnam, for example THE BOYS IN COM-PANY C (1977) or RUMOR OF WAR (1979), besides the better known DEER HUNTER or APOCALYPSE NOW. PLATOON is not so very different from any of these, yet it has become the focus of an unprecedented amount of public attention. It seems to tap into a sense of unease, an escalation of national guilt which has as much to do with Contra atrocities in Central America as with Vietnam. What is so interesting when President Reagan admits his 'error' over Irangate and arms for the Contras, is that the very fact of his 'confession' seems to absolve him of the guilt that, logically, it confirms. At a time when American imperialism seems just as amok as it ever did in Vietnam, PLATOON, whatever its avowed intentions, corresponds to some national search

for a discourse of purging and healing; a way of, precisely, confessing
and remaining innocent at the same time.

N.S. 1 May 1987

Carry On Up the Waterfall

The Mission
Latino

So worked up has this country become about British cinema that any
Puttnam-Goldcrest production appears not as a mere film, but, as the
trailer for THE MISSION grandly puts it, '*destined* to become the *motion
picture event* of the year'. The attention paid to Puttnam's films outside
the cinema is becoming par for the course: in this case, THE MISSION
(directed by Roland Joffé of THE KILLING FIELDS) is being linked with
Survival International, an extremely worthwhile campaign for the
rights of threatened tribal peoples, and the film's own missionary aura
of 'doing good' seems to be part of the general canonization of
Puttnam and his national achievement.

However, THE MISSION is not about threatened tribal peoples. The
film's advertising shows at a glance who its subjects really are: at the
top of a waterfall, in huge letters, 'Robert De Niro' 'Jeremy Irons' and
below, between inset pictures of them, 'THE MISSION'. (The ad is too
epic to bother with 'and' or 'in'.) In smaller writing, the film's plot is
accurately summarized: 'Deep in the jungles of South America two
men bring civilization to a native tribe. Now, after years of struggle
together, they find themselves on opposite sides in a dramatic fight for
the natives' independence.' (i.e. for the natives' continued dependence
on *them*). 'One will trust in the power of prayer. One will believe in the
might of the sword.'

And there you have it, with a lot of lush cinematography and the
kinds of virtuoso sequences (e.g. a whole army climbing a waterfall)
that distract you into wondering how they did it. In essence, the movie
is a kind of spiritual TOP GUN, with Jesuit priests Irons and De Niro
'up there with the best of the best' in a different sense. The intensity of

the relationship between these two white men (exchanging crosses instead of US army medallions) is the only real dynamic in the film — placing it in the current flood of homo-erotic movies.

In one memorable sequence De Niro undergoes a self-enforced penance by dragging his worldly goods up the sheer rock face of a waterfall. When he arrives at the top barely able to stand, an Indian cuts the rope and the whole load falls down the cliff into the water. Suddenly relieved of his burden, De Niro bursts into tears. At this key moment, after showing De Niro's weeping face, what does the film cut to? To the face of the Indian who has brought about this crucial symbolic release (an option which would have opened the way for more interest in, and interaction with, the Indians as characters, rather than camera-fodder)? No, to Jeremy Irons. It's hard to remember, at times, that we're not back in Brideshead, with Anthony Andrews, instead of De Niro, exchanging loaded looks with him. Like almost all films made by imperialist cultures about their pasts, this film goes deep into the hearts of the oppressors, while leaving the oppressed to figure as nameless pawns in the so-much-more-exciting story of individual white heroes. (The Indians in the 'threatened tribe' don't even warrant individual names in the credits.)

LATINO, Haskell Wexler's first feature since MEDIUM COOL, is a much braver and more intelligent attempt to show the effects of Western imperialism on a Latin American country, this time contemporary Nicaragua. Its protagonist is a Chicano US soldier, Eddie Guerrero, who becomes increasingly disenchanted with his role in aiding the Contras as he realizes what the US army is actually doing in Nicaragua. Overtly, both LATINO and THE MISSION face the problem of getting an audience to care what happens to a group of foreigners. LATINO does this in part by setting up some positive image of life in a Nicaraguan village *before* it is attacked — and by having Eddie become emotionally involved with two Nicaraguans: a woman whose father is killed by Contras, and a young boy prisoner who, despite all Eddie's efforts, remains loyal to his village. THE MISSION doesn't even bother to depict Indian life before European settlement, but deals with the same problem by having its Indians learn to sing chorales and play violins, so that their destruction can ultimately be symbolized by a violin floating down the river — along with other debris of *European* 'civilization'.

In both films the narrative is structured through the dilemma of those who perpetrate, rather than those who suffer, colonialism. In THE MISSION this takes the literal form of a letter, dictated by the papal envoy who ruthlessly seals the fate of the Missions and philosophizes his regrets very eloquently in the process. In LATINO the story is Eddie's change of heart. But this takes place through a kind of spurious racial solidarity: i.e. he is the same race as the Nicaraguans he's sent to destroy. When he takes a tortilla from one old woman's house, he says, 'that coulda been mama's kitchen' and, about a machine-gunned boy, 'he walked just like my kid brother'.

Obviously the important point being made is that those oppressed within the USA have much in common with those oppressed *by* the USA. But the device of the 'Latino' shares the same premise as THE MISSION: that similarity is a prerequisite of solidarity. The fact that the Indians are singing European church music as the army approaches to massacre them is meant to rend our hearts in a way that, supposedly, their making their own form of music would not. The Other has to be made the Same as ourselves. As the violins play in the jungle, and Latino tastes tortillas like his mother's, it is not a common humanity that is being asserted: that is just what is being denied, if it is only by seeing a mirror-image of our own culture that we can recognize the value of another.

N.S. 24 October 1986

Founding Father

The Mosquito Coast

Western culture, founded on the romance of exploration and funded by an economy of expansion, now faces the closing of its frontiers. There is scarcely a part of the globe where Coca-Cola — to use the obvious example — is not bought and sold; virgin territory, the stuff of both dreams and dollars, has run out. There are no new places to 'discover'.

Yet it is because exploration has been not merely incidental to our way of life but the means of its inception, that its mythology is so resonant even — or especially — at the point of its exhaustion. The enormous glut of travel writing currently in vogue, including the best-selling popularity of Lucy Irvine's *Castaway*, could be seen as one symptom of this. Another, perhaps, is the way the jungle looms ever larger in contemporary movie imagery even as it is being diminished daily in reality. THE MISSION, AGUIRRE WRATH OF GOD, FITZCAR-RALDO, APOCALYPSE NOW, and THE EMERALD FOREST are all examples from the last decade. Where once explorers dragged what were to become the means of economic exploitation up waterfalls and down great rivers, today movie equipment follows the same paths to provide us with the after-image of that great project of discovery and conquest.

The fact that CASTAWAY opens as a major film next week shows that the Crusoe image is a still popular part of our mythic repertoire. Robinson Crusoe has been such a tenacious figure in this culture because he represents its contradictory (if you think about it) ideologies of exploration and self-sufficiency: in this, Defoe's fiction was both symbolic and symptomatic of the moment of early capitalism. Allie Fox, hero of THE MOSQUITO COAST, is trying to return to that moment; a firm believer in American values, he just doesn't like the way they've turned out, and takes to the jungle where he recreates the early days of the industrial revolution with his wonderful ice-making machine.

If exploration is the 'pure' form of colonization, invention is the 'pure' form of industrialization; and before he turns explorer Allie Fox starts off as an inventor in a small rural community. The stress on his filing of patents in particular recalls that exciting period of the great steam and mechanical inventions whose impact on rural America is so vividly described by Sherwood Anderson in his novel *Poor White*. It is interesting that the Amish community, backdrop to director Peter Weir's previous film WITNESS, also exemplifies an early, 'pure' form of US frontier culture; at once pioneering and self-sufficient, both the Amish and Allie Fox's Mosquito settlement (at its best) are reminiscent of a 'good' township in a Ford western like MY DARLING CLEMENTINE. Indeed in his search for America's moment of innocence Fox follows the trail right back to the pilgrim fathers: his family celebrate their 'first Thanksgiving' practically *dressed* as Puritan settlers, in a strange drive to the pristine form of the very culture he tries to escape but comes, increasingly, to represent. For the great ice-making machine (a crazy symbol of the civilization of the ice-box) ultimately brings destruction and pollution in a microcosm of the history Fox tried to turn back.

Paul Theroux's book (adapted by Paul Schrader for the movie) was narrated by Fox's son, so these events had no narrative independence of the boy's point of view: seen at first from 'inside' Fox's ideology, they were only later described more critically as the boy's oedipal trajectory detached him increasingly from his father's grip. However, the film (despite intermittent voice-overs by the boy) is — inevitably — narrated through images, and while the boy's position remains a component of the story it is no longer its boundary. Where the novel's very structure was the boy's changing perception of his father's obsessions, the film signals from the start that Fox is 'nutty': for example, through the 'here he goes again' reactions of the DIY salesmen in the very first scene, or — also early in the film — where Fox's demagogic ramblings are drowned by the noise of a chainsaw, rendering him a comic rather than a powerful figure; and not least through the almost manic way Harrison Ford gets into the role, rather like Jack Nicholson at his most rampant.

This shift in perspective is an important one, for in its visual autonomy of the book's narrative structure the film takes on a more direct relation to us as viewers. And if the character of Allie Fox embodies the contradictions at the birth of our culture, in this dimension the film itself is symptomatic of the contradictions of its decline. By losing the narrative pivot of the boy's-eye view for our own as spectators, and by placing us outside Fox from the start, the film becomes less about changing *perception* than about a cumulative spectacle. We are presented with the lushness of the jungle and blond suntanned characters (the girl twins seem to have no function except to look like cute Coppertone ads): a *visual* return to the romance of exploration even while the plot is actually an undermining of it. Cut loose from the more subtle critique of Fox's values, the movie can be viewed simply as a good adventure story, where the interest lies in 'What happens next': it has become family entertainment.

Schrader's screenplay does re-emphasize the father/son relation with its obvious commentary on authoritarian patriarchy: another way in which Fox represents 'Founding Father' culture run riot. The point of view of the oppressed (the son) is only finally liberated by the death of the father. But to take the analogy between its content and the film's symptomatic level a step further: it will be another kind of liberation when the fascinating spectacle of our own civilization re-enacting its past finally accedes to the diverse points of view of those cultures which it 'settled' and 'explored'.

N.S. 13 February 1987

Burnt Offering

The Sacrifice
You Know It Makes Sense

It is a curious fact that the strongest supporters of competitive capitalism are the first to pay homage to spiritual values when voiced by a Soviet dissident (cf. Irina Ratushinskya). Similarly, many of those keenest on THE SACRIFICE are among those least prepared to make one: David Robinson raves about Tarkovsky in *The Times*; 'No other film-maker has a stronger sense of the moral purpose and necessity of art' he writes — from behind barbed wire.[1] The 'cry from the soul' (as leading actress Susan Fleetwood described THE SACRIFICE) is easier to hear from Siberia than from just around the corner.

Robinson's review is typical of many and its repeated references to 'genius' and 'destiny' show the extent to which Tarkovsky himself has become mythologized, until it is impossible to discuss the film without being dominated by the facts that he couldn't work in the USSR, and that he's dead — which makes any criticism seem sacrilegious. Tarkovsky's commitment both to film-making and to his own vision of his spiritual purpose are clear enough, even if his notion of his prophetic role is a little irritating. What is harder to account for is the concerted critical response which acts as if his vision weren't questionable.

Set in Bergman country THE SACRIFICE has the trappings of a Chekhov play, both in interior decor (strangely un-modern) and in its isolated group of protagonists. There is a philosophy professor, a postman, a doctor, and then the supporting cast of the philosopher's wife, daughter, two women servants, and his son, a key figure referred to throughout as 'Little Man'. The male characters say profound things, carrying the film's ideas: 'our culture is defective. . .', 'there is an imbalance between our spiritual and material developments'. The women, as so often, speak less and symbolize more (though the daughter's function, apart from balancing a pear on her knee and

---

1 *The Times*, along with other Murdoch-owned papers, was produced from 'Fortress Wapping' after large numbers of Trade Unionist employees were sacked in 1986. A literally violent dispute ensued; the newspaper building was fortified in military fashion while protesters and picketers were viciously attacked by police.

walking across a room naked, is hard to divine). The philosopher's wife seems to stand for the grasping materiality of 'defective' culture — she complains bitterly that he is no longer the famous actor she married — while his lowliest servant ('Maria') represents a 'true' spirituality. Tarkovsky never throws into question the sentimental sexism which underpins this tired 'religious' dichotomy, rather it seems to be that of his own sensibility.

The theme of sacrifice is introduced by the postman's expensive present to the philosopher, whose protestations he rebuffs with the central message: 'Every gift involves a sacrifice, if not, what kind of gift would it be?' Soon afterwards the group hear on TV of imminent nuclear war. The wife has a hysterical fit which involves a lot of waving and spreading of legs, her stockings falling down — an embarrassing and peculiarly humiliating vision of sexuality. She and the daughter are quickly given tranquilizers by the doctor, while the philosopher promises God that if he (God) will avert the catastrophe he (the philosopher) will sacrifice everything he loves, specifically his home and his son. The postman tells him he can prevent the disaster by sleeping with Maria, so he cycles to her house where they make love, her bed floating in the air like an altar. The next morning it is as if time has been reversed: there is no nuclear war. The philosopher keeps his promise by burning his house — to the distress of the family — and then getting himself carried off in an ambulance, leaving his son lying under the tree they planted together at the beginning.

Tarkovsky's dream-like style suggests a psychological rather than a literal sequence of events, so putting the plot like this sounds rather crude. Nevertheless, it is what 'happens' in the film, and is therefore material for analysis. THE SACRIFICE is without doubt finely made — in particular its slow-moving long shots and tiny flashes of black and white among the carefully controlled colour. But what is it really saying? According to Tarkovsky its key issue is 'the absence in our culture of room for a spiritual existence' and he has been quoted so often that it has become taken for granted that this is what the film is about. But without such statements, the film would be much harder to interpret. Is spiritual synonymous with sacrificial? If this is a message of redemption through sacrifice, who is meant to sacrifice what? It is hard to tell how one is meant to respond to the burning of the house, but it seems a completely pointless destruction, not just on a realist but on the film's own parabolic level. What kind of God is it that demands such loss? *Does* every meaningful gift have to involve a sacrifice (a curiously arithmetical notion which feeds into certain proto-fascist ideas)? Is suffering a good thing? And *why do Western critics practically worship this film?*

My own analysis is that it does, in part, appeal to values that are repressed in our culture — in particular, to some hazy sense of bourgeois guilt (how else could this house-burning be so popular among so many mortgage-holders?) while simultaneously, because of its real-life context, reassuring us that West is Best: He Couldn't Have Made This Film In The Soviet Union. And this much is true: it is typical of our society that the film can make so many well-fed people wax so lyrical about our lack of spiritual values at the same time as allowing them to feel that the system which feeds them is spiritually superior because people like Tarkovsky can make films in it.

Actually, Tarkovsky did have trouble in the West raising money for his films, though not in getting them shown. However, those trying to publicize the dangers of Aids and the means of preventing it have met with repeated censorship. A short, comic ad by young film-maker Ken Butler has finally reached the independent cinema circuit. This 2-minute film shows Margaret Thatcher (played by Gaye Brown) telling the country of her concern about Aids and holding up a condom — 'YOU KNOW IT MAKES SENSE.' It takes a few minutes before you realize that this is, in fact, precisely what the government *should* be doing.

Flippant as it may sound, there is a connection between these two items. The values of THE SACRIFICE give a meaning to suffering; and if you can make people believe that suffering has a meaning you have less reason to do anything about it.

N.S. 23 January 1987

Oh What a Beautiful Business

The Secret of My Success

If the fact of Brantley Foster's success is contained in the film's title, its source is contained in the opening scenes: the boy comes from a cornflakes ad, a small farm in Kansas (Dorothy country, as his mother's dress and the lighting remind us). We first see the hero behind an enormous heap of corn; and though the movie quickly follows his rainbow to New York, his origins are constantly referred to and play against the ethos by which he succeeds.

Brantley (Michael J. Fox) arrives at his first job to find the company subject to a take-over: executives are moving their belongings out of offices, an image of physical change that will be repeated endlessly throughout the film. Not deterred, he charms his way into the mailroom of a big company run by a distant uncle. On his first day in this lowly job, a workmate shows him a sacked executive crying in one of the offices; and the next day, on seeing the office empty, Brantley enters, sits down on the swivel chair behind the desk, takes in the view from this seat of power, then answers the phone when it rings. From this moment he invents another (impossibly Ivy League) name, Courtney Whitfield, gets a plate put on the door, has personalized stationery printed and starts to lead a double life as mailboy and executive, doing two jobs with positively Thatcherite zeal. This involves, more than anything else, an awful lot of dressing and undressing as countless times a day in office, lifts and cupboards he changes in and out of his executive suit/mailroom clothes.

This is more than a detail: it is one half of the film's ideology. Brantley's mailroom buddy refers to the executives as 'Suits' and, when Brantley asks why, his friend says, 'That's what happens to a man when he puts on a necktie.' This emphasis on clothes as both the vehicles and the signs of success works in relation to another theme, which is Brantley's conviction that 'deep inside I know I can do practically anything if I get the chance'. There is something existential in this idea that *being* a businessman is in fact looking like one and acting like one. Robert Warshow once wrote of gangster films that the hoodlum's means of success is also the content of his success: nothing could be more appropriate to the world of business where, if the means of success is talking on telephones and going to meetings, so is the content.

This sense of trappings is conveyed formally by the film's extraordinary visual and musical structure, which is basically like a series of ads with small plot links between them. For narrative alone seems unable to convey the *joy* of business; instead, at each step up in his rapid career, Brantley is the subject of a kind of breathless, orgasmic montage sequence where the accoutrements of his success are glorified to an uplifting music track. The day after he has secured his named office, he enters the building to the accompaniment of a song, 'I'm walking on sunshine': this is exactly what he appears to be doing since he could hardly be propelled through the ensuing montage on his own two feet. This medley of images consists of swinging through endless glass doors, slapping fellow executives on the back in corridors and gliding past rows and rows of secretaries who greet him sweetly as he pauses merely to say a special hello to the prettiest. His new familiarity with business is illustrated by his intimacy with its equipment as he nudges filing cabinets shut with his elbow, caresses desk tops and juggles with his briefcase — all to music. In a similar 'ad' sequence, two stages later, top financiers are assembled on the lawns of the MD's country house and we are given a montage of Brantley ('Whitfield') perched on top of a pavilion consorting with them to *Messiah*-like music: here, the very heights of business are shown as important men talking, gesturing and using calculators in not just wealthy but positively Edenic rural surroundings.

The ease of Brantley's rise in business is underlined by the equal ease with which others can fall; the crucial glimpse of removals men carrying pictures out of offices in the first company reminds me of *Vanity Fair*, where Thackeray has the same pictures and furniture moving in and out of auction rooms and ownership as the fortunes of mere people ebb and flow. Several conflicting philosophies are precariously blended here: while the film's visuals emphasize the slippery surface of finance, its narrative assures us that Brantley is a Good Guy, providing innate values and meaning in an otherwise postmodern world where the image of business refers only to business itself. For the elusive referent of all this 'business' is *factories*, and Brantley is the only character to mention them. When he becomes Courtney Whitfield the company is trying to sell off assets and contract: he is the saviour whose watchword is 'expansion', and he prevents closures by arguing that this is the soundest business sense. Brantley is an injection of corn-fed wholesomeness and 'common sense' into the world of city dealings: an impossible fantasy of the country and the city together, natural goodness and acquired competitiveness, creating the impression that not only is business glamorously ruthless but the good guys win and all is for the best in the best of all possible worlds.

The plot climax of the film is Brantley's and his girlfriend's and his secretary's and his mailroom buddy's eruption from the depths of the mailroom to the heights of the boardroom, as they reveal (à la TRADING PLACES) that they've bought out the company — a moment that has all the excitement of workers' control and when, significantly, Brantley doesn't wear his executive outfit but is revealed for the first time to the board as himself: underneath every Suit is the true self of Leisurewear. But once the film's narrative, which corresponds to its moral mode, has let us feel the deep righteousness of Brantley's success, it only remains for its montage mode to return us to the sensuous world of surfaces and let us *see* it: the visual and musical climax is a glittering sequence, in the genre of an up-market perfume or diamond ad, where the heroes and heroines dress up glamorously to go to the opera.

Our protestant culture is founded on a troublesome double-bind: 17th-century Puritans worried themselves sick about whether 'being' good was a state or an action. THE SECRET OF MY SUCCESS triumphs where philosophers have failed, offering up, through a combination of film's own forms, both original goodness and existential success.

N.S. 3 July 1987

Man for Our Season

Wall Street

There is a new, glossy magazine on the news stands at the moment called *Excel*. Aimed at the aspiring young businessman, it contains fashion, psychological tips about getting ahead, financial advice — but what is really a sign of our times is its glamour: a sort of *Playboy* with the sex taken out, it represents the extraordinary eroticization of money in this sexually troubled era.

The financial flow-chart is the centre-fold pin-up; looking good is for impressing clients, not lòvers; keeping fit is about performance at the office, not in bed. For the young and ambitious the flow of anxiety can now run seamlessly from the world of the Clearasil ad to the world of the clearing bank.

It is through this world that Oliver Stone's WALL STREET propels its fresh-faced investment broker Bud Fox (Charlie Sheen) — whose name echoes that of Michael J. Fox, hero of SECRET OF MY SUCCESS. Both films start with a young man trying to push his way into business: in SECRET this initially involves getting *any* job in a big company, while in WALL STREET the Sheen character is already a broker and the push is for a big financial client, Gordon Gekko (Michael Douglas). However, their equivalent scenes are extremely similar in that they show a young man using enormous ingenuity, sheer persistence and desperate *chutzpah*, just to gain an audience, in both cases, with an older and more powerful man. The energy that goes into 'being seen', in these scenarios, suggests a strongly oedipal relationship: but while SECRET OF MY SUCCESS is like a fantasy resolution of oedipal conflicts (sleeping with the boss' wife, taking over the business, then ultimately getting an acceptably non-oedipal girl-friend) WALL STREET's troubled story of two fathers (one of whom does indeed pass on a girlfriend to the young man) is not so neatly tied up.

In PLATOON Oliver Stone placed young GI Charlie Sheen between Good and Bad Fathers Sergeants Elias and Barnes; the former mellow and cynical about the outcome of the war, the latter obsessive and desperate to win. Not only is Sergeant Elias the repository of the film's own morality, showing compassion, courage, etc. — his view of the Vietnam war has been proved *right*: he is on the side of history. PLATOON struck a note that reverberated through American culture with the easy harmony of hindsight.

In WALL STREET, however, the Good and Bad Fathers are placed differently in history. Gekko, the charismatic and ruthless financier who takes Fox under his wing to make money for both of them, is clearly on paper the baddy. The Good Father is Bud Fox's (and Sheen's) own father, a mechanic and union rep with a small airline, who unknowingly provides his son with the inside information which lets him into the charmed Gekko set. The Conflict of the Fathers climaxes when Gekko's plan for buying the airline — masterminded by Fox Jr. — turns out to involve closing it down, selling off its assets, and spending the pension fund. When Bud finally crosses his mentor by switching the sale to a rival investor, Gekko, having covered his own tracks, lets Fox get arrested for insider dealing. However, ultimately Fox betrays Gekko by taping his 'I taught you everything you know' speech at their last showdown. He ends up true to his real father: 'I'm going to create, instead of living off the buying and selling of others.'

This distinction between producing, and merely buying and selling money, is stressed throughout: Gekko says, 'I create nothing — I own' and the occasional glimpse of the Fox father (Martin Sheen) in overalls, spanner in hand, provides the contrasting image. But the film isn't really about the opposition of labour and capital so much as that of industry and finance; and this is where its historical context inflects its imagery and values despite the 'ideologically sound' plot. With the near-collapse of the traditional manufacturing infrastructure, capital- ism — ever adaptable — has shifted bases from industrial to finance capital; father Fox represents a morality whose base is declining, while father Gekko represents an idea whose time has apparently come. The alignment of the film's subtext with this idea is probably unirten- tional, given Stone's strong 'message' — yet Gekko is the heart of the film, visually and in terms of energy: he gives out a kind of warmth despite his ruthlessness, while the real father is given very little screen time and no memorable lines (Gekko's 'lunch is for wimps' being my favourite). We are offered no insight into the Fox father's life or feelings, while Gekko is given frequent opportunities to explain himself and his motives.

The most powerful of these comes at the AGM of a company which he takes to task, in the middle of taking it over, for wastage and inefficiency. The speech he gives is the centre of the film and perhaps also hits something that illuminates the concept of 'being on the side of history'. In his impassioned plea to the shareholders Gekko invokes greed as not only good, but in tune with nature: 'Greed *works*, greed captures the evolutionary spirit, greed will save the USA. . .' and so on. It is the Darwinian evocation of evolution which suggests that at some level the film is very much concerned with being on the side of the times. Its energetic camera really gets off on the share price figures gliding across the screens of the broking room; there is an orgiastic little scene in Fox's new flat where a battery of electronic-age cooking equipment is used to produce home-made sushi, fresh pasta, advertisement-style food; there are even Gekko's endearing red braces, which somehow make him look as if he *is* a worker (Bud's ersatz son-ship is signalled by his own acquisition of braces). Early on in their relationship Gekko gives Bud money to buy a new suit; this is humiliatingly echoed when Bud gives his real father money for the same purpose.

Since people are going on about the sixties/eighties difference at the moment I'll throw my bit in: if this were the 1960s Bud's father *would* be glamorized — would be the repository of masculinity, strong, sexy, with that metaphorical muscularity which comes from being on the ascendant (think of Albert Finney, and the glamour and sexiness of being working-class in the films and novels of that time). The financiers and businessmen, on the other hand, would be — indeed were seen through sixties eyes to be — sterile, dry, weak, boring pasty faces behind the *Financial Times* on commuter trains. But the business drama is now the thriller of our times; the working-class hero (Gekko is non-WASP, a City College boy, Fox's father is a mechanic) rises and falls in what is essentially a gangster film without guns: the structure is the same. And both gangsters and businessmen really want one thing — MORE. 'How many yachts can you waterski behind?' Fox asks Gekko — but this drama isn't about use-value. It's about exchange.

For money, in exchange, *represents* value; and this is the great era, supposedly, of representation. The referent, the thing represented, slides off into history. If Bud's father *creates* value, nevertheless he has no part to play in the glistening world of its circuitry, where our present-day dramas take place. Stone's sixties morality is ineffectually acted out in the imagery of the 1980s: whose glossy seductiveness, more than any of the characters, is what really Succeeds in this film.

N.S. 6 May 1988

Up the Balls Pond Road

Prick Up Your Ears

Oh, for the days before Islington was fashionable. When rented accommodation was cheap, when a duffle coat was just a duffle coat, when you could have it away on the emergency staircase because the Northern Line lifts worked. '*London was still quite exciting then. Remember that? No, no, you wouldn't.'* (I do, I do!) *'That was when?' '1967.'*

ABSOLUTE BEGINNERS and DANCE WITH A STRANGER have brought us what we used to think of as the London of the future as the London of the past; now PRICK UP YOUR EARS taps the same time fault. I am as much of a sucker as anyone for seeing my landscape invested with both nostalgia and illicit sexuality: as the Holloway Odeon throws its red neon across my desk in the 1987 twilight, the image of Orton's 1967 *Evening Standard* award lying in the urinal in Holloway gents while someone sucks him off provides at once a hotline to the past and a transgressive thrill. *'A homosexual, Miss Battersby.' 'In* Islington?' *'Haven't you noticed? Large areas of the borough are being restored and painted Thames Green.'*

Leaving aside the intriguing fact that my Islington council block has just been restored and painted Thames Green, I can't help feeling that this rich vein of the film speaks to something more than my local concerns. Trying to unravel what it means for us today to see gay (except it wasn't widely called that then) sex on the Northern Line is not an easy matter, but this movie is as much about an obsessively self-conscious view of our own post-war past as it is about gay relationships during that time.

It is Alan Bennett's script (based on John Lahr's biography) that introduces this focus. The Orton story — up-and-coming playwright murdered by his older, increasingly neglected lover Halliwell — is well known. But its telling through the double flashback device of Lahr's investigation and Margaret Ramsay's (Orton's agent's) memories, places the entire story squarely in the realm of both personal and public memory. The Lahr character's American ignorance treats us to endless nostalgic re-interpretations: *'What was the Festival of Britain?' 'Oh, that was when it all came off the ration.' 'You mean food and stuff.' 'Life, dear. Sex. Everything.'* So Orton and Halliwell make love for the first time during the 1953 Coronation broadcast in their rented room in, of course, Islington, where the landlady bemoans the first greengrocers becoming an antique shop. The yearning for pre-bourgeoisification and the wish for something to transgress become hard to separate.

Interestingly, director Stephen Frears' last film, MY BEAUTIFUL LAUNDRETTE, invested what one might call post-bourgeois London of the 1980s with just such a thrill through gay romance. But in PRICK UP YOUR EARS, if there is one crucial point where his direction and Bennett's script seem to be at odds, it is in the presentation of Halliwell. Bennett's most interesting addition to the Orton story is his drawing out of the 'wife' theme — Halliwell's increasing frustration at washing the underclothes of his more famous lover, seeing his ideas unacknowledged in Orton's plays — and winding it into the outer narrative of Lahr, who also has a wife in the background, cooking, editing, acknowledged in the usual way in the preface: 'thanks to my wife Anthea without whom. . .' blah blah blah. This angle is clearly intended to give a 'wider', i.e. straight, application to the Orton/ Halliwell 'marriage'.

However, in its visual presentation of their uneven relationship the film makes Halliwell unnecessarily grotesque, an ageing queen hardly able to put his wig on straight. Judging by the photos available, Halliwell was chunkily good-looking. Yet the film externalizes his frustration and sense of failure literally on his overpainted face — you almost expect to see his make-up running à la DEATH IN VENICE — while Orton is cheekily cute and attractive throughout. Thus, in a way, Orton is salvaged for straight culture while Halliwell is sacrificed to it.

This caricature is not something written into Bennett's screenplay, but its tone is in keeping with another equally significant piece of distorting caricature which is very Bennett indeed. This is his apparent inability (cf. A PRIVATE FUNCTION) to envisage the 'lower' or working class as anything other than *lower middle class*. In a nostalgic haze which passes for social comment, lace curtains, rubber gloves, *Housewives' Choice* and white-collar aspirations become blended together in an all-purpose LMC which is like one great collective character in a Mike Leigh play. Orton grew up in a council house in Leicester, with a background that I would describe as working-class. Yet Bennett is working in a genre where the very word 'Leicester' can be used as a gag all to itself ('He can't have learned it in Leicester', 'I hope nobody hears about this in Leicester' are key jokes) and further laughs are raised by the mere mention of Epsom, East Croydon, Reading and New Zealand.

Purley may have been funny once in Pinter but this is closer to *Private Eye*'s overworked Neasden. These jokes aren't just snobbery, but *confused* snobbery: in a bizarre irony, the post-war working class is portrayed as a caricature of its own aspirations. Whatever problems Orton might have faced being gay in relation to this background are subsumed in the royal road to camp which leads apparently seamlessly from his mother's false teeth to his lover's false hair.

Camp class comedy has a history running back through *Monty Python* to the radio shows of my childhood (even today the thought of Kenneth Williams' rendering of the words 'Balls Pond Road' makes me giggle). But it doesn't seriously investigate either class or sexuality. Ultimately, perhaps the nostalgia invoked by PRICK UP YOUR EARS is as much for its own generic forerunners as for anything in its content. I enjoyed it; but searching that enjoyment I find a sort of municipal memory made up of stolen library books, *I'm Sorry I'll Read That Again* and Northern Line stairwells. *'Islington. Isn't that quite fashionable?' 'Not then, dear.'* Those were the days indeed.

N.S. 22 May 1987

Appearances are Everything

Wish You Were Here

Nothing in the press prepared me for the disturbing experience of watching WISH YOU WERE HERE. It was hailed everywhere as a delightful teenage rebellion romp and I went expecting something both funny and liberating, as, clearly, did the predominantly young, predominantly female audience which packed the Odeon Haymarket at six o'clock on a Wednesday night.

Perhaps I should have known better since David Leland, whose directorial debut this is, was scriptwriter on PERSONAL SERVICES, a film which by no stretch of the imagination could be called 'charming'. Nevertheless, that is one of the adjectives most consistently applied by critics to WISH YOU WERE HERE, and the publicity image of Emily Lloyd perched on a seaside railing seems to bear it out. At the same time the film is set up as 'naughty' since it tells the earlier part of Cynthia Payne's story, a prequel to PERSONAL SERVICES, following her adolescence in a small seaside town in the post-war years and charting her supposed rebellion against middle-class values.

The period is evoked by an excess of kitsch — the sort of fifties props like Craven A signs which now cost a fortune in Camden Market and the sort of wide-angle shots that Sunday magazines use to photograph the interiors of houses which couldn't possibly belong to their readers because the wallpaper is too horrid. Thus caught between the desirability and undesirability of what it depicts, the film is suffused with a sensibility of fashionable distaste.

This is exactly what kitsch is, but whereas usually it involves an ironic relationship to objects removed from their original context, here, objects returned to their historical period retain all the curiosity of their original removal. The past becomes a kind of retro-unchic boutique filled with what has been plundered from it.

If the props buyer is never quite certain whether the fifties are hip (now) or un-hip (then) what *is* quite clear in class terms is just how unpleasant its inhabitants were. I have gone on before about Lower-Middle-Class comic imagery, used to represent working-class aspirations in PRICK UP YOUR EARS; here, that all-purpose LMC is used, if possible even more perniciously, to represent what critics have unanimously called *middle*-class values. This slippage is supposed to make the rebellious Linda into a kind of revolutionary working-class heroine fighting off middle-class hypocrisy (mainly by saying 'Up your bum' incessantly).

But the film's aesthetics (and looks are its main form of comment) say otherwise. The sense of comic distaste that constitutes kitsch is fundamentally a form of snobbery: in loosely symbolic terms, those yukky people with shiny suits and net curtains aren't the *middle* class (heaven forbid) but a sort of generalized 'lower class'. (Of course, a film like MAURICE is about small-minded middle-class morality, but nobody in it *looks* so horrible, and certainly no one in it is *funny*.) WISH YOU WERE HERE, however, is peopled with characters whose big noses, red faces or sticky-out ears (which produced a good laugh) turn them into cartoon characters, and who, while they supposedly represent middle-class mores, really represent all that the middle class despises. Linda, in contrast, has a directly-presented prettiness which places her, in the film's visual hierarchy, above them: like the only real character in a comic strip, she up-your-bums her way through the small-town world whose problem becomes, not its social codes, but the fact that it is uglier than her.

This is epitomized in the film's opening sequence when a fat, middle-aged woman in an ill-fitting short dress tap dances on the promenade. It is meant to be funny: but of course if she were young and pretty it would merely be cute. The inseparability of these values is something the film never comes to grips with, since it employs cuteness (Linda's) as its radical term.

But besides being a form of displaced snobbery, this device is ultimately self-defeating since the comic disgust which is the film's only consistent mode of representation also pervades its chosen ground of rebellion — sex. In a film where a fat woman dancing and a dog chewing a Durex are high points of humour, sexuality appears as grotesque as the lower middle class which represses it. Sex is supposed to be subversive but is presented as absolutely horrible: the red, panting face of Linda's bus-conductor boyfriend as he comes too soon on their first night; the verbal abuse of her father's friend Eric (Tom Bell) as he gropes in her knickers — these are among the most upsetting scenes I have ever had to watch in the cinema.

So when Linda jumps on a chair in a restaurant at the end and yells, 'I like willies,' it is quite impossible to see why. The film's central confusion is that what the narrative presents as her 'liberation', the imagery and mise-en-scène present as humiliation. When she lies on a bed begging Eric to put his arms around her while he pulls her dress off, you could have heard a pin drop in the previously giggling, whispering, sweet-wrapper-rustling audience. The distress was palpable.

This is partly because Emily Lloyd does act as if she had real feelings. Yet the film never explores the contradictions of her situation, it merely exploits them. If there is one adjective *I* would use to describe the film it is *painful*. This applies — in different senses — both to the gruesome distortions of its clichéd humour and to the depiction of some of the truly hurtful moments of adolescence. Most of all, it is the product of their combination. Neither charming nor naughty, what is as depressing as the film itself is the fact that no one has thought even to comment on its one binding quality — the perception of sex, class and history entirely in terms of grotesque appearances. If this is invisible to our national press it only shows how disturbingly deep in the British sensibility such perceptions lie.

N.S. 18 December 1987

And the Coloured Girls Go. . .

Something Wild

It is interesting that in this time of social polarities, as the gap between rich and poor widens, one of the most fashionable American movie themes is the excursion from the safety of boring old middle-class affluence to see 'how the other half lives'. DESPERATELY SEEKING

SUSAN, AFTER HOURS, BLUE VELVET, now SOMETHING WILD, and the soon-to-be-released BLIND DATE, are all concerned with a foray made by a middle-class person into an 'otherness' represented by the other side of town — and into which they are flung, in each case (even Rosanna Arquette's) by a woman.

In SOMETHING WILD Jeff Daniels plays Charlie Driggs, a rather weedy-looking, clean-cut executive who is pounced on by 'Lulu' (Melanie Griffith), a wild and wacky woman with a Louise Brooks haircut, lots of African jewellery (more of that later) and the obligatory stockings. Having noticed him slipping out of a diner without paying, she instantly recognizes him as a 'closet rebel' and kidnaps him for a night of funky sex — a kind of 9½ WEEKS in reverse — pausing only to rob a liquor store. This initial scenario has much in common with AFTER HOURS, where the 'weedy' hero is propelled through Bohemia by women; and, like AFTER HOURS, SOMETHING WILD also ends up at its starting point with the characters returned to the location in which we first saw them. This circular structure suggests it is a psychic rather than a social geography that has been traversed; and the elision of the two is one of the most problematic aspects of this whole group of films.

BLUE VELVET wears its psychoanalytic intentions very openly on its sleeve: the scary side of town is where the nice boy's oedipal drama is played out (sleeps with older woman, kills older man). Much has been written about BLUE VELVET along seething-underbelly-of-small-town-America lines, but the point is that this seething underbelly is mainly presented as the vehicle for a voyage into the male psyche (or what is supposedly the male psyche) with Dennis Hopper functioning not only as evil father but also as out-of-control alter ego to the young man. DESPERATELY SEEKING SUSAN has an even more explicitly *doppelgänger* format, with Rosanna Arquette and her 'wild' counterpart Madonna wearing identical jackets.

SOMETHING WILD plugs the same point; its most quoted line is Lulu's 'What are you going to do now that you know how the other half lives? I mean *the other half of you.*' This slightly top-heavy piece of scripting pushes the movie — almost against its own grain — towards the psychic voyage category; shortly after this remark, the final confrontation between Charlie and his counterpart, Lulu's husband and ex-con, Ray, is filmed so that they could literally be mirror images of each other — both in bloody white tee-shirts, locked in identical and opposite positions as if there were a pane of glass between them. Like Jeffrey's battle with the Hopper figure in BLUE VELVET, this Ahab and the Whale struggle in his own bathroom is the culmination of Charlie Drigg's journey.

Other connotations of Moby Dick are pertinent, given that in this little genre of films (as in pop psychoanaylsis) *sex* is the gateway to the other world/underworld/inner world. And it seems important to these scenarios that the sex be seen as kinky — hence the handcuffs Lulu uses to seduce Charlie. But SOMETHING WILD poses a challenge to the nice girl/sexy woman dichotomy represented by Sandy (blonde)/ Dorothy (dark) in BLUE VELVET: as, with a simple switch (also in the bathroom) from dark bob to blond curls, Lulu is revealed as Audrey, an ordinary small-town girl.

This middle section of the (highly episodic) film brings us the small-town America of which BLUE VELVET is meant to be the underbelly, but here it's neither idealized nor completely parodied; for a while the polar opposites so necessary for the psychodrama are dropped and we are presented with both a complex and a funny social scene. For pulling away from the symbolic dimension of the film is Jonathan Demme's habitual penchant (particularly evident in his CITIZENS BAND) for unravelling the rich and crazy tapestry of life among ornery US folk. The irritatingly repeated theme-phrase of BLUE VELVET — 'It's a Strange World' — (used in that film in a universal and internalized sense) could appropriately be applied to the external, specific world of Demme's film, whose strangeness is exemplified by a dog in shades riding on the back of a motorbike.

This image is especially resonant because SOMETHING WILD is fundamentally a road movie, full of loud music (John Cale/Laurie Anderson) and fast cars. Instead of crossing town (AFTER HOURS, BLUE VELVET, 9½ WEEKS) we cross country — to Virginia. And if the 'Walk on the Wild Side' of this genre represents the sexual part of the middle-class psyche, the wild side walked on is itself represented — as indeed in Lou Reed's song — by black people. The opening sound track of SOMETHING WILD, accompanying gorgeous circling shots of Manhattan, turns out to be coming from a ghetto-blaster carried by a black kid, who is the first figure the camera focuses on in the whole film. Its last image is a black woman rapper, also in the street. Between these points the rich backdrop of wildness/laidbackness/ cameraderie/funkiness is made up of some black buskers Lulu offers a ride to, black rappers outside a gas station, a black harmonica player, and the literal backdrop of a gospel choir as Charlie parks his car in front of a church. His new-found wackiness is shown by his easy, hand-slapping relationship with Nelson, the black gas station attendant; the small progress in wackiness made by his dumpy colleague is measured through an identical gesture when he sees Charlie off at the end of the film.

This is where the conflation of social and psychic does matter. For if sexy women and laid-back blacks can be made to stand for repressed facets of the middle-class psyche — what of their own social reality? And if they are merely props in the white middle-class male's psychodrama — what of his place in *theirs*?

N.S. 10 July 1987

Soundtracks

Round Midnight
Crossover Dreams

Music movies might not be the first place you would expect to find morality tales. However, in different ways both this week's music releases focus less on music itself than on the moral life of musicians. This is seen as enabling ROUND MIDNIGHT to '*transcend* the confines of a music film' (Derek Malcolm, London Film Festival programme), while CROSSOVER DREAMS is precisely *about* the prostitution of a music form through the mechanisms of mass media. On a more fundamental level both films hinge on a colonial relationship: ROUND MIDNIGHT conceals this beneath its theme of 'personal dignity'; CROSSOVER DREAMS makes it explicit. Despite their diametrically opposed conclusions, the moralism of both films grates, being in the one highly insidious, in the other a bit crude.

ROUND MIDNIGHT was this year's hit at Venice, with the press convinced that its failure to win a prize was an injustice on the scale of an international conspiracy. But, elegant as the film is, its story is insultingly simplistic. Dexter Gordon — himself a great saxophonist — plays Dale Turner, a veteran jazz musician (amalgam of Bud Powell and Lester Young) starring at the Blue Note in fifties Paris and, for the first section of the film, sinking deeper and deeper into alcoholism, addiction and degradation. The middle-aged black man is saved by a young white Frenchman, Francis Borier (François Cluzet), whose admiration for true art makes him dedicate himself to rehabilitating the musician. Dale Turner's recovery, once lifted from his black

Parisian milieu, is remarkable. Repeatedly, Turner gets blitzed, ending up in police stations and hospitals; repeatedly, Borier bails him out like a baby, until he straightens out and starts composing again.

You may wonder what the white man gets from his burden: which is close to asking what the audience gets from the film. The black artist is shown simultaneously as a great 'genius' and as hopelessly weak — opening the way for his appropriation by our on-screen representative Borier: a colonization which allows the music to seem as much the product of white European, as of black American, culture. Indeed, towards the end of the film the renovated Turner hankers (unsurprisingly) to return to his family and friends in New York, and there the two of them go (to be greeted by a wonderfully sleazy Martin Scorsese as Turner's manager). All too soon the evils of the black community are apparent — Turner's young keeper has to fend off black drug pushers — and it's evident that Turner will degenerate again under the influences of his own people. In case the point isn't quite clear, the minute Borier goes back to Paris, Turner dies.

I am stressing the offensiveness of the 'white man's burden' theme because the movie has been so highly acclaimed by mainstream critics with no mention at all of this at best naive, at worst patronizing and racist structure. ROUND MIDNIGHT has been hailed on all sides as wonderfully 'human' (usually a danger signal): Derek Malcolm writes that the 'warmth and affection of the movie is (sic) its greatest asset'; but no one has cared to ask why a predominantly white art-house audience should *find* this particular scenario so warm and affectionate. The idea that a young white designer (and, charmingly, single parent with a cute pre-teen daughter) can save the out-of-control black artist and thereby indirectly 'give' the world great music certainly makes us all feel warm and cosy. Add to this the film's exquisite photography and fine layering of narrative — using in part the home-movie reels that are Borier's (and our) souvenir of the man he saved — and you have no doubt the most 'watchable' art film of the year. Add to this also a truly excellent soundtrack, arranged by Herbie Hancock, and you have the most listenable as well. But the film's lack of irony and failure to recognize the contradictions of its central relationship are, sadly, among the reasons for its success — especially in the context of the current jazz come-back on the mainly white club scene.

Equally topical, in terms of music fashion, is the Salsa film CROSSOVER DREAMS: a low-budget picture starring Rubén Blades — the excellent Salsa singer, composer and activist — as Rudy Veloz, a singer on the NY Salsa circuit who wants to 'cross over' into the mainstream pop world. While ROUND MIDNIGHT suggested that the

only way for a non-white musician to survive was to cast off his own
degraded culture for the cosmopolitan scene, CROSSOVER DREAMS
shows how the aspiring Latin singer comes to his downfall by trying to
escape his background and hit the big-time.

Politically, I have much more sympathy with this film: it is about a
refusal to be colonized, just as ROUND MIDNIGHT provides a subtle
justification of colonial relations. Yet its morality is so predictable as to
make it less exciting than its music deserves. Much of the plot is
carried through clichés: when Rudy signs up with an American record
producer he suddenly starts having orgies in bubble baths with white
girls, abandoning his nice Latina girlfriend who represents the integrity of his roots. Finally, however, on the brink of making a drug run
for a white pusher, the memory of his old Salsa teacher and mentor
sends him back to his own music and people.

It seems unfair to compare CROSSOVER DREAMS' rather pedestrian
mise-en-scène with Trauner's stylish design in ROUND MIDNIGHT;
instead of being made with an eye to the art-house audience it comes
over as a film with an urgent message to its own community. The
slightly creaky narrative is bolstered with street shots of East Harlem
and montage sequences of the Manhattan skyline: these, and the
lingering shots of Brooklyn Bridge in ROUND MIDNIGHT are enough to
hold my attention in themselves. But in the end, both films make you
want to go out and hear music — *without* the morals.

N.S. 28 November 1986

Skin Trade

Soul Man

It must be tough being a white, middle-class male. Not only is it
politically fashionable to be oppressed like women or blacks, but
subordinate cultures seem like so much more fun; what's more, the
very idea of positive discrimination makes some of those in tradition-

ally dominant groups actually feel anxious about being discriminated *against*.

This bundle of feelings may account for what might be called the Tootsie Syndrome: the wish to be in an oppressed group rather than that of the boring old oppressors. On one level the film TOOTSIE can be read as an exposé of sexism: by 'becoming' a woman, the Dustin Hoffman character experiences sexual discrimination first hand (he's called demeaning names like Tootsie, for example). This could be seen as a way of drawing attention to the whole issue.

But if films, like dreams, also function as the expression of a wish, then the desire to 'take over' being a woman (and make a better job of it than real women do) can be seen as the film's underlying dynamic, and this wish has much to do with the advances made by feminism. For women have a justification for righteous anger denied to their oppressors, and to 'be' one provides one way of expressing the sense of unfairness which, in the plot of TOOTSIE, the male actor feels at finding there are no male parts available for him.

SOUL MAN takes the Tootsie Syndrome into the realm of race. Its central character, Mark Watson, is a white boy whose wealthy parents refuse to pay for him to go to Harvard Law School and who darkens his skin with suntan tablets in order to win a black scholarship. At Harvard he meets the young black woman Sarah who should have been the recipient of the scholarship and is working to pay her way through school and support her child. Mark falls in love with Sarah, eventually owns up, goes through a mock 'trial' at the Law School, punches the WASP preppies who make racist jokes in the canteen, and finally overcomes Sarah's resistance to mixed marriages; as in TOOTSIE, romance is offered as the ultimate resolution.

And, as in TOOTSIE, SOUL MAN's narrative takes us through an enormous number of situations where the details of day-to-day prejudice and discrimination are shown up vividly and effectively. As a black student, Mark is an unwelcome tenant and his landlord tries to find excuses to evict him, while his daughter Whitney chases him with all the colonizer's avidness for a bit of the Other, claiming to have felt 'four hundred years of anger and oppression in every pelvic thrust' after they make love. When basketball teams are picked, everyone wants Mark on their side.

While all this appears to expose a variety of racist attitudes, the film functions partly through the very assumptions it purports to condemn. Mark, really white, *isn't* good at basketball; the 'real' black player is. After being black for a while, Mark's taste in music changes: when his best friend asks, 'Do you really hate the Beach Boys now?' he replies,

'Well, I guess I still like some of their funkier stuff.' The film certainly draws attention to crudely racist assumptions (there is a surreal dinner sequence where each member of Whitney's family is shown to have a different fantasy about Mark — the mother sees him as a rapist, the father as a pimp, the son as a pop star) but these only serve to conceal its own.

For while the film's overt narrative function is to show what black people are up against, its deeper theme — the Tootsie analysis — is that of envy. The movie contains a structure of parallels and comparisons which suggest that it *is*, in many ways, nicer to be black and poor than white and rich. Mark's well-off Californian parents are presented as total neurotics, swayed by the dictates of his father's grotesquely parodied therapist. Sarah's family, on the other hand, are warm and supportive, care for her child, and are enormously proud of her achievement. This may on one level be a realistic comparison but the way it is structured into the film leaves one in no doubt that Mark is a 'poor little rich kid'. The fact that the only scholarship money available for the school is for blacks further fuels the sense of envy, while his desire for Sarah also, in a sense, puts him in the subordinate, pleading position, at her mercy.

Mark's underdog role continues at his trial where his best friend pleads for him: 'Can we blame him for the colour of his skin [i.e. white]? Despite his upbringing, my client may still become a useful member of society. . .' The language usually heard in liberal defence of the underprivileged is here mobilized on behalf of the white man. The combination of all these factors seems to echo a quite real feeling, both of an emptiness in the dominant culture and a sense that some of those within it have of being hard-done-by.

SOUL MAN is interesting precisely because of the contradictory relationship between its 'message' of anti-racism and its driving emotion of envy. The device of pretending to be in a particular group in order to highlight its oppression has a long history. In Elia Kazan's 1947 film GENTLEMAN'S AGREEMENT Gregory Peck plays a gentile journalist who pretends to be Jewish in order to research anti-semitism; more recently the German journalist Günter Walraff has pretended to be a migrant worker in order to write about the experience from the inside. Yet, somewhere in this drive to *be* (rather than *listen to*) the oppressed, is yet again the impulse of the colonizer to take over whatever he is not.

In both TOOTSIE and SOUL MAN it is the white male who is the source of knowledge about women and blacks respectively, allowing him to remain bang at the centre of things while also appearing to understand perfectly the situation of those who are not. Which goes for the audience too. For of course SOUL MAN invites a white audience to identify with Mark identifying with a black kid, who is the object of discovery rather than the subject of the film. Well-meaning as this movie may be, what it really reveals is the reluctance of dominant social groups to let go their control of knowledge. Or, more simply, how hard some people find it just to shut up and listen.

N.S. 20 February 1987

Strategies

The columns in this section all investigate, in one way or another, how people have used the medium of film across a range of political and aesthetic strategies. It is an important task of criticism to consider what a film's strategy or project *is*, before discussing whether it 'works' or not, because some enterprises are more suited to the medium than others, and this is a different critical issue from that of whether or not one endorses (e.g. politically) the enterprise itself. As a critic one may end up showing how a film works in its own terms even if one may, simultaneously, criticize those terms; equally, one may feel sympathy with a film project but at the same time point out that it is not, for whatever reasons, working. Alternative or independent film-making has always been caught between the urge to experiment visually with politically radical themes and the wish to reach audiences and achieve success with more conventional treatment of those themes. At the same time, an experimental or out-of-the-mainstream handling of quite conventional subject matter may actually jolt our perceptions at least as much as the 'politically subversive', carefully right-on film. There can be no resolution to these tensions, but they can be much more productive in a film culture where there is real discussion about them.

Examining these issues brings us back, ultimately, to the same central concern as the previous section: what are the capacities of film, what are the effects and experiences that cinema can produce, and for whom does it produce them? If 'Symptoms' asks those questions from the viewpoint of the cultural observer, 'Strategies' asks them from the viewpoint of film-making itself.

The Interpretation of Dreams

'Syncopation Animation'
'The Hard Cell — Politics and Propaganda'
Basil the Great Mouse Detective

The way film works as a visual language is to a large extent disguised by the fact that its images happen to be produced by means of photography, and that the things photographed are 'real'. Thus whether or not a film sets out deliberately to be 'realist', the viewer tends to see its meaning as lying in *what* is depicted, rather than as being constructed within a two-dimensional frame. Animation, however, presents us with film stripped of its symbolic relation to reality, reminding us instead of its generic links with graphic design and other forms of two-dimensional art.

I introduce the BFI's 'Syncopation Animation' and 'Hard Cell — Politics and Propaganda' programmes in this context because far from being a sort of sub-form of film, of interest only to children and specialists, animation could be seen as essential film, exploiting its unique capacities for movement and meaning unhampered by photography. Obviously the most exciting films do this whether through animation or not; the first piece in the 'Hard Cell' selection is a 1924 animation by experimental Soviet director Dzigha Vertov, called SOVIET TOYS, in which many devices common to his live-action work can be found. Early films by other Soviet directors like Eisenstein, Dovzhenko and Pudovkin also have close links with the poster forms of their time, and use the graphic dimension of cinema to the full.

As Freud pointed out in his analysis of dreams, a visual language works with almost childlike simplicity: if something is big it is important or powerful, if small the opposite and so on. In SOVIET TOYS Vertov's giant capitalist 'pig', eating up Russia's resources, towers over the worker and peasant until they join forces and finally deflate him — literally. Scale is treated entirely as a conceptual, not a realist tool. This vocabulary is extended in Norman McLaren's powerful anti-war animation HELL UNLIMITED (1936), which has much in common with John Heartfield's work, montage being another of the essential components of cinema. People are shown being fed into a mincer to produce weapons, a munitions 'plant' being watered by arms dealers, words from a radio going 'in one ear, out the other' — all these (again, as Freud says of dreams) translating thoughts into images, making concepts concrete.

Another area where animation draws out the inherent capacities of film is in the relation of movement to music, and the 'Syncopation Animation' selection shows this particularly clearly. From the abstract movements of shape and colour in Len Lye's, Norman McLaren's or Oskar Fischinger's non-representational work to the slipping and a-sliding of Looney Tunes or Betty Boop, the best of this work is characterized by a liberating disregard for narrative in favour of rhythm, movement and metamorphosis.

Betty Boop was originally created for Max and Dave Fleischer by the great animator Grim Natwick, who went on to do the figure of Snow White herself for Disney. What is particularly interesting about BETTY BOOP IN SNOW WHITE (1933), one of the classics in this collection and predating the Disney feature by only four years, is its anarchic fluidity both as regards plot and in the extraordinary metamorphoses of the characters themselves. The obligatory 'mirror, mirror' story rapidly gives way to a funky underworld where the characters change forms entirely and, as it were, metamorphose to music — 'St James Infirmary' by Cab Calloway. The abandonment of character and plot is extreme in this instance, but the slippery shifts in shape and the overtly sexual quality of Betty Boop (the only animated character to be banned by Hollywood censors as 'lewd') are character-istic of much early animation and are still seen in the best of the Disney features — SNOW WHITE, an extraordinarily fluent and graceful film, being a case in point.

However, one of Disney's achievements was to introduce a greater 'realism' into his animated characters, and part of that realism was consistency of shape, matched on another level by consistency of character. Model sheets laid down the limits to movement by particular figures (it would be inconceivable for, say, Mickey Mouse to change form) and the bodily anarchy of some of the Fleischer oeuvre is replaced by coherent identities, which ultimately function outside movies altogether (Disneyland, Mousketeers).

In recent Disney productions — e.g. MICKEY'S CHRISTMAS CAROL and BASIL THE GREAT MOUSE DETECTIVE — this process goes even further, with animal 'characters' in fictional human 'roles': Scrooge, Tiny Tim, or, in the case of BASIL, Sherlock Holmes and Dr Watson. There is none of the wild elasticity of earlier animation and BASIL deliberately employs a repertoire of genre film scenarios: the characters perform musical numbers, solve crimes, and there is even a Hitchcockian chase across the face of Big Ben. Animation is employed merely to make the creatures move: if mice could act, the film might almost as well have been photographed.

But the most striking aspect of the reactions of the innumerable small children in the audience was that they laughed almost exclusively at points of physical destruction or disintegration: since this hardly happens to the *characters*, they had to be satisfied with Basil crushing his violin, for instance, which they liked better than anything except an untypical moment when Basil's face is flattened by a smashing cymbal.

Children have an ecstatic fascination with violent physical transformations, which can roughly translate (Freud again) as symbolic aggressions to the body, without real effects. (This is surely part of the great delight for adults too of Tom and Jerry etc.) What appears to be an increasing censorship and morality in contemporary Disney features results from mistaking the symbolic for the real — a bit like sending someone to prison for having a violent dream. Which returns to my starting point: animation is a vivid reminder that film itself is not only a visual language, but one whose grammar is that of our own unconscious.

N.S. 7 November 1986

Tricks of the Light

The Magic Toyshop

Writing and filming are completely different ways of unfolding a story. Books tell; films show. This makes the transition from book to film much more complicated than simply filming the things that 'happen' in a book, because while the writing itself is the voice of the book, the film's voice is not the story, but its staging: the way the camera moves, the spaces shown and not shown, and the editing of these slices together either to give or withhold an illusion of depth, place, continuity, point of view.

Angela Carter's writing is more than just stories; much of her work — and *The Magic Toyshop* is a particularly good example — deals with the process of storytelling itself and with its historical genres. The short story on which COMPANY OF WOLVES was based was a deliberate reworking of the Red Riding Hood tale, a sort of post-Freudian, feminist foray into the forest of femininity, which sets out to speak not only about female sexuality but about the genre — the fairy tale — which it so cunningly twists and turns. *The Magic Toyshop*, too, is a kind of fairy tale combined with Gothic romance in which a heroine encounters her own sexuality in a strange, at first frightening, environment. The particular atmosphere of fantasy in the book comes in part from its way of combining this heavily referential symbolism with its quite ordinary, girl's story kind of voice, and from its contemporary setting which gives as strong a sense of South London in the 1960s as of Gothic sexual territory in literature.

But not only is film's way of telling different from literature's, its conventions and generic traditions are different and its weighting of words, settings and symbols creates quite different inflexions on similar material. I found the COMPANY OF WOLVES film peculiarly *literal*, for a fairy tale. The story was intriguing, but its telling didn't really use film's own tonal range, so that while fantastic things happened *in* it — men turning into wolves, etc. — these owed more to the repertoire of the Special Effects department than to the subtler fantastic effects that film language is capable of. It seemed event-heavy; while film can be light, mysterious, not just a bundle of tricks but a dream-like form itself. Not many writers are adept in this medium, but Cocteau's LA BELLE ET LA BÊTE is a brilliant example of

fairy story turned into film; full of sexual symbols — the breaking of
the glass skylight at the end being one of the most obvious — its misty,
mysterious ambience draws you into its telling just as a storybook
soaks up daydreams on a rainy day.

This is the quality THE MAGIC TOYSHOP lacks as a film. Directed by
David Wheatley from Angela Carter's own screenplay, it is a fairly
'faithful' adaptation of the book, yet with important differences. In the
book, inevitably, time is spent on description, on slowly moving the
reader through experiences as well as between objects. But the film
seems top-heavy with *things*, symbols, meanings; within about ten
minutes its heroine has got locked out of the house wearing her
mother's wedding dress, climbed an apple (geddit?) tree in it thereby
getting blood (geddit?) on it, whereupon her parents are killed in a
plane crash and she is sent with her brother and sister to live in the
magic toyshop. In writing, all this seems a little less knowing; you can
at least make your own space to breathe. But the film just shows,
shows, shows; its range of devices for being magical are, precisely,
tricks: ships appear in the sea-obsessed brother's glasses, the parents
in the wedding photo move, a broken statue — 'she's a fallen woman,
poor thing' — cries.

Lines like this feel awkward to me. 'Dreams — they're not catching,
you know' and so on are phrases that, though poetic in themselves,
seem over-pointed when inserted into a film which is not itself very
dreamy. In books, dialogue seems less weighty; it is written in the
same medium as the story is told in. In film, dialogue like this stands
out, cut adrift from the words on the page, floating awkwardly among
the spectacle.

However, the most significant effect of changing the mode of an
adolescent-sexual-awakening story from book to film is that, instead of
the experience of the heroine, we are presented with the vision of her.
The film is successful in avoiding a voyeuristic presentation of
Melanie's sexual explorations, yet inevitably we watch rather than
share them, for again, film's way of expressing point of view is different
from writing's and instead of being folded into Melanie's vision
through filmic devices she becomes a focal point of ours. In fact, all the
characters seem at once emptier, and more symbolic, than in the book;
which is not a problem with the acting, but the turning inside-out
process of the adaptation. Tom Bell as the puppet-like puppet-maker
is really excellent, as are many of the other performances.

But what I feel is neglected is the film itself, as a film. No writer
would treat a book as a mere vehicle. And the writer's passion for
words, for layered memories of other words, other books, the ability to

conjure imaginary spaces out of print on the page, all this has its —
different — equivalent in film. The two dimensional can open (and
close) imaginary spaces; images, not words, and not things *in* images,
can move you through time at a pace you can't choose. Film isn't a
medium you can just bung something into — a story has to unfold *out*
of its flat surfaces; and THE MAGIC TOYSHOP, absorbing as a book, just
doesn't.

N.S. 31 July 1987

Pomp and Circumstance

Ivan the Terrible
(Part One and Part Two)

A Christmas treat for anyone interested in cinema must be the
re-release (with new 35mm prints) of Eisenstein's IVAN THE TERRIBLE
Parts One and Two. Originally released fourteen years apart they
have rarely been shown together and between them they chart a
bizarre history — not only in their own increasingly ornate representation of a powerful populist ruler but, more broadly, of the crisis of
representation in Stalin's USSR.

By the 1930s the Stalinist regime's insistence on 'Socialist Realism'
— healthy, heroic dramas endorsing the social order of the day —
made it increasingly difficult to pursue the kinds of freewheeling
formal and conceptual experiments that had characterized film-
making in the years after the revolution. Eisenstein was out of favour
for a variety of reasons at this time and, in 1937, was prevented from
finishing BEZHIN MEADOW: accused by a critical committee of formal-
ism, over-stylization at the expense of narrative clarity, and abstract-
ing themes rather than particularizing. Having submitted to these
criticisms he was allowed to direct ALEXANDER NEVSKY the following
year — under the rather humiliating condition of strict supervision by
his assistant, whose task was to keep him to a clear narrative line and
away from any stylistic experiments.

This single-track historical drama about a popular hero defeating

Teutonic invaders met with official approval (though it had to be withdrawn on the signing of the 1939 German-Soviet pact) and Eisenstein was allowed slightly freer rein in directing another big historical drama with the same leading actor, Cherkasov, about the unification of Russia by Ivan the Terrible. Part One, finished in 1944, won Eisenstein, Cherkasov, Tissé (Eisenstein's longstanding cameraman) and Prokofiev (who composed the music) a first class Stalin Award. Part Two, however, appalled Stalin and was not released until 1958 — five years after his death and ten years after Eisenstein's.

This history of IVAN THE TERRIBLE helps to make sense of the film visually. The story itself offers exactly the kind of grand patriotic drama favoured by Stalin: the opening title declares 'This film is about the man who united Russia in the sixteenth century.' Ivan — in the extraordinary figure of Cherkasov — is presented as a magnetic, majestic personality and, in the first half at least, as a rationalist in the face of superstition, a populist in the face of elitism. Given all this, what is striking is the intense use of imagery which, far from Socialist Realism, gives an eerie, almost expressionist edge to the monolithic saga of Ivan's exploits.

Under orders not to stray into conceptual devices like montage, Eisenstein channels stylization and conceptualization into forms quite different from those familiar from STRIKE, OCTOBER and BATTLESHIP POTEMKIN. It's as if all expansion on the material becomes flattened into the image itself, giving a frieze-like quality to the mise-en-scène. The period and setting provide ample material for formal richness, for example in the memorable opening scene in Part One, Ivan's coronation. Even here there is some scope for Eisenstein's old methods of generalization: after the opening title calls Ivan the 'First crowned Tsar of all Russia', the first image of the film is a shot, not of Ivan, but of *the crown*: in this one moment Socialist Realism is defied as Eisenstein focuses on the concept of the ruler rather than his person. In the next instant, as the crown is placed on Ivan's head, the film begins its uneasy marriage of the specific and the general, the personification of power and its visual conceptualization.

Eisenstein has always had an eye for the paraphernalia of office — in OCTOBER, the feather beds, classical statues, decorative glassware and cutlery of the Winter Palace — but, denied access to any imagery outside the story itself, his representation of iconic forms becomes almost baroque. An army marching with scythes forms the shape of scythes on the landscape; the line of the people's march from Moscow to beg Ivan to return forms the shape of his profile as he surveys his subjects. In interiors, candles abound and shadows prefigure every entrance; movement becomes balletic, symbolically choreographed, as when Ivan steps repeatedly on the trailing robe of his priest friend, pleading with him to stay.

This visual formality is present in Part One, but its narrative line is straightforward to the point of singlemindedness: Ivan being truly monomaniac. However, in Part Two it is the representation which becomes almost manic — culminating in the near-abstract, swirling colour sequence of the Oprichniks' dance — as if, unable to expand outwards, the imagery implodes. The story of the strong hero seems to crack open — in part from the very pressure to hold together. The character of Ivan becomes more complicated and contradictory, with a sort of Freudian childhood sequence that attempts to offer some explanation of his personality, and the multiplying of angles on his character is matched by the accelerating diversity of camera angles until the imagery seems to overtake the story: the stunning red, gold and black dance has no overt narrative function at all.

This insistence on the plane of the image produces some consideration of representation in the political sense as well. Vivid examples of this are the visualization of the Polish court as a giant chess board at the beginning of Part Two, and the counting of soldiers with coins in Part One. For the film is both a product of, and addresses, a crisis of historical representation — how to portray a powerful, despotic leader — and of visual representation, of how to speak *about* the subject matter through images. Ultimately what is fascinating both inside the film and outside is the way the political restrictions on Eisenstein's earlier visual techniques result in a film at once so rigid and yet so ornate; and then how this convoluted opulence itself functions as an ideological threat to the narrative message, which led to the film being banned. In watching both parts today we can trace the bizarre tension between the single view of the dictator — both Ivan and Stalin — and its splintering in this strangely frozen, fragmented film, Eisenstein's last and never completed.

N.S. 19 December 1986

Once More with Feeling

Swan Song

SWAN SONG opens with a shot of the narrow Canton street where Ou
Laoshou, an old composer, lives; the image of its roadway winding
between high walls is repeated over and over in this economical film,
which spans a period of about thirty years and leaves a lasting
impression of being hemmed in on both sides.

SWAN SONG's director, Zhang Zeming, is one of the generation of
Chinese film-makers whose work has developed in the decade since the
re-opening of the Beijing film school in 1978. While there is still some
Party censorship (the most recent example of a film which was altered
is THE BIG PARADE), these 'fifth generation film-makers', as they are
known in China, have been able to address the problems of the
Cultural Revolution (and Party bureaucracy, cf. THE BLACK CANNON
INCIDENT) extraordinarily frankly.

Zhang Nuanxin's SACRIFICED YOUTH — which opens here in the
summer — speaks, as its title suggests, both of and from that 'lost'
generation which grew up during the Cultural Revolution's dominant
years and whose formative experience was the clash between traditional, regional cultures and the uniform official cultural line. SACRI-
FICED YOUTH is very much a 'growing up movie', narrated in the first
person and delicately tuned through the sensibility of its heroine. But
SWAN SONG too, though its subject is the music of an ageing composer,
charts in a more disturbing way the confusing experience of his son.

The son, Guanzai, lives alone with Ou Laoshou — whose wife, a
much younger professional singer, divorced him after the Liberation
and went off, taking her daughter, to make a successful career with the
State Opera. The film lets us learn this information gradually and
unobtrusively, placing less emphasis on the telling of a story than on
the emotional import of scenes which give a sense both of the
complexity of relationships and the texture of life as it is lived by the
main characters. At the beginning of the film it is the early 1960s and
Ou Laoshou has just composed a new piece; he plays it to the local
amateur orchestra of blind musicians whose traditional instruments
produce the sound he desires and who cherish his work in their small
community. The piece itself, with a particularly haunting, poignant
theme, is repeated throughout the film, part of whose function is

literally to do what it is about — preserving a traditional musical aesthetic (just as SACRIFICED YOUTH's lush cinematography preserves an image of the colourful Dai culture discovered by its heroine).

While his little band loves Ou Laoshou's music, he is not allowed to publish any of it; Party officials tell him it's too 'mournful' and command him to produce something rousing. Meanwhile, he is teaching the boy Guanzai to play traditional music, and father and son are close despite occasional rows as the unworldly composer forgets to buy food, spending his money at teahouses. As times become harder the conflict between father and son becomes harsher, until the height of the Cultural Revolution when Ou Laoshou is viciously harassed and punished and Guanzai, seeing this, runs away from home.

The way this scene is presented is typical of the film's sparse aesthetic: we never see the harassment of his father but see Guanzai looking over a high wall, and hear the violent questioning. The next shot is simply of the wall, filling the screen, and the small boy walks past. There is something dramatically unsentimental about the way his experience is handled; whatever pain is internalized in his rejection of the father is entirely implicit, and therefore in a way internalized by the film itself, suffusing its entire tone. Years later Guanzai returns to find his father even more broken and responds with anger, even when the old man tries to make reparation by cooking special meals: he sells Ou Laoshou's beloved (and banned) lute, to get money to go away again. Meanwhile an old colleague now living in Hong Kong visits them and Ou Laoshou entrusts some precious compositions to him, begging him to get them published. A few months later he hears them performed on the radio — and attributed to the dead, officially recognized composer He Dasha.

The scene where Ou Laoshou hears his work credited to someone else is traumatic enough, but when he burns his still unpublished manuscripts on his deathbed it is almost unbearable to watch. Yet as he dies the local band plays his music, so that it actually becomes the film's own accompaniment to this most moving and distressing scene. Like everything else in the film, its emotional effect derives from understatement. We are simply forced to watch manuscript after manuscript flaring up in the tin basin until only ashes remain, and even then the shot is held on the embers snaking in the bottom.

This is another striking aspect of the film's visual style — its use of natural light. The new Chinese cinema is producing an aesthetic with colour film that is as textured, and as graphic, as that of the most highly shaded black and white. SWAN SONG is to contemporary Hollywood's flattened colour as expressionism or film noir is to the brightly-lit studio set piece of the 1930s. In Ou Laoshou's tiny apartment the overhead light bulb brings a small pool of the room to the screen just as the film itself selects its few exchanges and incidents from the bigger, darker history it draws on. The film actually becomes gloomier as Ou Laoshou goes downhill; after he dies, Guanzai seeks the bright lights of the city, but the Western way — lit by Coca-Cola and Marlborough signs — merely creates the other wall that bounds his path. The long-lost sister makes contact and copies out drafts of Ou Laoshou's music, promising to make him famous. But Guanzai watches on TV the concert where she performs it in grossly western-ized style, on a grand piano — and claims to have composed it.

The film ends with Guanzai listening to a distant street vendor's song, something his father used to copy down. The suggestion is that traditional culture lives on in the vernacular: neither 'reformed' nor westernized. Yet it also lives in the film itself, which, like the other new films coming out of China, succeeds in producing a powerful sense of what the Cultural Revolution damaged, while avoiding Western forms and developing a distinctive aesthetic of its own. Rain, light, the roofs of buildings, the ground — the frame holds these, I was going to say surfaces, except I've been writing too much about surfaces recently and besides, the surfaces of roof, walls, water, close-up and filling the screen, are shown precisely not as surfaces but as pattern, texture, depth. There is a materiality to this kind of film-making that eludes the supposedly 'materialistic' West. Money-grubbing as it is, a film like WALL STREET (the current No. 1 here) is pure idealism: the financial remoteness of what it shows, to its popular audience, is matched by a kind of remoteness in the image, that window through which we gaze longingly. SWAN SONG, by contrast, makes you feel things in the two senses of the physical and emotional combined. The route that new Chinese cinema is steering between Party line and the West is not nearly as narrow as that of our own box office.

N.S. 27 May 1988

Into Africa

Sarraounia

African cinema is rarely seen in this country. An entire colonial relationship is written into this fact. Africa as a backdrop for the goings-on of white colonialists is an increasingly popular feature of mainstream films like OUT OF AFRICA and the forthcoming, inanely-named WHITE MISCHIEF, while even the telling of the 'other side' of the story seems to be the province of well-meaning white liberals, as with CRY FREEDOM. We have managed to colonize not only Africa, but the image of that colonization — like children, we love to tell about how naughty we have been.

Yet if Africa is such a popular subject for first-world films it is worth considering in more depth the apparent paradox that its own cinema is so invisible here (except at festivals and in specialist seasons). The question can best be answered by asking, conversely, what is it that makes the 'Out of Africa' genre of films like those above so appealing to us?

Their most obvious feature is that they manage to star white heroes and heroines, thereby allowing predominantly white, first-world audiences a viewing position which, no matter how African the *setting*, does nothing at all to disturb the structures of identification of mainstream cinema. Linked to this simple fact are issues both political and aesthetic: the presentation of African history from an African point of view challenges the politics even of a liberal cinema (which is still obsessed, ultimately, with vindicating the oppressors — us) and simultaneously challenges the Hollywood aesthetic of a neatly sealed narrative, which it is the film's function to manoeuvre us through as imperceptibly as possible. The Ethiopian critic Teshome Gabriel has written, 'In the Western movie, the theme of the story is the style of the form; in other words, it is the tools, the camera and the sets, that move the story around instead of the story moving the tools.' On a literal level it is always the tools which move the film, for it has to be shot, cut, etc., but Gabriel's description suggests a difference between a cinema whose point is merely the gratifying deployment of its own processes, and one whose cinematic processes are driven by the purpose of the story itself. Story-telling and the forms of popular memory which support it are an important part of much African cinema, particularly because they have been suppressed — or, more subtly, dismissed — by the Western bourgeois aesthetic in which telling is invisible and plots seem magically to resolve themselves, reassuring us that history can be organized equally to our satisfaction.

History and memory are both the point and the process of Med Hondo's SARRAOUNIA. It opens with the image of an army marching from the misty distance, across the plains of the wide (CinemaScope) screen and out of the frame; led by white soldiers on horseback, the seemingly endless trail of black figures following behind evoke one strand of African history, a history of oppression and subordination. The film ends with a matching image, as its heroine Sarraounia, the queen who resisted the French colonizers, leads a loosely united stream of African people who, similarly, move out of the frame into the future — until, at the very end, the costumes of the film's 'period' give way to modern clothes, baseball hats and tee-shirts.

This use of space to evoke time is part of the film's extraordinary achievement in telling a tale *of* the past, *in* the present. It is an epic: a story of history, but one which we are invited to watch from our own place in history. To maintain interest and excitement in such a story without resort to illusionistic structures — in other words, inviting us to watch it as a true story, rather than a realistic fiction — requires a sustained cinematic skill which most of our own film-makers are totally deficient in. Where Hondo wants to make a historical point he does it graphically: as with the incredible image of Africa literally carved up by the Europeans and bleeding along every boundary. The light-handed and yet vividly concrete way in which concepts like 'the march of history' become real on the screen is part of the film's use of technique (perhaps this is what Gabriel meant) to *say* something: it is not just telling a story, it is also telling its audience something about itself.

For the film speaks to Africans in the present. Its story of Sarraounia's resistance to the French colonizers is full of points with resonance today. Villages which try to placate the invader are destroyed as savagely as those which are defiant; it is divisions among the African people which allow the Europeans to conquer. Their army consists almost entirely of black mercenaries; far outnumbering their white leaders, this discontented band is enlisted in one part of Africa to fight in another. The message is clear: to fight off white imperialism some sinking of differences among the African nations is necessary. It is also clear that the manic invaders are the 'savages' in this story — demanding hands cut off bodies as proof of the numbers of villagers killed, etc. The whole discourse of barbarism is turned back on its users.

In contrast, the film uses the scope of its aesthetic to give a strong visual sense of the beauty and space of Africa, which in turn contributes to the depiction of the strength and dignity of African cultures pre-colonization. The Europeans appear pale, petty and corrupt against the great sweep of ancient land and ancient customs; the shamefulness of those who give in to the invader is felt not as a 'political weakness' in modern terms but as a lack of pride and, most of all, historical short-sightedness, since, as the film's songs remind us, ultimately only names survive.

The last song in the film, as Sarraounia leads the people forward, invokes popular memory directly: 'What would happen without our musicians? He who dies without a name dies forever.' The film is not only about resistance, it is about remembering resistance; and, like COMRADES or BLOOD RED ROSES, places itself in this process, its very title keeping Sarraounia's name alive, along with the memory of the culture she defended. In depicting this culture the film's beauty is part of its purpose; the pleasure of its aesthetic, like the tune of a song, is inseparable from the way it is remembered. At the same time, the end, far from appearing completed, drops us off in the here and now. This is a radical film: and yet there are no 'difficult' avant-garde techniques, no references to exclusive texts. As with Hondo's last film, WEST INDIES (unfortunately not in distribution), we are offered an alternative to mainstream cinema which is both exhilarating and accessible. Film-makers in this country who are interested in Brechtian forms could learn an enormous amount from it; cinema-goers will be surprised how much they enjoy it.

N.S. 8 January 1988

A World of Difference

The Passion of Remembrance

The more power any group has to create and wield representations, the less it is required to *be* representative. Those in dominant social groups are rarely called upon to represent anything more weighty than themselves: as I tried to point out recently about Tavernier's ROUND MIDNIGHT, the fact that a film is made by a white European 'art' director is enough to induce a mass myopia about its inclusion of any racial themes at all. In the dominant cinema, stereotypes can masquerade as 'individuals'.

The problems facing the black film-maker, however, are almost exactly the other way round. As one of the characters in THE PASSION OF REMEMBRANCE says, 'Every time a black face appears on the screen we think it has to represent the whole race', and another immediately replies, 'But there is so little space — we have to get it right.' This central exchange raises one of the key issues for those whose very access to representational forms is seen as being 'representative'.

It is an issue which runs through the history of Sankofa, the black film workshop who are collective authors of THE PASSION OF REMEMBRANCE; and this history has as much to do with urban politics as with film-making itself. The 'disturbances' in Brixton in 1981 caused a number of institutions to rethink social policies: one of these was the GLC,[1] whose commitment to cultural pluralism resulted in their funding of groups like Sankofa and Black Audio Film Collective (whose new film HANDSWORTH SONGS opens shortly). These were important additions to the already growing workshop movement, which successfully negotiated the historic ACTT Workshop Declaration with the film technicians' union, allowing independent films to be made at lower rates (hence on lower budgets) than the usual union minimum. These developments plus the arrival of Channel Four and its commitment not only to fund one-off projects but to give revenue funding to certain workshops, in particular to encourage 'multicultural' programming, have all contributed to an independent film culture which, despite an extraordinary lack of interest from the

---

1   Greater London Council (disbanded by the Conservative Government in 1986).

mainstream press, is expanding and flourishing.

However, for a group like Sankofa none of this lifts the burden of representation, as the invisible demand to 'speak for the black community' is always there behind the multiculturalism of public funding. What is courageous in Sankofa's project is that they have chosen to speak *from*, but not *for* black experience in Britain; and rather than fighting simply for black visibility, they are forcing the recognition of other issues which have themselves been invisible within that campaign. At the heart of the film is an insistence on the problems of sexuality and gender which question the priorities and style of the black power movement: 'You can't hide behind your little black fist for ever', says a young woman to a male activist — challenging not only a politics but, more specifically, its representation.

This challenge is made partly by the form of the film itself, which completely eschews agit-prop or 'community drama'. Its own aesthetic places it firmly in the avant-garde tradition: there is a shifting between tenses and persons (from 'she' to 'I' and back again) reminiscent of Duras; a use of dialogue for didactic rather than narrative function reminiscent of Godard's 'political' films; a mixing of day-to-day situations and formal devices (like the 360° pan) that characterized certain intellectual experiments of the seventies, such as the Mulvey/Wollen RIDDLES OF THE SPHINX. This is a stylistic heritage which the film-makers combine with a quite different heritage — that 'passion of remembrance' which throws up the contradictions within black British culture.

Against a plain red backdrop, a black woman tells 'her story': a story of oppression within a movement against oppression. Then in a 'no-man's land' (or perhaps a piece of common ground) she argues out the unspoken conflicts within that movement with a black man: in a deserted sandpit they shout and circle, the bizarre landscape standing for an unknown political territory, possibly a place not yet found.

Between these strangely abstract exchanges a more everyday story is told, as the film presents scenes from the lives of members of a black household, the Baptistes, and traces their differences and desires. A third visual thread repeated in the film is produced through Maggie Baptiste's montage of video images recording moments of struggle and solidarity — marches, rallies, fights and embraces — distanced by various visual devices until they become drained of their naturalistic meaning and take on an almost dream-like status.

Throughout the film, images are under discussion: there is the viewing of Maggie's video ('Maggie, is it true you're a lesbian? What have gay marches got to do with black struggle?'); there is the whole family watching a TV show where the black couple fails to win a prize; there is the heated debate about the black athlete's clenched fist at the Olympics. The film's own imagery is most successful in its more casual moments — as when Maggie and her friend Louise start dancing while getting ready to go out. At this point the film makes you *feel* something that, the rest of the time, it tells you.

The difficulty with the film is exactly this: there *is* so much to tell and so much to be said. This makes the dialogue rather top-heavy — it carries too much of the meaning — while the diversity of rhetorical devices sometimes distracts from, rather than reinforces, the complexity of the issues, and makes it hard to take away a visual sense of the film as a whole. But these are some of the problems of breaking new ground; which the film does, not so much stylistically — despite its stylistic self-consciousness — but politically. What is new within this (so often evasive) avant-garde format is the extraordinary boldness of the film's challenge to heterosexuality; the directness of its articulation of conflict between black women and men and between generations; the strength of its subjective voices to speak for no one but themselves.

N.S. 5 December 1986

Signs and Meanings

Rocinante

When I was at film school in the seventies, narrative forms were regarded as reactionary. Those using film for directly political purposes worked mostly in documentary — Cinema Action were a key group in this genre — while those who thought any form of 'realism' was bourgeois eschewed the representational qualities of film altogether.

This meant that no one either learnt, or learnt to value, the skills of directing actors, writing dialogue, sustaining action, or in any way using film as an exciting or pleasurable fiction medium. Films by theorists Laura Mulvey and Peter Wollen exemplified this non-art of film-making: worked out on paper beforehand, their attempts to say radical things through schematically constructed narratives proved wooden and unfilmic — that is, with the ideas easily separable from the image.

I introduce ROCINANTE in this context because as Cinema Action's first fiction feature (and their accession to Art Cinema) its problems are relevant to a much wider movement within independent film-making, a turn from documentary to fiction that in many ways parallels the left's more general abandonment of its old clothes for what it thinks to be smarter or more popular.

ROCINANTE — one of those names you always feel you are pronouncing wrong, which is *not* very popular — is the name of Don Quixote's horse. The film is described in the production notes as 'a journey through the English countryside and a re-examination of Britain's cultural and social history'. What happens *in* it is that Bill (John Hurt) who lives in a derelict cinema projecting images of the English landscape, crosses paths with Jess, who, we finally discover, is involved in a plot to disrupt the Coal Board computer. Together they travel through the English countryside (beautifully photographed by Thaddeus O'Sullivan) on their different missions. A 'Jester' (Ian Dury) provides intermittent comment and quotes from English history and poetry.

The narrative is obviously meant to be quite engrossing because there are regular 'clues' to Jess's plan of action, people appear and reappear, and oblique references made early in the film are explained later on. But the real 'clues' are, in fact, not clues to the plot but to the film's intellectual structure; which instead of being organic within the film has to be perpetually found in translation between film and ideas. In this sense it isn't really a fiction and the characters aren't really characters — they are representatives of particular positions and values. Jess doesn't actually do much in the film but clearly stands for political activity. Bill, equally clearly, stands for Romantic idealism. Thus every encounter becomes an ideological essay, until even dialogue like 'what's your name?' comes to sound painfully meaningful, while phrases like 'was it a crime, or was it just In the Nature of Things', said with heavy innuendo, speak to an audience already smugly versed in the ideological import of 'the nature of things'.

The self-consciousness of its 'meanings' is one of the film's biggest failings. The script itself is always ready to provide metaphors, with characters saying things like 'I suppose we all light matches in the dark' and 'Do stowaways know where they're going?'. Or they translate each other, as when the old projectionist helpfully outlines the conceptual significance of Bill's speech about land: 'Oh, you mean like in RED RIVER, all people remember is the prairie.' This over-labouring of the dialogue is characteristic of many films of this kind — another recent example being THE PASSION OF REMEMBRANCE.

These two films are hailed together in the BFI's prestigious *Monthly Film Bulletin* as 'an exciting new wave of British independent film-making' and have been lauded in the usual fashion outlets, *The Face*, *New Musical Express*, etc. But watching ROCINANTE (twice) made me think, in retrospect, that it was doing the less experienced makers of THE PASSION OF REMEMBRANCE a disservice in the long run not to point out more harshly the dangers of being boring and pretentious. In last month's review I allowed my sympathy for their *project* to soften my criticisms of their *film*. But a film really has to work as a film — not as a text to be translated into political concepts. This is a common problem with political film-makers turning to fiction: there is no investment in the story, only in what it stands for. If you really want to say something it is still usually better to make a documentary and *say* it than to put it into the mouths of puppet 'fictional' characters.

For somewhere in this new drive to 'fiction' there is a fundamental mistake. The analysis and deconstruction of classical Hollywood films in the seventies revealed narratives as the vehicles for powerful ideological messages — this was what the film criticism of *Screen* was all about. But these messages weren't thought out on purpose and then craftily wound into the plot: no one sat down and said, 'let's make a film about bourgeois values', they said 'let's make a film about a wartime romance' or whatever. The fact that we can 'decode' the film later to discuss its values doesn't necessarily mean the process can be reversed. You can draw ideologies out of a fiction, but you can't nearly as easily put them in.

What we now analyze in Hollywood films is usually 'put in' them unconsciously; and something on this level exists in all creations. What is striking about the weightily self-conscious contemporary fictions is their attempt to control all the meaning, as if nothing would come over without massive plugging.

But if there is something to be drawn out of ROCINANTE that its makers are surely not aware of, it is a terrible humorlessness. Lack of humour has always been a problem for the left, and one quality the right-on documentaries of the seventies share with the Art fictions of the eighties is precisely a lack of self-irony, a level of humour that prevents affectation.

It is not easy for me to say these things about films produced by groups I know and support, in a context of independent film-making to which I am firmly committed. But from that very commitment arises the need for debate and real criticism, and at a certain point someone has to say — look, this really doesn't work. ROCINANTE is full of good ideas and stunning images: but then, so is a good art history lecture. What makes a fiction film work is something else, and we have to learn what it is and how to do it.

N.S. 16 January 1987

Riddles of the Robot

Friendship's Death

The most powerful image in FRIENDSHIP'S DEATH is also the most familiar: newsreel of a plane going up in flames on a Jordanian airstrip. 'Pure spectacle', the script reminds us, through the mouth of Bill Paterson playing a British journalist, Sullivan. Sandwiched between two handy slices of such newsreel, the rest of the film (except the closing sequence) is set in two hotel rooms in 1970 Amman and consists of filmed dialogue between Sullivan and Friendship (Tilda Swinton), a robot designed as a woman and named after the aim of her mission from the galaxy of Procyon.

Friendship was programmed to arrive at the US MIT station but having lost contact with her control base finds herself left to her own devices in the Middle East. Initially bemused, Sullivan befriends her and ultimately tries to persuade her to return to England with him. However Friendship, adrift herself, identifies increasingly with the Palestinians and stays to fight their cause. Years later Sullivan, presuming her dead, is left with only the memento of a strange crystal which she has told him contains jottings in image form; his teenage daughter, a scientific genius who bears a strong resemblance to Friendship, finds a way to play her 'notepad' on video and it consists of a jumble of image-memories and what seem to be close-ups of blood cells.

This scenario is adapted from a short story written by director Peter Wollen some years ago. It's an interesting story, because it contains some interesting ideas: less about politics, despite its fashionable location, than about the relation betwen humans and machines, and the possibility of non-biological life forms. Its details raise intriguing philosophical questions about what it is to be human, and what aspects of humanity machines can replicate.

But there is one question I find unanswerable (except in terms of expedience) and that is why Wollen has chosen to do this as a *film*. There is another, indirectly related, question which is whether the film would merit much attention if Wollen himself were not already well known in the world of independent film, and particularly the world of film theory. I found FRIENDSHIP'S DEATH pretty flat, yet have chosen to write about it for the very reason that Wollen is an important figure in this world and therefore to some extent represents, as well as influences it.

Wollen's outstanding contribution to film studies was the book *Signs and Meaning in the Cinema*, published in 1968, which pioneered the application of semiotics to film. Since then he has made, with fellow film theorist Laura Mulvey, a succession of films attempting to put into practice their notions of an anti-mainstream film-making; this is his first solo directed feature.

I have discussed elsewhere what I see as some of the problems of the Mulvey/Wollen oeuvre, and more recent films in that tradition: a tendency to construct film by a sort of deconstruction in reverse, and an over-reliance on script to carry the meanings. The over-scripted quality of many British intellectual films is not coincidental. There is a much stronger literary than visual tradition in this country, and a great many of the influential figures in the independent film scene come from a background in English — in particular, English at Cambridge, with its Leavisite stress on both text and morality.

One of Wollen's key essays in the seventies discussed the 'two avant-gardes' in film-making: the aesthetic avant-garde, whose politics are those of form, and the more content-based avant-garde, whose politics are more located in the social realm. FRIENDSHIP'S DEATH is neither of these. Wollen seems to have moved — like so many erstwhile 'avant-garde' film-makers — to a pretty conventional use of narrative imagery, while retaining that dominance of the verbal that characterizes much of the didactic avant-garde genre.

For the images in FRIENDSHIP'S DEATH seem like mere vehicles for the spoken word, carrying streams of literary and philosophical aphorisms: 'politics has nothing to do with people, and all to do with maps — a war is the romance of territory' or 'I thought ruins are the past, but now I see that they belong to the present.' The characters given these lines hover uneasily between roundedness — for both Paterson and Swinton are excellent actors — and vehicle status, since basically they have to be made to say everything Peter Wollen wants to say.

Since the meaning seems almost totally confined to the script, FRIENDSHIP'S DEATH could work as a radio play (or, as it started out, a short story). But since for some reason it has to be a film, the characters have to be filmed talking and stuck in two rooms; the test the film poses itself is how many ways to shoot the two characters in this confined space. But this comes across more like a film school exercise: a scheme devised for some extraneous reason rather than for any reason integral to the film itself. Rather un-modestly, in an interview with the *Monthly Film Bulletin*, Wollen describes this as part of his penchant for 'virtuoso film-making', as exemplified by the 360° pan in RIDDLES OF THE SPHINX. But just bunging in fancy shots (like the overhead angles which refer to Hitchcock) isn't enough: virtuoso film-making implies at least a kind of energy. Passing over the fact that the female Robot provides a classic art-cinema Iconic Woman to look at and that the Palestinians are merely gunmen who occasionally rush across the room — or on second thoughts, inextricably linked with these stereotypes — the key problem with the film is that, like Friendship, it lacks precisely that indefinable quality which gives out warmth, which bleeds, sweats and cannot be entirely programmed — in short, humanity. Or, to put it Bob Dylan's way, its sin is its lifelessness.

N.S. 20 November 1987

To Haunt Us

Handsworth Songs

As 1986 closes, our national film critics look back on British Film Year and discuss the problems of Goldcrest, the failure of REVOLUTION. As 1987 opens, their eyes are turned to the major international releases, with Tarkovsky's death drawing added attention to THE SACRIFICE, and a new Coppola movie (amongst others) opening the same week.

Meanwhile, new steps in British film production, distribution and exhibition continue — the product not of a Year but a decade's work setting up the structures that allow independent, low-budget films to be made (the ACTT agreement outlined here recently) and, just as important, to be seen. After years of agitation for a central London exhibition venue by the Independent Film-Makers' Association, the Metro cinema was started a year ago by independent distributors The Other Cinema, with funding from the GLC's Arts and Recreation Committee. Its opening of THE PASSION OF REMEMBRANCE last month marked the first ever West End run of a film from a black workshop. Now, hard on its heels, comes the release of Black Audio Film Collective's HANDSWORTH SONGS.

Much of the so-called British film revival has hinged on pictures about our colonial past; now, one of the most vital strands of British film culture both arises from and addresses that same past (and its legacy in the present) from the other side. This movement owes something to the development of cultural theories which are changing the lines of debate about ideology, race and class: both PASSION OF REMEMBRANCE and HANDSWORTH SONGS pay tribute in their credits to Stuart Hall, a human landmark on the field of cultural studies in which the political language of both films has taken shape.

'There are no stories in the riots, only the ghosts of other stories.' This line from the extraordinarily poetic script of HANDSWORTH SONGS is at the heart not only of the film's meaning, but of its structure; or rather — and this is true of all successful films — the two are inseparable. Described by its makers as a 'film essay', HANDS-WORTH SONGS is a montage of images, sounds and words that simultaneously explore the surface of the 'civil disorder' in Handsworth and South London as presented through the media, while raising the ghosts, the histories political and personal, that hover behind that surface. Yet the film makes no simple distinction between the 'superficial' and the 'real'; its images are very much felt as such — from archive footage of colonial labour to the TV picture of Thatcher's 'alien customs' speech — and on one level it is *about* the images it's made of, at once impenetrable and resonant. The familiar shots of burning cars, the giant headlines, newsphotos of 'looters' on the run: jostling those pictures of urban debris are the ghosts of other *images*, fifties newsreel of Caribbean immigrants waving from the decks of ships, families with suitcases and the promise of work, images of hope and expectation whose very existence as old news gives them an added sense of lost innocence.

It is in the tension between image and story that the film really pushes the boundaries of documentary. Though none of the material is simple, the contemporary sequences take recognizable forms as interviewees speak, politicans argue. But with the 'ghost stories' the film-makers have taken a risk, shifting to intimate, individual narratives, feelings, recollections — 'that night I moved from an idea to a possibility' — so that the voice-overs provide an interiority which contrasts poignantly with the documentary footage of the time. And after the endless imagery of black 'violence' — always rioting, always running — different pictures: wedding photos, dances, the lifetime of dreams and desires whose shattering lies behind those unrevealing shots of fire and rubble. The risk taken with this unusual and beautifully written script pays off, for by creating these interiors, clearing room among the images as it were for some of the quiet passion and pain of the past, childhood memories, uncertain identities, a space is created for the viewer, one which also makes possible a kind of echo as meanings reverberate across and between the images.

This is the film's great achievement: it manages to produce a sense of what it is about, not just by telling but by doing it. The film is accessible — but not didactic; there is room to breathe. The opening image of the black, uniformed museum attendant surrounded by giant wheels of machinery, with the ominous gong-like knell of the sound track, has a meaning that can't be defined verbally but can be sensed by anybody; as birds gather on twilight telephone wires, a mechanical clown in a shop window turns his head and stares unseeing from side to side — who needs to be told what these images mean? They work in their own right, along with the brilliant soundtrack which plays a crucial part in distancing the familiar, referencing the past (for example in a version of 'Jerusalem') and creating literal echoes to match those of the pictures. It is no coincidence that Black Audio come to this — their first film project — from making tape-slide work, for they are strikingly skilled in overlapping sound and images both new and 're-used'. And, as Eisenstein pointed out, in the process of montage something new is created: this is both an analogy and a part of the process they describe, 'by which the living transform the dead into partners in struggle'.

N.S. 9 January 1987

Pictures of Pictures

The Last of England
The Belly of an Architect

I have sometimes complained in this column about the lack of formal
experiment in recent British films. Here are two features from
directors with backgrounds in the avant-garde, both of whom have
retained that investment in the image characteristic of their experimental short works. Both are now marketable as art film directors:
these two features are both funded by Channel Four and British
Screen in co-production with another European company (in Jarman's case, German, in Greenaway's, Italian) and clearly hold some
prestige value for their British producers. But, in stretching certain
avant-garde or 'art' concerns to feature length, it becomes apparent
that these are not, on their own, enough.

Derek Jarman's THE LAST OF ENGLAND is a layering of images
whose frequently impenetrable quality makes you constantly aware
that they *are* images. Grainy, murky, often seeming like 'found
footage', different thematic strands are overlaid: Jarman writing what
appears to be a diary in his room (which makes up the voice-over),
ruined streets in a newsreely present, home movies from the twenties
and fifties and a fantastic, apocalyptic future where masked soldiers
round up people on the streets.

This excavation of images from future, past and present is exciting
for about twenty or thirty minutes; for, as in scratch video, the way the
images are piled up, slowed down, repeated, makes something else out
of them, just as a poem can make something else out of words. The
exhilaration of seeing film used as a surface in this flickering way
recalls Brakhage (even though Jarman is much more obviously in the
line of Kenneth Anger, with his drugginess, his soldiers screwing on a
Union Jack, etc.). One of the richest visual moments is when the
swirling image of a woman trying to tear out of an interminable
wedding dress actually seems to thicken into solidity — as if the film
itself was being stirred like setting toffee.

The very act of taking techniques like these beyond the bounds of
the short is important in itself. But the weakness of the film is in what
the imagery's *of*. Jarman seems to have had this apocalyptic vision for
so long — IN THE SHADOW OF THE SUN, JUBILEE — that it suffers

from overkill and loses its political meaning: the derelict young men shooting up in empty buildings and ragged post-punks dancing round fires are becoming familiar trademarks. And shoving 'Land of Hope and Glory' on the soundtrack doesn't really work as a political gesture: despite an oblique parody of the Royal Wedding, the film offers no insights into the end-of-empire destruction it depicts.

But the real problem is that we've already moved into our own *fin-de-siècle* period where images of urban decadence and decay are so modish that they refer to each other as much as to any social actuality. Half of the imagery in THE LAST OF ENGLAND is like a Heroin Screws You Up ad; the aggressive-litte-boy-lost looks glower out from every album cover. There is a stylishness about all this dereliction which makes it meaningless politically. This isn't entirely Jarman's fault; he is, in fact, able to suggest an atmosphere entirely through non-transparent images culled from this *Face*-like repertoire; they *connote*, rather than denote anything specific. A shopping trolley in water isn't so much a realist image of our streets as an image of the emptiness of a culture. But the film partakes of this emptiness itself; it riffles through the visual thesaurus of our time but adds no new meanings or inflections. In particular, the home-movie imagery is part of a new shorthand for a fifties-esque, suburban normality, now superceded by our own superior knowingness: we can already see beyond those happy, shy smiles which, for a whole generation, merely confirm our cynicism. The fact that those fifties faces now grace not only Biff cartoons but British Rail ads detracts from the impact of this juxtaposition in Jarman's film. Yes, the cute little boy in shorts is now a guy in a leather jacket, but so what?

Those two horrible words, or rather, their twins, Big Deal, were frequently in my mind during this film. 'Naked guy eats raw cauliflower by burning bin — big deal.' 'Guy wanks on Caravaggio picture — big deal.' A response, perhaps, to the film's own lack of humour; lines like 'tomorrow has been cancelled owing to lack of interest' or 'The *A-Z* clamped a grid on despair' are so desperately redolent of adolescence, it felt as if the diary was being written by a sort of camp Adrian Mole. It is a pity that, in carrying visual experiment into a major production, this film is without a wider context of similar work which might help knock the edges off its clichés.

Peter Greenaway's latest, THE BELLY OF AN ARCHITECT, is, though very different, also highly invested in its visual surface. Sacha Vierny's photography, capturing both the liquidity of Rome's light and the solidity of its buildings, gives the film an aesthetic quality that it would be churlish to deny.

Like Greenaway's other films, it is clever but cold. However, unlike Greenaway's other films, it has someone who can act. Brian Dennehy as Kracklite — the middle-aged American architect with stomach cancer whose great project is taken from him by the same man who seduces his wife — gives a deeply moving performance, quite against the grain of the film's own heartlessness. Where Greenaway seems to use this massive, dying man merely as part of an intellectual formula, Dennehy turns him into a living, raging being. The sense that he is struggling, not only against his illness but against the coolness of the film itself, heightens the poignancy of Kracklite's position; in particular the emphasis on the male body, one of the film's neat architectural analogies, becomes peculiarly moving, the folds of stone flesh on the great statues forming a counterpoint to Kracklite's own pasty bulk. But while Dennehy almost pushes the film into being about the fragility of the male body and ego, the formulaic plot pulls us back into the realm of ideas, and this uncharacteristic injection of humanity only makes it clearer that the rest of the characters are merely counters on the Greenaway board.

N.S. 23 October 1987

Dirty Linen

Sammy and Rosie Get Laid

SAMMY AND ROSIE GET LAID couldn't have had better publicity than that provided by Norman Stone's by now notorious article in the *Sunday Times*, attacking recent oppositional films like THE LAST OF ENGLAND, MY BEAUTIFUL LAUNDRETTE, EAT THE RICH, EMPIRE STATE, BUSINESS AS USUAL and, of course, SAMMY AND ROSIE GET LAID which he specially notes for 'general disgustingness'.

Stone's dislike of these none too similar films seems to hinge on two main factors: first, their 'disgustingness', which in a Jarman film might take the form of explicit sex while in EMPIRE STATE it is the 'revolting sadism' of the fight scene where two men tear each other apart; second, their political attacks on the state of Britain under Margaret

Thatcher — the only reason a film like BUSINESS AS USUAL, which I wouldn't hesitate to take my mother to, can be included in his list.

There have been many considered responses to Norman Stone, including one in the *Guardian* by SAMMY AND ROSIE's scriptwriter, Hanif Kureishi. Stone is a prophet of the far right and I need hardly say that politically I align myself with those fending off his hysteria about any film which portrays present-day Britain as less than perfect. But while Stone himself is easily dismissed, it is all too easy, as the lines are drawn up around this issue, to dismiss any misgivings one might have about any of these films, for fear of appearing to be on the wrong side. Yet I too found, for example, the level of sadism in EMPIRE STATE disturbing and unnecessary. Kureishi talks in his article about the suppression of criticism in Britain today. But a sad feature of this Britain is precisely the fact that, so busy are those on 'our side' attacking/defending themselves against the Right, there is precious little real cultural criticism on the left *of its own products*. Since, however, I have no fear of being mistaken for Norman Stone, I will come right out and say that I found SAMMY AND ROSIE GET LAID an extremely irritating film — and I'll try to explain why.

It is revealing that much of the publicity has centred on Kureishi (his diary of the filming is published by Faber along with the script) because this is yet another British film where the script is all-important and everything else — actors, camera, the lot — is basically there as its vehicle. The very fact that the script is published simultaneously with the film's opening seems a tacit admission of their equal importance. On their last project, MY BEAUTIFUL LAUN-DRETTE, Kureishi and director Stephen Frears seemed better able to hold at bay this quality of script-self-consciousness; here it runs rampant. The title couple invariably speak as if they know their words come from a controversial scriptwriter: 'naughty' lines are delivered with a truculence reminiscent of the pseudo-careless voice children use to swear in when they want to shock their parents.

And it is in the mixing of sexual 'daring' with political criticism that the film perfectly fits *both* of Stone's despised categories. But do they necessarily have to go together? It takes a different kind of courage to make political criticisms than it takes to bung in lines about 'cunty fingers'. Within the plot characters use sex deliberately to shock, as when the obnoxious lesbian couple (are they *meant* to be so creepy?) kiss in front of Sammy's father, Rafi, simply to embarrass him; there is no sense of desire. The film itself seems to employ a similar mechanism: its use of sex is not erotic, but full of its own permissiveness, daring you not to be embarrassed.

The sex scenes would only matter if one cared about the characters. There is some engaging material in the film: the opening sequence when police shoot a black woman in her home, as with Cherry Groce, is the most emotionally shocking episode, but sadly this sinks into a backdrop for the horrible Sammy and Rosie, who live their horrible yuppie lives somewhere around Ladbroke Grove. The heart of the story — raising its key political questions — is the return of Rafi: a freedom-fighter turned dictator in his native Pakistan, fleeing to London, shocked by his son's lifestyle and, ultimately, rejected by his long-left-behind suburban lover, Claire Bloom. Bloom, Shashi Kapoor as Rafi, and Roland Gift as Danny — the black itinerant who provides the other characters' rather token link with the urban 'underclass' (it is typical of the new leftism that there is no *working class*) — provide the film with what warmth it has, even though Claire Bloom is given some ridiculously didactic lines. The rest of the time the characters merely seem to stand for things, so that their interweavings produce complicated socio-political alliances, but you are left wondering if the film-makers really intended them to appear so two-dimensional and cold.

Leaving aside right-wing paranoias, I think negative responses to the film partly arise from the fact that two kinds of bleakness are present, mixed up together: the bleakness of 'Thatcher's Britain', which the film vehemently attacks, but also the matching bleakness of its own sensibility. It *tells* us things, but cannot make us feel them: lines like 'the city is a mass of fascination' and 'what is going to happen to all that beauty?' shouldn't be necessary because the film should be able to evoke beauty, fascination and the sense of their loss by means of its own imagery and narrative structure. That its coldness is not fully intentional is clear from the fact that its narrative ploys don't work. As bulldozers move in to crush Danny's and his friends' homes, the film cuts to the faces of Sammy and Rosie as if to evoke feeling. But the characters seem so empty that there is none.

This is a film standing on important territory, confronting important issues, and trying to say important things. But its supreme failure *as* a film is that, frankly, I don't give a damn whether Sammy and Rosie get laid.

N.S. 29 January 1988

The Rules and the Game

Hermosillo Season:
Doña Herlinda and her Son
Deceptive Appearances
Matinée

There is something profoundly self-conscious about the concern of both mainstream and oppositional cinema with sex and 'sexuality' at the moment. Gay sex in particular is usually subject either to an irritating coyness, very noticeable at the more mainstream end of the market, or to an equally irritating tendency to statement-making, usually found in the more deliberately political sector. In a society where homosexuality isn't taken for granted, it *is* very hard to present sex between men or between women as a simple fact of life on the screen.

This makes it all the more interesting that, 'from the land of the margarita, the taco and the macho' as the publicity puts it (i.e. from Mexico), the work of Jaime Humberto Hermosillo has an extraordinary directness which makes films like PARTING GLANCES and MY BEAUTIFUL LAUNDRETTE look precious by comparison. Hermosillo's most popular (and most specifically gay) film, DOÑA HERLINDA AND HER SON, is currently playing the independent circuit here and has been widely reviewed; but its opening has been accompanied by a retrospective at the National Film Theatre, which has given an unprecedented opportunity to get a wider sense of his work.

The most striking aspect of Hermosillo's films is their matter-of-factness, not only about sex but about death, bodily functions and the sources of money, aspects of life which most films either gloss over shyly, or conversely, act wildly proud about including. (Of course that look-at-us-we're-so-upfront tone is only the flip-side of the don't-look-now.) In DECEPTIVE APPEARANCES (whose plot is extraordinarily like that of Balzac's *Sarrasine*) the owner of the family fortunes is a wheelchair-bound old man, whose infantile state of incontinence and frustrated emotions are presented in a way that's neither patronizing, sentimental nor 'political'. (It's almost impossible to imagine an English film in which somebody is found to have shitted their pants that didn't provoke either hysterical comedy or a concerned social worker response.) The treatment of this one detail speaks for the tone of the whole film, in which sex, sickness and the making of money are treated explicitly but never self-consciously.

The film's sexual plot — in which a straight man is forced to realize, finally, that the 'woman' he desires is a man too — may sound wacky but what is truly unusual is that it's presented in a completely affectless manner. It's not that the *characters* don't have feelings — but Hermosillo presents them without a structured appeal to ours. MATINÉE, for example, is a film which could have been very cute: two little boys, obsessed with gangster comics, get embroiled with a real gang when one of them stows away in a van which the robbers have hijacked from the other boy's father. The kids end up living with the gang, befriended by their captors, until one of them tips off the police.

This sounds like material for a charming comic movie: yet one boy's father is killed, and the film refuses to switch tone for his death so the audience is left with no clues about how to take it. Two of the gang appear to have a gay relationship, but since they are not shown actually making love this emerges as an emotional fact, through the jealousies that ensue when one of them becomes particularly close to one of the boys. The men die in each other's arms, dressed as priests, while attempting to rob a cathedral; but, again, this episode is signalled neither as comic nor romantic.

Which is not to say the film isn't funny or emotional; but that's not the same thing. We are so steeped in the modes of conventional narrative that we expect a film not only to tell a story but to tell us how to respond to it. It becomes literally hard to imagine love outside of a romantic mode or sex outside of a 'sexy' mode. And it is precisely cinematic conventions which coincide with and reinforce the social conventions that translate the raw materials of physical and emotional life into ways of thinking about them. We are accustomed to films providing us with some ground on which to make moral judgments, and Hermosillo refuses to offer it. What is subversive about his films isn't the fact that you see, for example in DOÑA HERLINDA, men undressing and making love (as if they meant it, for once); it's that the *audience* are stripped, left without the comfortable clothing of cinematic codes which, like their social counterparts, provide structures of meaning which keep a vision of the world secure.

The shifting of these structures reminds me of Renoir (one of Hermosillo's favourite directors) with his liberatingly amoral quality which, ultimately, is an expansion of morality rather than its denial. Hermosillo doesn't have anything like Renoir's visual style; yet a film like MATINÉE has very much the same absence of conventional moral tone as, say, BOUDU SAUVÉ DES EAUX, and their off-beat endings are strikingly similar. DOÑA HERLINDA AND HER SON, in which the conventions of a patriarchal society are shown as completely at odds with actual sexual feelings, yet strangely able to contain them, is reminiscent of LA RÈGLE DU JEU, where the very fact of portraying the ins and outs of desires becomes subversive.

For film is a medium better suited to showing things than to saying them; and in this lies its specific capacity for challenging social assumptions. There is no *obvious* 'sex-pol' in Hermosillo's films; and yet they liberate the viewer from an enormous number of preconceptions, by showing the supposedly abnormal in an unconcernedly normal way.

N.S. 26 June 1987

Man, Myth and Maggots

Gothic
The Fly

Ken Russell has always had a penchant for the wild and wacky doings of creative folk. Composers, dancers, sculptors, painters: in his films their work is scarcely as fascinating as their strange sex lives and bizarre behaviour. But with the romantic poets he must surely have found his most sympathetic subjects, for Byron's exotic views on the lifestyle of the Artist seem to tally remarkably well with Russell's own.

GOTHIC is a dramatization of the night in 1816 at Byron's villa where he, Shelley, Mary Godwin, her half-sister Claire, and Doctor John Polidori passed the time cooking up ghost stores, out of which eventually came Polidori's *The Vampyre* and Mary Shelley's *Frankenstein*. The film draws attention to the creative processes through heavily scripted remarks about the vastness of the imagination and the force of fantasies from within; the period is hailed by Byron as 'an age of dreams and nightmares'.

However, if the imagination is so vast, it is a pity that Russell's repertoire of effects for evoking this internal sea of seething sexuality and terror is so limited. The inventory of pigs' heads, leeches, rats, skulls, snakes, creaking doors and trailing cobwebs makes the film resemble nothing so much as a ride in an old-fashioned ghost train. The key to the Gothic mode was the externalization of inner drives and fears; and none of the film's effects is subtle or suggestive enough to give a sense of internality. 'It's no good, you can't run away from your own fears', someone tells Mary, and this is rendered rather grossly in a scene where she finds herself in an octagonal room with weird scenes taking place behind every door — a *Steppenwolf* kind of notion, suggesting that this scenario has its roots as much in sixties culture as that of the early 19th century.

All this horror is used to psychologize Mary's creation of the Frankenstein story: the dead baby with the Boris Karloff face and her apparent premonition of Shelley's death by drowning are rolled in to explain or interpret her tale of a creator whose creation goes out of control. The application of this idea to Artists is played on endlessly: 'We are the gods now . . . we call ourselves creators . . . but the punishment is . . . we have created — what?'

One is tempted to answer: a banal film. For the problem with GOTHIC is its inability to get beyond the graphic level — as if the only way to evoke the terrifying or sublime were to bung in more maggots.

A further liability is the self-consciousness of the dialogue — 'For God's sake, Mary!' 'But God is already dead, Shelley!' — and the bizarrely anachronistic line, as his friends notice Shelley hitting the opium again: 'I can handle it.' The film could work as an extended anti-drug ad. It also works as kitsch: there was much audience hilarity when I saw it. But the camp level is spoiled by the portrayal of Polidori, whose homosexual love for Byron is turned into an orgy of self-mutilation and disgust. Ultimately, GOTHIC is not very Gothic; it is too sexually explicit. If the repressed positively *flaunts* itself down every corridor, it is hard to get a sense of that frisson between the inner and outer which characterized the Romantic modes.

I say modes because the Gothic was extremely close to its less currently fashionable sibling, the Sentimental, which evoked pity where the former evoked fear. The tenacity of Romantic discourses in our present culture can be seen in, for example, our responses to disease (and specifically Aids) where pity and terror are two sides of the same coin. Cronenberg's THE FLY is another curiously graphic film, most interesting for its suggestion of a different response to bodily sickness; though in its preoccupation with a range of disjunctions between inner and outer — with particular reference to sexuality — it is placed firmly on Gothic territory. Its hero, Seth Brundle (Jeff Goldblum) is a scientist whose single-minded involvement in his work makes him appear 'pure', almost non-sexual at the start of the film, when he invites a science journalist (Geena Davis) up to see his extraordinary invention, a computerized teletransporter, and over- comes her scepticism by transporting one of her black lacy stockings.

These transporting chambers bear an intriguing resemblance to Reich's orgone machines; and indeed a Reichian sense of the energiz- ing properties of sex echoes throughout the film. In his 'virginal' state Brundle is at an impasse with his project, being unable to understand 'flesh' — as the script carefully tells us, several times. However, after sleeping with his new woman friend he finds he can transport living matter: sex has an enabling function. At the same time it is the darker side of sexual entanglement that transforms him more radically; in a rage of (unnecessary) sexual jealousy he transports himself and fails to notice a fly in the machine, with the result that he becomes genetically merged with it. The immediate effects of this are, again, strangely Reichian: Brundle finds enormous reserves of energy and strength, wants to fuck all the time and becomes very self-assertive, ultimately aggressive, stomping around bare-chested in a leather jacket instead of the shirts and ties that made him so charmingly 'straight' at the beginning. He has swapped science for sex: knowledge has been the gateway to his sexual relationship and sex the gateway to completing his scientific invention. The final outcome of the two together is his hideous transformation into a giant fly.

Of course, what this fable most resembles is the Frankenstein story — but with a twist. For Brundle is both inventor and monster; the two roles are elided, neatly bringing back together the two sides of 'human nature' that Gothic literature split. Mary Shelley thought that the inventor would recoil in horror from his presumptuous creations. Brundle, however, after initial despondency, becomes remarkably exhilarated: 'I'll become something that never existed before', he enthuses, flinging himself into his disease with great humour, bottling the parts of his body that fall off, video-ing his eating habits for future science lessons. There is something not Gothic, but existential, in his excitement at becoming his own creation; and even if the film's simpler level of horror brings us back to pity and terror in the end, this momentary glimpse beyond Romantic self-loathing is both timely and refreshing.

N.S. 27 February 1987

In the Pink

Lesbian and Gay Film and Video
'The Lesbian Vampire in Film'
'Underground Canada'
November Moon

Where, in a culture which suppresses homosexuality, do lesbian and gay concerns surface in cinema? A diverse collection of events during the next month provides answers to this question in different ways. Mainstream cinema frequently deflects 'deviant' sexualities into the corners of genre forms; whether sublimated into the male buddy movie, or, more overtly, into those genres whose stories and symbolism allow for stylized representations of sexuality, like horror or vampire movies.

It is well known that within the latter genre 'initiated' women will prove as avid as Dracula himself in pouncing on nubile female bodies: this is practically the only area of popular cinema where lesbians are seen at all — ambiguously portrayed as at once strong, independent, and predatory. The lesbian vampire film is the subject of a presentation by Andrea Weiss at the Tyneside Festival and the Ritzy Cinema next week, with screenings of a variety of films including THE HUNGER; one issue under discussion will be the extent to which genre films can be re-read, reinterpreted subversively by lesbian and gay audiences. This kind of appropriation has been a crucial aspect of the relationship of gay culture to mainstream cinema, a topic explored most richly in some of Richard Dyer's writing on film (*Stars, Heavenly Bodies*).

Appropriation also works the other way. Straight romance is becoming rather threadbare in opportunities for the kinds of obstacles, misunderstandings, parental and social disapproval that used to fan the flames of traditional movie romances, but now, with films like DESERT HEARTS, or MY BEAUTIFUL LAUNDRETTE, the thrill of transgression can be rekindled as gay romance against the backdrop of a repressive society.

MAURICE, the Merchant-Ivory version of E.M. Forster's novel, fits this formula nicely; though with its central affair never consummated, most of the love-making is done by the camera to the accoutrements of upper-class life — Cambridge colleges, well-kept lawns and sherry decanters. It is interesting to compare this film, or ANOTHER COUN-TRY, with PRICK UP YOUR EARS: working-class homosexuality can be offered up as 'Carry On' camp comedy, but upper-class sex lives must be shown as unbearably sensitive and serious. (Of course, the bearer of 'earthy' sexuality in MAURICE is, as in *Lady Chatterley*, the game-keeper.) Interesting in its portrayal of a repressed, Platonic love between men, the film's sensibility remains rooted in class, rather than gay, culture.

On the other hand, the lesbian and gay section at Tyneside (repeated as the NFT's 'Gay Lives' season) brings us a collection of film and video from within gay cultures around the world. THE OUTSIDERS (Yu Kan-Ping) is an extraordinarily moving film from Taiwan, following the story of a young man thrown out of home for 'unnatural acts'. Ah-Ching finds refuge in the city's gay scene, and along with other stray boys forms a kind of substitute family under the kindliness of an older gay man and his sympathetic landlady.

The film's use of lighting and colour gives it a very particular aesthetic, rather like the quality of neon seen through rain. The gay scene centres on a park, where, as lovers seek and are sought, blue, cavernous light falling in shafts through the trees gives the feeling of being underground — a feeling reinforced less metaphorically by the police raid. But although the 'outsiders' are, most of the time, literally outside, the film's visual effects leave you with a sense of the softness of the park at night compared to the harshness of conventional family life.

There seems to be greater scope for campness and tongue-in-cheek in films from the more established gay cultures. From the US West Coast two shorts by Gus Van Sant (who made MALA NOCHE) combine humour and poignancy — I particularly liked MY NEW FRIEND, a sort of one-home-movie stand. Most gut-wrenchingly funny are the shorts by David Weissman, BEAUTIES WITHOUT A CAUSE and 976-DISH. As the dial-a-gossip Dish says, 'Can you *believe* David Weissman *still* makes these cheap 2-minute films?' Yes, and it is the witty use of their cheapness — as when the Beauties 'drive' in a stationary car — that makes them so exhilaratingly camp.

Another strong centre of lesbian and gay film-making is Toronto, and three excellent programmes of film and video called 'Under-ground Canada' play at Tyneside, before coming to London. These include Midi Onodera's chic TEN CENTS A DANCE, which neatly shows the gaps in sexual communication through visual devices, and Marga-ret Moore's FRANKLY, SHIRLEY, which follows a lost lesbian affair through Toronto's winter streets. Also at Tyneside is THE LAW OF

DESIRE, an extraordinary film by Spanish director Pedro Almodóvar. Its tone recalls Hermosillo's work: the film confronts not only sexuality in every form but also death, and yet remains wildly, crazily funny.

An important project of gay film-making has always been to claim its own eroticism, and the Tyneside/NFT programme gives an airing to the cult film PINK NARCISSUS, an extended erotic fantasy which shows that sexiness doesn't mean just sex. A close-up of a blade of grass trailed across skin, a hand caressing beads on a string — the repertoire of imagery is both inventive and, again, funny.

Humour is something that feminists, particularly lesbian feminists, are supposed to lack, but Caroline Sheldon's 17 BEDROOMS OR, WHAT DO LESBIANS DO IN BED? proves otherwise. What *do* lesbians do in bed? Read, eat breakfast, sleep, play Scrabble — this film denies the voyeuristic pleasure that sex between women has so often provided not only within porn genres but within art film. As Mandy Merck has pointed out in an essay on LIANNA, love between women can provide the thrill of the forbidden *and* the satisfaction of being 'progressive' required by the art movie genre.

Alexandra von Grote's NOVEMBER MOON manages to avoid any such smug voyeurism as it follows the emotional and social lives of two women, one of them Jewish, in occupied France during the war. The film is elegantly if conventionally made — from the Virago Modern Classic school of film-making. But not only does it sidestep glib formulae about fascism and sexuality, its key images send out resonances which go beyond their immediate place in the plot.

November, the Jewish woman, is forced to go underground in her lover's apartment, hiding in an excruciatingly small cavity under a sofa when guests — including Nazis — come round. To avoid arousing suspicions, her lover also takes up with an old admirer who writes for a Nazi paper, pretending to be both straight, and sympathetic to the new order. The painful concealment of an actual woman who literally can't 'come out', and the social cost — her lover has her head shaved after the war for 'collaborating' — hits a note of fear that must have meaning for anyone who has ever been in the closet.

N.S. 9 October 1987

Post-Sex Cinema?

The strange sequence of words above (without the question-mark) was the title of a seminar I attended last week as part of the Piccadilly Festival, whose theme this year was 'Living Dangerously'. As always with words, one tends to assume that they refer to something: but it is hard to determine whether there is, in fact, a referent for the phrase 'post-sex cinema'; or, if there is, what it might be.

The most immediate connotation of 'post-sex' is Aids — unfortunately, given that Aids doesn't spell the end of sex. However, the phrase does have currency in the USA as a trendy way of describing the enormous readjustment Aids has demanded. You would expect to see evidence of this readjustment on the screen; but in mainstream (or particularly in what I think of as 'mainstream independent') cinema such evidence — either as encouragement to safe sex or as anti-gay backlash — is hard to find. Far from being *post*-sex, there seems to be a particular obsession with sex, or, as it's fashinably called, 'sexuality', at the moment. Any crude notion that Aids must result in a general repression of sexual concerns in film must be belied by a glance at recent hits.

On one tack we have BLUE VELVET, 9½ WEEKS, BETTY BLUE, SOMETHING WILD — all of which suggest that sex is very much in vogue. But *what* sex? One strand of meaning in the phrase 'post-sex' can be found in its very structure: that prefix of the moment which makes it so easy to dismiss whatever (by a sequential irony) comes after it. And if there is a 'post' which accurately describes the films named above it is surely 'post-feminist'. There is a new, 'liberated *and* sexy' woman on the screen at the moment whose persona is a bit like a combination of *both* the images in the 'Underneath They're All Lovable' lingerie ad: tough, smart and independent (like the big picture) yet invariably clad in sexy underwear (like the inset). Indeed the trend marked by these films is the very same that has produced the striking expansion of the lacy/frilly/funky camisole/suspenders/french knickers market at the moment, evident from a quick dip into any high-street chain store.

This woman is visually indistinguishable from the old-style sex-object except, with plots which hinge on her new aggressiveness of spirit, she is miraculously turned into the new-style sex-*subject*. And alongside this increasing fascination with the sexually active (straight) woman, there is the increasing number of successful 'mainstream

independent' movies with gay and lesbian subject positions: MY
BEAUTIFUL LAUNDRETTE, DESERT HEARTS, PARTING GLANCES,
PRICK UP YOUR EARS. One could hardly claim that Aids was making
homosexuality taboo at the moment. Rather there has been if anything
an increasing eroticization of the male body in mainstream Hollywood
film (Richard Gere, Tom Cruise) and an increase in gay subject-
matter in up-market independent film. Then there is the smash hit of
Spike Lee's SHE'S GOTTA HAVE IT, one of the few financially successful
black films about sex.

I am not holding these films up as positive examples of anything —
most of them have been heavily criticized in this column — but
pointing out that there is an increasingly mainstream interest in what
have hitherto been the 'margins' both socially and cinematically. This
has moved in tandem with current theoretical work on 'difference',
'the Other' and so on: there is a sort of general exploration of
colonization going on at the moment (with the exploration and the
colonization often collapsed together).

But ultimately the issue must be not merely *what* (or who) is
represented in film, but *how*. Mainstream cinema is always in search of
new and more thrilling material, but it is usually absorbed into
familiar structures; so that, for example, the gay romance of BEAUTI-
FUL LAUNDRETTE or the lesbian romance of DESERT HEARTS are
highly palatable to an audience accustomed to straight screen
romance. However, while these films pack out the Art House cinemas,
what is going on at the margins of film production itself?

One of the great achievements of the Piccadilly Festival was to
juxtapose the mainstream with the low-budget/short/avant-garde end
of the independent sector, and their comparison is very revealing.
Some of the most interesting material was found in the Canadian film
and video programme 'Prime Cuts', compiled by John Greyson, whose
own works combine gay politics, sex, humour and narrative — in YOU
TASTE AMERICAN, for instance, Michel Foucault, visiting Tennessee
Williams, gets arrested in the 1983 wash-house raid in Orillia,
Ontario. Other pieces like Kim Tomczak's SEE EVIL and Vera
Frenkl's SIGNS OF A PLOT deal directly with the issue of censorship;
which is a major part of the climate in which all this work was made.

For while the very project of the mainstream independents is to
appear totally liberated, it is here, in the semi-underground, that
oppression is dealt with. It is in this context that Rosa Von Praunheim's
vehement, vicious (to women), irreverent, angry A VIRUS KNOWS NO
MORALS turns Aids into a form of revenge. It is here that Paul Bettell's
ILLEGAL TENDER defies the 'criminality' of 'under-age' homosexuals,

that Greyson documents the persecutions of Apartheid in A MOFFIE
CALLED SIMON. It is here that Isaac Julien's moving THIS IS NOT AN
AIDS ADVERTISEMENT has to repeat the message, 'feel no guilt in your
desire'. It's not *sex* that mainstream cinema can't confront — but
homophobia, fear, suppression. It is left to those on 'the margins' to
confront these.

N.S. 5th June 1987

Death in the Family Way

The Stepfather

So many people have told me how disturbed they were by FATAL
ATTRACTION that I feel I must publicize an ideological antidote,
guaranteed to cut through that sick creepy feeling it left you (and me)
with. This antidote is THE STEPFATHER: a concise low-budget film
with a little-known director (Joseph Ruben) and no stars. As a thriller
it is taut and well acted, every bit as suspenseful as its opposite; but
here what is monstrous is not the single woman but precisely the
idealization of family values in which a film like FATAL ATTRACTION
so cloyingly deals.

The film opens with a perfect suburban street: trees line the
sidewalk and a paper-boy cycles between them, throwing his bundles
onto kempt front lawns. Taking this all in, the camera, disturbingly
smooth and mobile, glides through an upstairs window where a man is
washing and shaving off his beard. He packs his old clothes and
wedding ring into a suitcase and walks downstairs — pausing to tidy
some toys into an over-full toybox and push down the lid. He moves
past a scene of mayhem in the front room, where a woman and child
lie hacked to pieces, straightens a chair, and passes through the front
door into the sunny street, where he picks up the paper and walks off,
whistling. Taking the ferry into town, he drops the suitcase overboard.

The next thing we see is another sunny street lined with trees; a girl
cycles along casually, and a caption tells us this is 'One year later'.
Everything is as smooth as before; but as the girl unmounts in front of

one of the neat suburban houses, we experience the first sudden movement of the film, as someone bursts out at her from the back garden. It is her mother, throwing a bucket of leaves over her head, and the two begin a mock-fight. Their game stops abruptly when a man comes home: it is the newly-shaven character from the first scene.

Where this film differs from many conventional thrillers is that we know, from the opening, who represents danger: it is the stepfather, whose obsession with family life, totally 'normal' in a film like FATAL ATTRACTION, is thus neatly pathologized from the very start. His patriarchal values — 'father knows best' — take on a more macabre tone the 'nicer' he gets in his efforts to turn his new wife and stepdaughter into a perfect family.

That the film's attack on patriarchy is more than an accidental effect of the plot is shown by the way its script and imagery constantly take us beyond the particular. Mr Murderer works for American Eagle Realty and feels that his job is 'not just selling houses but selling the American Dream'. His language comes straight (and straight is the word) from the Reagan/Thatcher script computer; and his clean-clean-clean appearance makes him look all the time like a man in a lawn mower ad. However, the most subtle and disturbing aspect of his psychology is his obsessive measuring-up of each new family against the Ideal; he kills from *disappointment*. In a spine-chilling piece of self-righteousness he muses that a man could be '*driven* to do something like that' (my italics). This testing of real relationships against a normative blueprint makes a vivid political point: the man is a kind of walking Clause 28,[1] his mission being to clean up any domestic situation that deviates from the ideal.

This is emphasized in the film by the way the plot's Goodies are *im*perfect: it is the Baddy who, apart from his few murderous outbursts, is always calm and smiling. This says something about repression: its flip-side is violence. Here is the importance of the mother-daughter fight scene, and a similar 'friendly' fight between the daughter and her boyfriend: the truly frightening people are those who never let go. The film's sub-plot, involving a reporter on the murderer's trail, shows that Goodies can be unshaven, rude, drive un-smart cars, and — in the lead-up to the climax — can even be a rowing, adulterous couple in the middle of splitting up.

Because the other point about repression is that it doesn't work. The image of the toybox being forced shut is exactly reversed in the first

1   See footnote on p. 68.

moment of eruption with the new family: the girl goes into the basement to get icecream from the freezer and as she lifts the lid she hears her stepfather having a violent fit. Another sub-plot, with the girl's analyst, reinforces this point as he, of all people, makes a 'Freudian' slip; after inventing a fake identity in order to investigate the stepfather he forgets to keep it up and lets himself 'show through'.

When the murderer finally flips, *he* forgets who he is 'this time': it is appropriate that his stepdaughter stabs him with a broken mirror. In a climax that smartly invokes Hitchcock (a shower, birds on a wire) only to subvert his typically sadistic voyeurism (nothing happens in the shower, the birds just sit there) the two women, mother and daughter, succeed without male help (sorry for spoiling the plot) and moreover one of the mother's shots hits the picture of an eagle, shattering that image of American Patriarchy into a thousand pieces.

It is this kind of symbolism which, though obvious, is so enjoyable for us ideological misfits. During the film the stepfather has been building, with his violent tools, a cute little birdhouse which stands on a high pole: in the closing scene the girl cuts down this emblem of phallic domesticity and the camera follows it to the ground.

This overturned representation summarizes the whole film; and also explains why it is unlikely to be a sell-out. For what is frightening about FATAL ATTRACTION is less the film itself than its popularity. A brave cinema would programme these movies together: and leave audiences to ponder why, of two thrillers, one which monstrosizes the single woman should be a hit, while one which monstrosizes the ideal family is not.

N.S. 12 February 1988

Short Circuit of the New Man

Making Mr Right

The key fact about the New Man is that he doesn't exist. Variously a
marketing concept and a projection of modern women's desires, the
emotional, sensitive, tender Loving Hunk is no more real than the
Living Doll who was, similarly, an amalgam of consumer products
and male fantasies. Of course, no one really noticed at the time how
postmodern the Living Doll syndrome really was — that the swinging
chick was primarily an image — because pop culture didn't jar,
fundamentally, with the male point of view that has never stopped
being socially dominant. On the other hand, the Ideal Man, to most
women today, is palpably unreal, no matter how many baby-faced
new male models in pink sweaters pout out from the pages of *The Face*.

So it makes perfect sense that the 'New Man' in Susan Seidelman's
MAKING MR RIGHT is, literally, new: a robot. While it has not been
warmly received, the film has been widely reviewed and most people
must have got the gist of the plot: Frankie Stone (Ann Magnuson), a
PR agent, lands a publicity contract for an android, Ulysses, designed
for space travel and made in the exact image of his scientist creator,
Jeff. When she spends time with Ulysses as part of his social
programming they gradually fall in love.

Both Jeff and Ulysses are played by John Malkovitch (in a witty
visual aside the film acknowledges THE PARENT TRAP, where Hayley
Mills plays identical twins) and on the face of it this echoes the
doppelgänger theme of Seidelman's DESPERATELY SEEKING SUSAN,
where Rosanna Arquette finds the wild side of herself in Madonna.
Here, however, the interest lies less in Jeff finding (and hating) the
'softer' side of himself — the two are never reconciled, least of all in the
surprise ending — than in Frankie, or indeed the other women
characters, finding a decent date. The film opens with a TV item
where Frankie's current boyfriend Steve, who is running for Congress,
is shown kissing a beauty queen. Frankie watches from her couch and
kicks him out the next morning when he turns up feebly apologizing.
This deft pre-credit sequence ends with her hurling a lifesize card-
board model of Steve (from his publicity campaign) out of the window
and the smiling, waving, two-dimensional man floats onto the road
beneath the wheels of her car.

All through the film there is an emphasis on Man as Image: Frankie's friend Trish checks out her actor husband's girlfriends by watching how realistically he kisses his co-stars on a soap opera. Both men and media are seen through *women*'s eyes: suitably enough since, as Frankie points out in a business presentation, 'women control most of the nation's TV dials and buy 72 per cent of magazines'. While Seidelman has always had an eye for the transformations of femininity — Frankie switches from tousled tee-shirt to boardroom glamour as she drives to work — the stress here is not on women switching images (as in SUSAN) but on women as *consumers* of images — and of men, in relation to whom the film functions like a *Which?* guide.

And all the real models are found lacking. When Frankie arrives at the space lab for the first time, she has to deal with the over-smarmy director on the one hand and the cold, uptight Jeff on the other, carefully steering a route between the familiar poles of harassment and rudeness. It is in this context that she meets Ulysses: and, unlike all the other men in the film, he is open for programming. This offers a fascinating opportunity for Helen Gurley Brown-style training in reverse: Frankie teaches him to make prolonged eye contact and to listen to what his companion's saying 'as if it was the most important thing in the world', while from Steve's TV campaign ad he learns concepts like *It takes a man this sensitive to know your needs*. Ulysses is like a feminist RoboCop: instead of an unreconstructed male mind in a newly mechanical body, we have a newly constructed open mind in a traditionally good-looking male body. Like RoboCop Ulysses is blond and baby-mouthed but unlike RoboCop he is perfectly suited to female (inasmuch as this is a straight scenario) needs: he combines these features with emotional openness, complete sincerity and, as Frankie finds out by accident, an enormous penis.

On this level the film functions very much within the realms of Girl Talk, i.e. the kinds of things men like to think women *don't* talk about. Frankie and Trish lounge about in bed despairing and giggling — 'It was hard enough to find him, and even then he wasn't hard enough' — and the film itself exists within that space between giggling and despair. It takes a woman's point of view completely for granted: unlike, for example, BROADCAST NEWS, which makes a big palaver about its working heroine, it matter-of-factly shows Frankie addressing meetings ('I'm always late, but I'm worth it'), zapping around in her adorable little jackets, giving orders to and getting support from her nice, dumpy male secretary — and this is not the film's *action*, but the *backdrop* to its action. MAKING MR RIGHT doesn't pathologize its female protagonist because she can't find a suitable man, but shows how inadequate the men available actually *are*. Frankie is often exasperated, but doesn't go around crying: both emotional *and* professional, she is the most sympathetic heroine I've seen in any film for a long time.

. Which is all the more interesting because the film (again, unlike BROADCAST NEWS) makes no pretence at realism. (William Hurt in BN is indeed rather like the blond, soft-hearted android — and both films are very much about contemporary media.) But Seidelman's film is *within* the postmodern media idiom: it playfully (never disdainfully) partakes of the surface of modern life. Frankie's punkish sister's wedding, an extravaganza of purple and orange frills, takes place on a beach; for the photos a beach backdrop is set up in front of the real sea, while the reception takes place round an indoor pool. Colour is used boldly and purposively: Frankie's red car and bright outfits are contrasted with the cold blue interior of the lab. References to other films abound: 'Nobody's perfect' are Frankie's closing words to Ulysses (who short-circuits when he kisses her) — a phrase whose full meaning derives from the echo of their famous prequel, 'I'm a man'.

So why has this smart little movie failed to catch on? It shares with the successful DESPERATELY SEEKING SUSAN a witty, sex-comedy plot, neat acting and a generally postmodern style (which it also shares with the cultish ROBOCOP). But the point about MAKING MR RIGHT is that, unlike many 'modern woman' films, it really is a Women's Picture. Forget post*modern*: this is post *men*. No wonder critics have so fervently dismissed it.

N.S. 20 May 1988

Permanent Revolution

Blood Red Roses

History and class are funny things. When critics not known for their left-wing views emerged from the preview of ROSA LUXEMBURG murmuring appreciation, I couldn't help feeling, with perhaps rather crude logic, that something was wrong. But once your revolutionary is in the past, allowing your film the delightful production values afforded by period costume etc., practically anything can be forgiven by the class enemy. Not that there was a lot of class consciousness in ROSA LUXEMBURG: the maid was a character of even less significance than Luxemburg's cat, and the crucial question of reform or revolution seemed to be thrashed out mainly at dinner parties.

BLOOD RED ROSES is — on one level — also a story of a woman's commitment to the struggle against capitalism at considerable cost to her personal life. Like ROSA LUXEMBURG, it centres on one figure throughout a significant period of history. But the history it tells is the history of working-class activism, and its period is not of the kind that requires golden-brown or misty-grey tones: it is the period of our own lives. Although on the face of it the two films have similar subjects, BLOOD RED ROSES shows, as ROSA LUXEMBURG never attempted to, what political struggle really means in the lives of the people for whom it is a matter of survival.

The structure of BLOOD RED ROSES is, until the very end, that of a long flashback: at her father's funeral, Bessie Gordon looks back over her life, from childhood in the forties, adolescence in the fifties, her involvement in factory politics, marriage to a shop steward, the birth of her children, and then notoriety as — a shop steward herself, her husband now a union rep — she and her workmates take on the multinational corporation which owns their small works in East Kilbride.

In charting the history of a class (and a country, Scotland) through the saga of one woman, director John McGrath draws on the great realist tradition: realist not in the sense of being realistic, but in the sense that, say, *Middlemarch* is the story not only of individuals but of the classes they stand for and the social forces that affect them. Much in BLOOD RED ROSES seems clearly representative in this way: Bessie's husband becomes the union official, she the shop-floor activist; one daughter (born during the Macmillan election) becomes a Trotskyist, the other (born around the time of the Wilson election) becomes an apolitical punk. The birth of a third daughter, in the eighties, seems to suggest the start of a new future. Equally, the geographical shifts are representative: from their cottage in the highlands, Bessie and her father move to East Kilbride: she says, 'As we grew up, so did the new town all around us.' By the end, they have moved into Glasgow, to the inner city of the 1980s.

BLOOD RED ROSES shares its concern with working-class lives and problems with many realist dramas of the Loach/Garnett genre (KES, PROSTITUTE, THE GAMEKEEPER, etc.); it does not, fortunately, share the irritating naturalism (e.g. hard-to-hear dialogue) of their pseudo-documentary style. Instead it tells a story through short, detailed scenes, often years apart, yet giving a vivid sense of everyday life. But the other major difference is that this film goes on far beyond the point that would make a conventionally rounded-off drama (e.g. the story of a childhood, the story of a marriage, the story of a particular strike) and as it keeps steadily on it gathers weight until you realize that it is not a drama but an *epic*: the epic story of post-war capital told from the other side.

This gives it something of the feel of Edgar Reitz's HEIMAT; but while his epic of German daily life in history was totally compelling, it was disturbingly detached politically. BLOOD RED ROSES is like a HEIMAT *with* politics: the sense of time passing through generations, parents dying, children growing up, is merged with class history so that the profound emotions of loss and continuity are felt not just on an individual but on a social level. In this sense the film does the exact opposite of mainstream ideology, which attempts to channel emotions away from the social and political realm and limit them to personal relationships.

In some circles on the left, 'class politics' are desperately out of fashion (and so, in film theory circles, is realism). But this film isn't a piece of grainy nostalgia. It leads to the brink of the future, giving the exciting sense of our own lives as history still in the making. Bessie's father dies during the 1984–5 miners' strike, and at the end of the film the flashback gives way to an image of the present in which she and her eldest daughter take the new baby on a Nicaraguan solidarity march. As union banners blaze in the wind, music from Chilean exiles Inti Illimani fills the soundtrack with the poignant but persistent sound of courage in the battle against imperialist capitalism. It is the memory of the cost of that battle which gives the banners their meaning: a memory which the film has supplied. For, rivetting as BLOOD RED ROSES is, its true function seems neither to entertain nor to inform. Rather — as its title suggests — it is a testament, a profoundly moving record of a real history which must be remembered and made visible, not to convince others but because memory is necessary to keep going for those whose history it is.

N.S. 7 October 1986

Music While You Work

Golden Eighties

The musical has always been my favourite film genre. It has the
peculiar capacity to create bubbles in time: there people are, going
about their business, then suddenly erupting into song and dance in
extravagantly expanded moments of emotion while the narrative
stands still. There is something thrilling about this device for magnifying the instantaneous; it seems to open up chinks in the surface of daily
life, tapping energy usually used up in merely keeping going, as
passions explode with a pattern and logic of their own. Through music
and spectacle the invisibly charged moments of existence flash into
form.

If a temporal dichotomy between narrative and emotion is the
structure of all musicals, there can be no more fitting material for it
than the relation between work and love. Having complained recently
that contemporary films rarely deal with ordinary work, here is an
exception: Chantal Akerman's latest film GOLDEN EIGHTIES is a
musical for our times. Set in a shopping mall, its surface is the working
lives of hairdressers, shop assistants and barmaids; and its eruptions
are the loves and desires of those working girls and guys whose days
are spent among the sinks, shampoos and clothing rails.

Traditionally, Hollywood musicals show us work by taking us
backstage, and the theatrical context provides a 'natural' excuse for
spectacle and display. But what better setting for spectacle today than
the shopping mall, the theatre of consumption? And Akerman's cool,
economic style is perfectly suited to this glass world of artificial
lighting which, even in reality, bears a striking resemblance to a film
set.

I haven't much liked any of Akerman's films since her early NEWS
FROM HOME, where the camera's calmness combines with the sentimental demands of the soundtrack (her mother's letters, read out
loud) to create that mixture of surface and longing which produce
passion in a film. Her better-known JEANNE DIELMAN deals in a
different combination of narrative and feeling as it follows a housewife
and prostitute through the details of her day in 'real time', a four-hour
marathon. More recent works have seemed indulgently self-
referential, like LES RENDEZVOUS D'ANNA, about a woman film

director. But now Akerman returns to daily life in a genre where — as in the very different NEWS FROM HOME — organized style and channelled passions produce an effect both poignant and aesthetically sharp.

The stylistic economy of GOLDEN EIGHTIES is epitomized in the very opening shot, a fixed frame of the mall's mock-marble floor, crossed and re-crossed by hurrying feet — an image complex and clear at the same time. This shot is a paradigm for the restricted setting, where the film's visual expansion comes not from moving outwards to new locations but from multiplying the combinations of characters, objects and emotions within its fixed bounds, of salon, shop, bar and lobby. The musical always seems to fill all available space: a graphic version of the libidinal economy whereby desires fill the world around them. As one character in the film says, 'The heart has got to love somebody', and GOLDEN EIGHTIES floods its small, artifically-lit world with the emotions of its inhabitants.

Love is discovered in ready-to-wear, jealousy simmers beneath the hairdriers; comic as the style of all this is (and unlike Jacques Demy's more sugary confections, rude too, as in the hairdressers' chorus, brandishing blow-driers) there is an undertow of serious emotion, particularly in the central and most understated relationship, between Delphine Seyrig's shop-owner in partnership with her husband, and the customer who emerges from her past (John Berry). What makes it so moving is the discrepancy between the trivial but necessary demands of the day-to-day grind, and the momentous but economically superfluous demands of the heart. Without the slightest realism in its style, the film articulates something very real indeed: the tension between the wish to break from, and the need to conform to, the patterns of material existence, which Akerman's script (she wrote all the song lyrics) places firmly in the 1980s, the age of marketing and monopolies.

As Richard Dyer has pointed out, classic musicals have a utopian quality; they offer a sense of community, abundance, exuberance, in a universe where feelings are transparent and love always finds a way. Akerman's film reinflects these qualities for the contemporary world; a world where bills are many and customers few, where love may be betrayed and caution triumph. It leaves you with that life-must-go-on feeling — the flip side of the 'show-stopper' — and when we finally leave the underworld of passions and plate glass for the daylight of the street, we enter the normal world of denial; though the ending has already changed so many times that nothing seems totally closed.

A musical of restraint might be a contradiction in terms, but restraint implies its opposite, and in bleak times fantasies too must work hard to muscle their way into the cold air of a competitive existence. GOLDEN EIGHTIES are not words that go together well; but this film plays out the tensions between them in a world of work and consumption at once intimate and public, whose fantasies are familiar to us all.

N.S. 27 March 1987

Career Opportunities

Working Girls
War Zone

There is a certain glamour in claiming yours is 'a job like any other', but only if it isn't. Bus conductors, teachers, cleaners don't need to make this assertion; however, it is striking that, unlike the sixties when both social realism and comedy offered some visibility to jobs which really are like any other, ours is an era where work on the screen is mainly represented by extraordinary jobs which nevertheless pretend to be ordinary.

Prostitution has always held a fascination for film-makers. For a start, the curiosity many people feel (what exactly do they *do*?) meshes with the inherently voyeuristic nature of film (it offers to *show* you) so that what can appear to be a demystifying social project in fact perpetrates the audience's sexual curiosity about the women them-selves. Tony Garnett's film PROSTITUTE comes into this category, presenting some very disturbing sex scenes as if the context of social realism made them completely unproblematic. Other directors like Godard see prostitution merely as a *metaphor* for exploitation — making it 'a job like any other' in a different sense, the idea being that we are all prostituted under capitalism anyway.

Of course, if prostitution really is just another job, it is hard to account for the decision to make a film about it. Director Lizzie Borden claims that WORKING GIRLS 'is about prostitution as work, not as a moral or psychological problem'. And the film is very successful in producing a sense of the mundane detail of work in a middle-class brothel. We follow Molly, a college graduate and photographer (easy for a middle-class audience to identify with) from the moment she wakes, with her black female single-parent lover, through her day in the small apartment in mid-town Manhattan where she and a few other 'working girls' await their clients. The routines become familiar: 'Can I fix you a drink?', 'Please make yourself completely comfortable' — the phrases of a hostess at a cocktail party. The women's relationships with one another and with Lucy, their 'madam', are closely observed and our interest might well be the same if they were working in a typing pool.

But it *isn't* a typing pool. In claiming to have made a film just about 'work' Borden is sidestepping the issue of what this kind of work means, and more specifically what it means in this film. Her last production, the fantasy BORN IN FLAMES, offered a radical feminist perspective on an imagined 'social democratic' future; so radical that many people found it extremely threatening. Now, with her apparent lack of comment on her subject matter in WORKING GIRLS, you are left looking for some sexual politics.

For me, the most striking aspect of the working girls' routine is the *verbal* pandering that must be kept up at all times, a tone of appreciation and admiration: 'How's your job going?' 'Really, that's *great*'. It may be sad that the men have to pay for that buttering up of their egos, but what is even more depressing is how close the mechanisms for pleasing men inside the brothel are to those for pleasing them outside; as is made particularly clear by Lucy's own relationship with her boyfriend, a married man. The fact that Molly is a lesbian appears almost casually incidental but must presumably be read as a further comment on the heterosexual relationships presented in the film: for the clients aren't sleazy old men in raincoats but include college lecturers, a young musician — again, not a million miles from the film's audience.

However, the film itself doesn't invite you to search for comments on sexual relations; rather it offers a tone of almost documentary matter-of-factness which, while certainly demystifying prostitution, also defuses the drive to understand it as a job which is *not* quite like any other.

The job most in vogue on the screen at present is without doubt that of journalist/photographer. I have pointed this out so many times in recent months that I feel I'm becoming repetitive, but then, so are the films. We've done Nicaragua and El Salvador — now WAR ZONE takes us to Beirut; in this decade of living dangerously the only question seems to be where another war can be dredged up to provide a backdrop for caring, daring journalists. WAR ZONE is an entirely formulaic movie along the lines of UNDER FIRE or SALVADOR: Christopher Walken plays a US journalist embroiled in an intrigue involving an imaginary PLO leader who denounces 'terrorism' (surely US wish-fulfilment). He ends up with a brilliant scoop by being in a Palestinian camp during a massacre, allowing him both to care very, very deeply and to get a world exclusive on the photos of dead bodies. However, since his tape is confiscated at the border, he leaves with merely another layer of concern added to the rugged geology of his professional persona. It's all in a day's work.

N.S. 20 March 1987

Arms and the Men

Salvador
Boy Soldier

The journalist/photographer has become the battle hero of our times. Where there are political objections to a war, as with Vietnam, a figure like Don McCullin can provide an acceptable peg for the displaced values of male heroism. In movies, the seeker after facts and photos has become the staple of almost every 'political' thriller (DEFENCE OF THE REALM) or 'political' war film (UNDER FIRE). We are becoming accustomed to experiencing the devastation wrought on other cultures through these heroic representatives of our own.

What is unusual about Oliver Stone's SALVADOR is that it appears to offer *anti*-heroes in that slot usually reserved for goodies like Redford. Its main protagonist (James Woods) — whose exploits are based on those of real-life photojournalist Richard Boyle — and his friend Dr Rock (James Belushi) are a couple of freeloaders living hand-to-mouth and driving down to Central America in search of work and women. These unsavoury sexist slobs spend the road-movie to Salvador discussing the price of Latin 'pussy' and the advantages of

Latin women: 'the best thing about them is that they don't speak English.'

This crude misogyny is — as always — the flip-side of a sickly sentimentality and it turns out that the Boyle character has a good woman in Salvador: the dirt'n'grit talk of the road turns to dumb romance. His 'real' love for this woman he never appears to have a conversation with is central to the plot, as it makes him 'care' about conditions under the repressive regime they have tumbled into more than he would merely for his own safety.

The best part of the film is the way the slob duo do become aware of what is happening: the film's racy style combines with an all-pervading sense of fear — starting with sudden arrests and ending with brutal murders — to turn their easy-rider trip for a quick buck into a journey through terror and oppression, which they increasingly realize is perpetrated with the collaboration of their own government. The fact that such *objectionable* characters make this discovery could produce some fascinating ironies, in which case SALVADOR would be a very sophisticated film indeed. For its heroes personify precisely the aggressively racist macho values that put US troops in Central America in the first place.

But the film doesn't distance itself from its male characters, rather its whole structure appears complicit with their world view, particularly as regards women. The only good women in the film are Latin women with long hair who wash clothes in rivers and don't speak English; and nuns who, with the nice young woman missionary, are horribly raped in an unnecessarily graphic, titillating scene. The only woman who is the guys' professional equal is portrayed as a silly bourgeois creep, and they play some rather disgusting tricks like dropping acid in her drinks (with the film's tacit approval). Finally, there is a woman from the FMLN resistance movement shown 'callously' shooting prisoners in the head (this is also part of the film's liberalism — the other side *kill people too*!).

Between raped virgins, sexy foreigners and careerist bitches, this does seem to suggest that, like its protagonists, the film is unable to treat women as equals. It may seem churlish to stick on this point when the film is a strong indictment of the repression in Salvador, but it matters, and not only to women. For, despite the film's narrative message, on a deeper level it recycles the ideologies that underlie what it purports to condemn. Any boy that likes war films will get off on this one. The scene where the heroes take photos in the crossfire of a battle — in torn khaki, loading and reloading their cameras noisily like guns, bang bang bang — is like any other war movie. If you must give your characters the sensibility of Rambo, it is at least better to be aware of the contradiction.

A film like Wexler's LATINO attempted to draw out this contradiction by using a member of the army itself as 'anti-hero'; and this is the device at the heart of BOY SOLDIER, Karl Francis' Welsh-language film produced for Channel Four. Its protagonist is a young squaddie in the Welsh Guards, charged with murder while serving in Northern Ireland and used by politicians as a scapegoat for the army's policies and actions there. The film functions halfway between realism and psychodrama, as in solitary confinement Private Thomas remembers his training and violent initiation into army life, while finding ever more extreme ways to resist his jailors' violence and turn it back on them. The mix of flashbacks and claustrophobic prison scenes creates a convincingly traumatic atmosphere against which the coolness of political manoeuvering appears as most brutal of all.

The *bildungsroman* theme is Thomas' slow realization of the connection between the derision of 'micks' by the soldiers and his superiors' equal derision of his own language and culture. In one memorable scene he has to translate a letter from his father 'in case it contains political secrets'. The halting inadequacy of the letter's real contents leads us to the most poignant aspect of the boy's life — the lack of any real home besides the army, which makes its power over him all the more complete.

The film deals effectively with all these issues, and the 'boy soldier' is never glamorized; he is at once unpleasant and pitiable. But the atmosphere is so overwhelmingly tough and male (hardly surprising, given the subject) that you sense first-hand the brutalizing effect of the army: the film functions — very effectively — like the macho forces it attacks. I feel I could forgo this experience, since I am already opposed to what the British army is doing in or out of Ireland. However, as an anti-recruitment film BOY SOLDIER would be hard to match.

Both these films are attempting to preach to a wider audience than the already converted, and to do so in a popular way, using the language of violence to challenge its ends. There are many problems with this project, and SALVADOR is far from resolving them. Nevertheless, the project itself is an important one; if anti-war films could be made to appeal to precisely the RAMBO audience, then their ideological function might come into its own.

N.S. 30 January 1987

Let Their People Go

Cry Freedom

I have used a lot of space in this column criticizing films which heroize white journalists, and my expectations of CRY FREEDOM were low. Yet I left the cinema as a movie-goer filled with righteous anger at the regime which tortured and killed Steve Biko and so many others; while at the same time, as a critic, pondering over this feeling and the devices which aroused it. For CRY FREEDOM is a powerful film; far more political than it needed to be (if it were just another journalist-in-danger movie), it is an impressive example both of the strengths of a liberal mainstream cinema, and of its limitations — and of the strange way in which these are bound up together.

The immediate context of the film is well known. Directed by Richard Attenborough, it tells the true story of Donald Woods, white South African newspaper editor whose attempts to expose the circumstances of Biko's death in detention led to his being banned, followed by a dramatic escape with his family. Woods' book, *Biko*, smuggled out with him, had a wide-reaching effect in focusing attention on Biko's case and on the torture and murder carried out routinely by South African 'security' forces. The Woods have acted as advisers on the film, which in many respects goes out of its way to de-heroize them.

For the Woods are not radicals: they have a black live-in maid and at the start of the film Biko accurately calls Woods 'a white liberal who clings to all the advantages of the white world'. But it is this which allows the film its central persuasive device, the gradual exposure of Donald Woods' flawed liberal position and his education by Biko and by events which lead to a total undermining of his belief in South African 'justice'. The mechanism is exactly similar to that of MISSING; a conservative view which may be that of a general audience is inscribed in the film in the form of a sympathetic character who is then confronted by a reality — representing the *film*'s bottom-line political view — which forces him or her to change it. This is by no means a stupid way of challenging deeply held 'neutral' attitudes: MISSING, for all its faults, took conscious aim at the dominant US ideology of the time. And CRY FREEDOM, especially in its first half, takes some pretty good swipes at the kind of ludicrously 'balanced' conservative-liberal position which contains the concept 'black racism'.

The part of the film in which these criticisms really come alive is where Woods first explores the world beyond white privilege and tests out his ideas on Biko and his friends. It is from their mouths that attacks on liberal hypocrisy work best, because they carry all the force of an utterly different experience. Surrounded by Biko's political buddies in a black settlement, Woods' comments on 'black racism' come across as laughable, and in one memorable scene where Woods anxiously tells them that he may be imprisoned for six months, they laugh and say it will do him good. Their criticisms come across sympathetically because the film has taken care to show from the outset the far more extreme dangers blacks are subject to all the time. The opening sequence is a violent raid on the Crossroads settlement: so by the time we first meet Woods, state brutality has already been established — itself presented, significantly, after first establishing the peacefulness of the camp just before the dawn raid. Thus the film's own bottom-line reality pre-endorses Biko's speech and comments and we eagerly anticipate the realignment of Woods' views in accordance with this reality.

The second half of the film provides, in a sense, a retrospective justification of his changed perceptions, because the dramatic chase and escape create a sense of danger (as in any thriller) and we start to feel the oppressiveness of the regime not through image and political argument, as in the sections where Biko is still alive, but through the different narrative device of suspense. When Woods is 'banned' (as Biko was, but with less dramatic impact) the film's devices shift into a different gear, that of the race-against-the-clock. Yet the film ends with a considered attempt to counterbalance the drama of the white family: at the moment of their greatest danger, flying unauthorized over South African airspace, it cuts to an extended sequence of the Soweto massacre and ends with a long list of all those killed in detention, Biko merely one among many, whose deaths are accounted for with imaginative explanations like 'fell against chair'.

This measured counter-weighting is not only part of the film's politics but of its *appeal*. For at heart it represents a kind of improved liberalism: if the plot is in a way the white liberal's *bildungsroman* — a story of growing and learning — the movie itself is its product. Donald Woods' flawed liberalism is exposed, not to be replaced by radicalism, but to be made whole again. In a period of change, liberal ideology must let go certain positions — 'de-territorialize' — in order to re-form or 're-territorialize' in ways more appropriate to the times: a process Barry Curtis has likened to putting down a suitcase so as to get a firmer grip when you pick it up again. This is almost exactly what CRY FREEDOM does — which is why its first half is so genuinely powerful, representing as it does the undermining and letting go of a liberal racist position, and with its positive presentation of black leaders (Denzel Washington as Biko successfully conveys the enormous charm and personal charisma that Biko reputedly had).

This half of the film provokes a political anger, as indeed it should. But by the end, why am I feeling so righteous? Is it the immense narrative relief as Woods reaches a British Embassy and is offered a cup of tea? Is it perhaps the very fact that Britain is where Woods escaped to? Is it the certainty that the film is right, that *I* am right, that all right-minded people are right, in opposing apartheid? This feeling, to return to my original point, is simultaneously the strength and the weakness of the film: a strength, because of course apartheid *is* wrong and the more people convinced of it the better; a weakness, because in leaving a glow of indignation about South Africa, the film never undermines our ultimate faith in the fairness of its updated liberalism (it endorses only *non-violent* black struggle) and, by implication, our own traditions. Perhaps some day someone will make a big-budget mainstream film about police violence to blacks in *this* country. If that seems hard to imagine, it is interesting to consider why.

N.S. 4 December 1987

Do You Want to Know a Secret?

Empire State
T. Dan Smith

Power is a difficult thing to visualize. Partly because it is not, in fact, a thing but an operation, a relationship; very hard to 'see', though certainly felt, its invisibility is easily confused with secrecy.

In recent years our filmic vision of state power has been channelled through the thriller format (DEFENCE OF THE REALM, BBC's *Edge of Darkness*) where secrecy is essential if the hero is to have anything to find out. On a slightly different but related tack there have been the investigations of urban power in underworld thrillers like THE LONG GOOD FRIDAY and MONA LISA, where the 'old' London, as represented by Bob Hoskins, confronts a new ruthlessness in a world where secrecy is a visual climate of neon-lit alleys, gloomy railway arches and smoke-filled nightclubs.

It seems important to outline this territory because it is becoming a given that we visualize the evils of power in this deliberately film noir way; and the phenomenon itself seems to say something about our times. 'Film noir' refers both to a visual style and a content; it is usually used to describe those thrillers of the 1940s and '50s where heavy use of contrast and shadow in the image went hand in hand with shadowy subject matter and plots so murky they often hardly made sense. Films noirs are now seen as expressing the deep social unease of their era. Yet what is interesting is that the term *film noir* was coined retrospectively — it wasn't used by the makers themselves — and the focus on this sub-genre in film theory and education has reached an almost obsessive pitch in recent years as our own times become harder. 'Down these mean streets a man must go. . .' and the meaner the streets, the more men (and it is men) seem to go down them.

Both Ron Peck's EMPIRE STATE and Amber Films' T. DAN SMITH are about urban corruption — development schemes, corporate wheeling and dealing — and both self-consciously engage with the film noir format. The resonantly-named EMPIRE STATE starts off almost as pastiche, blood on the typewriter keys as a young woman in a torn dress remembers what the journalist told her — 'Write it!' — and true to form the story is told in flash-back with a convoluted plot of gay pimps, boxers, businessmen, symbolic figures representing the change from the old East End to the new. Social comment is never more than a few lines away — 'a new leaner Britain needs a new kind of city' — and in the ring of the underworld what we watch is the battle between old-fashioned working-class bandits and new yuppie brutality, exemplified by the pimp. 'You haven't got class; everything you've got is bought,' the old gangland boss tells him; as in THE LONG GOOD FRIDAY everything is a paradigm for 'Thatcherite' Britain, and there is a vivid sense both of social decay and the 'new breed' of entrepreneur who feeds off it.

Yet there is almost too much in it, too many ideas, too many characters representing too many things; the boxer, the reporter (for once, thank God, he isn't a hero), the barmaid, the cute gay prostitute, the boy-just-arrived-from-the-North, the pimp's oriental PA — all seem to stand for something yet their weight as characters isn't enough to carry whatever else they mean, so that as the film accelerates it becomes a sort of postmodern mêlée of meanings about post-modern, post-industrial, multi-racial Britain. One of the film's greatest problems is its acting: people emphasize odd words in their lines, like airplane announcements (*'at* this time we *do* request. . .'), and this makes the characters seem more cipherlike than necessary. The style hovers between the tongue-in-cheek of Peck's WHAT CAN I DO WITH A MALE NUDE and the urban realism of NIGHTHAWKS; these come together most powerfully in the claustrophobic night club where confusion, excitement and violence culminate in a particularly shocking scene that seems to place the film itself in an ambiguous relation to the ruthlessness it depicts.

This brings us back to power, which, clearly, can be expressed through violence; and in a sense the cultural clash that EMPIRE STATE addresses *is* violent, a clash between political and economic forces — and styles: old working-class versus new urban upwardly-mobile. T. DAN SMITH also deals in a clash of political styles, as well as power, as it raises the story of a working-class radical caught up in suaver, secreter big-time politics and ultimately sacrificed to save bigger and more upper-class fish than himself. The film is half documentary — its subject is a real character — and half fiction — a dramatised contemporary version of the Poulson/Smith affair — wound together in a film noir style. This partly involves things like venetian blinds casting their shadow in the cutting-room; for the investigative heroes of this film are the film-makers (or two male members of the group) themselves. Since they disagree on their 'angle', this device allows for a multiplicity of views (sometimes rather simplistically presented as a multiplicity of video screens) and so, unusually, no single conclusion is drawn from the material. Yet the dramatization of the two men as they walk the mean streets of Newcastle becomes rather irritating.

The reasons for this (to me, anyway) lie ultimately in the same cultural clash that EMPIRE STATE deals with through its 'new-style' poncey pimp-dealer versus old solid beer-drinking working-class gangster. The makers of T. DAN SMITH locate themselves firmly in the latter category, eating fish and chips under railway bridges, drinking endless pints in endless unrenovated pubs to the extent that the film has the nostalgic aura of a brewery ad. In contrast to this, the trappings of power are characterized as *effete*: the upper-class MP and the Home Secretary speak mincingly and sip sherry on leather sofas (while Labour councillors confer in the gents, without a hint of Orton in the air).

It may seem picky to stick on this iconography of the effete and the macho when, as a documentary, the film works well on many levels. But it *does* matter; and it also matters that the understanding of power is generally presented today as the unravelling of secrets (of particular fascination to boys, it seems). I am reminded of the characterization of power in DEFENCE OF THE REALM, ministers in sinister panelled rooms, journalists (and now film-makers) in dark streets and shabby elevators. Is film noir the best way of representing power? Is what's wrong with the state really its secrecy? Despite working on a magazine whose recent reputation has centred on discovering 'secrets'[1] I am inclined to think not. EMPIRE STATE and T. DAN SMITH are among the most interesting and socially relevant of contemporary films, and this point may be something of a sideline. Yet the renovation of film noir, exciting as *film*, seems less effective as *politics*, precisely because it dramatizes power as plot and focuses, ultimately, on its discovery rather than its effects.

N.S. 29 May 1987

Causes Without a Rebel

At the Edinburgh Film Festival we're now halfway through the Scottish Association of Workshops' 'Any Voices Left' event: a series of screenings and discussions of work from film and video workshops throughout the UK.

The workshops have become the main infrastructure of independent film and video production in Britain and owe their current strength to two particular achievements which have been the result of years of organization among the independent sector. One is the ACTT agreement allowing workshops to waive union rates (which would otherwise push production costs out of their reach), and the other is the franchise system whereby certain workshops — about twenty in all — receive revenue funding from sources such as local authorities, the British Film Institute and Channel Four, thus enabling their members to

---

1   The *New Statesman* was widely known for its investigative
    features about undercover government/military projects.

function on regular salaries and maintain equipment, etc., indepen-
dently of the production of any particular film.

Not all workshops are fortunate enough to be enfranchised in this
way and that in itself creates enormous differences between, at one end
of the spectrum, small local groups trying to produce, for example,
community video, and at the other, workshops who, with Channel
Four money, are making full-length feature films aimed at a much
wider audience both on TV and in the cinema.

What has struck me most forcibly over the last year, and now at the
festival, is the way in which the enormous and valuable efforts put into
setting up the workshops — plus the fact that they spring from the
most consciously 'political' (i.e. left-wing) part of British film culture
— have led to a situation where being in a workshop seems such a
right-on thing in itself that criticism of their aims and methods, and of
their products, is both hard to make and — it seems — to take.

Not that there is any obvious uniformity throughout the sector; on
the contrary, the gap between the wealthier workshops now producing
fiction features and those struggling with small-scale productions is
enormous. This is particularly evident at Edinburgh, where a feature
like Frontroom Workshop's THE LOVE CHILD is showing in the main
festival while, so far, the 'Workshops Event' screenings have consisted
of documentary and campaigning films (though the two areas are
straddled by a film like T. DAN SMITH which is billed in both). At a
time when the top and bottom seem to be pulling apart in our society
and culture, this is happening in independent film too. At the 'top' end
of the sector there is a drive towards increasingly 'respectable' forms
aimed at wider audiences; at the other end the drive towards
community access and low-budget campaigning projects produces
more downmarket work whose look and purpose are utterly different.

Yet these two ends of the spectrum have one thing in common: a
lack of formal innovation. I am well aware of having criticized various
attempts to produce formally innovative work — Sankofa's PASSION
OF REMEMBRANCE comes to mind — but this was not for the attempt
itself: and in fact the rarer attempts at formal experimentation are, the
less likely they are to be successful, precisely because the necessary
environment of shared experiment and critical debate is missing. For
the fiction work which many groups are now making is fairly
conventional, albeit interesting and/or 'political': I would put THE
LOVE CHILD, a successful comedy, in this category. Especially with so
much TV money going into bigger-scale workshop films, the pull
towards conventional structures is strong. And there is also the feeling,
in this late eighties climate, that giving up 'avant-garde' notions of

experimentation is somehow *grown-up*: the 'New Realism' is permeating the cultural, as well as the economic arena.

In a different way, the worthy low-budget campaigning films are also all too often conventional, indistinguishable from the more uninspired TV documentaries full of talking heads and shaky footage of political events. (A notable exception at the Workshops Event was the Glasgow Film and Video Workshop's witty and accessible housing campaign tape ABOOT THE HOOSE.) Where these function in an *immediate* political context, their lack of formal interest is a minor issue compared with their polemical role: at this moment, for example, the most boringly filmed talking head interview with a black South African miner would have enormous political power. But perhaps the value of this kind of work is in the timing: spend too long in the cutting room with your strike/demo/uprising footage and the moment will have passed where simple reportage has a dramatic role to play. Equally, 'community videos', while often providing a valuable experience for the people involved, may be less interesting when taken outside the immediate context of their making.

In a bizarrely contradictory session, we watched Ceddo's powerful documentary THE PEOPLE'S ACCOUNT, redressing the media reportage of the 'riots' on Broadwater Farm (itself a good example of a conventionally made work whose political *un*conventionality has been strong enough to get it banned — the IBA refused to screen it). Later in the same session we saw a community video from a Welsh housing estate, which had been made by tenants with help from a local workshop, Red Flannel, specifically to redress their sense of grievance at being compared to Broadwater Farm on a TV programme. Such was the feeling of achievement that the video had actually been made, that attempts to pinpoint the political contradictions of its relation to Broadwater Farm were met by a walk-out of the (understandably) hurt video-makers.

If this conflict made anything vividly clear, it was that access *is* important — whether by small groups or wealthier workshops — but it is not *enough*: what you make is as important as the fact that you make it. Maybe a festival, with its self-congratulatory atmosphere, is hardly the place to say this; but somehow it makes me want to say it all the more.

N.S. 21 August 1987

Single Issues

When the Wind Blows
Rate It X

Nuclear holocaust is the great unrepresentable of our time. Govern-
ments rely on its unimaginable nature to prevent us thinking it could
happen: not because we don't know, intellectually, that nuclear war is
possible, but because we literally can't picture our daily world not
being there.

This creates certain problems for any visual representation of
nuclear war. How can you make believable something so unbeliev-
able? Anything too horrific appears merely as science fiction, anything
too 'normal' fails to present the terrible dangers. Realist films like THE
WAR GAME or, more recently, THREADS, do give a sense of the horror
that could follow nuclear exchanges, but their very realism links them
too closely to the life we are used to, almost as if TV cameras would
still exist after the bomb dropped.

For all these reasons the idea of an animated film about nuclear
destruction is a promising one. WHEN THE WIND BLOWS, based on
Raymond Briggs' best-selling cartoon book, relies on a range of
complicated animation techniques to present us with the drawn
characters of Jim and Hilda Bloggs (voices by John Mills and Peggy
Ashcroft) in the three-dimensional setting (based on photographs) of
their house. Strangely, it is the two-dimensional simplicity of the
Bloggs which gives the stronger sense of 'normality' as they have all
the cosiness of familiar cartoon characters, whose personalities are
fixed. They talk in an exaggeratedly homey way of the 'here's your tea,
dear' kind, which is clearly meant not so much to be realistic as to
represent the stability of ordinary life, and in particular the well-
meaning, gullible natures of the Bloggs.

This gullibility is central to the film's one basic device: which is to
show the Bloggs doing in complete faith ('This must be really
authoritative, it's from the County Council') exactly what the government pamphlets tell them, down to the last letter. The film's poignancy is intended to lie in the naivety with which they dutifully build
their shelter of old doors and lay in their supplies — as if preparing for
another World War Two air-raid.

A sort of ancillary to this device, which is repeated so often as to lose its charge, is the Bloggs' unperturbed dialogue in the devastation *after* the bomb. There must be a dozen lines of the 'I'll pop out to the chemist tomorrow for some suppositories' . . . 'I promised old George I'd see him in the Half Moon for a game of darts. . .' variety. Once would have been enough; the point is made.

And it *is* made: the film does succeed in suggesting that mix of the everyday and the unimaginable, through its picture-book simplicity — a bit like setting Chernobyl in Noddyland. But the fact that there is basically a single script idea makes it hard for the material to hold up for full feature length. The combination of attention to realist detail in the photography-based depiction of the house, with the crude (if affectionate) caricature of the figures in it, feels bizarre and feeds into the key problem of our relation to these characters. It is obvious that we are expected both to laugh at them, and feel real concern for them, and the two responses don't mesh. There is a patronizing note to any amusement they might provoke (though it is hard to feel that any of this could be really *funny*); on the other hand, the necessity of the characters' simplicity for these 'jokes' to work prevents the production of real feelings about them.

Ultimately, it is hard to get a sense of who the film is for. Is its audience CND supporters, or is it aiming to convert those wedded to nuclear defence policy? Is it for adults or children? Will people see it for entertainment or education? These questions leave one with a curiously disjointed relation to the film, even while sharing its aims.

RATE IT X by Lucy Winer and Paula de Koenigsberg is another film with one basic device: in this case, that of giving individual men (ranging from a baker who makes cakes shaped like women's torsos, to the author of *Hustler*'s grotesque 'Chester the Molester' cartoon) enough rope to hang themselves, letting them reveal their own sexism, while the film-makers appear as discreetly gloved hands holding microphones. The simple economy of the device produces far from simple results: some of the men, particularly the editor of a black 'men's' magazine, grapple with the contradictions of their positions; some happily expound grossly misogynist attitudes; some strive to find what the interviewers want of them ('Oh, I see what you're getting at,' says one old war veteran, with relief).

What the film lacks is any mediating concept of ideology. These men don't just 'have' sexist attitudes; in a more complex way, 'being a man' itself involves layers of — for want of a better word — sexism, and this is structured into both consciousness and society. Instead of exploring those connections, the film-makers act rather like teachers, who ask you questions to which they already know the answer.

Perhaps this is what gives the film its slightly irritating tone.

The question 'who is it for' applies to RATE IT X as much as to WHEN THE WIND BLOWS. It makes most women feel righteous anger; I'm not sure how it makes men feel, but by focusing on particular individuals I would imagine that it tends to let any 'sympathetic' man going to see it off the hook. Can an ideology be revealed merely by letting it speak for itself? A good device is a good device, but it cannot make an entire film. Perhaps for film-makers *this* is a message to be learned from the forms in which these films put their own, important messages across.

N.S. 6 February 1987

Alain who will be 71. . .

A Flame in My Heart
The Unbearable Lightness of Being

A lot of people see Art Movies as simply all the films that are left if you take away Hollywood and other mainstream products, a sort of pure cinema unhampered by the constraints of popular genre structures. Yet the Art Movie is itself a genre; one whose components are often as readily identifiable as those of the more obviously generic Western or Thriller.

The two obligatory themes in the thinking person's Art Movie are politics and sex, usually in some sort of clever combination. HIROSHIMA MON AMOUR (and this is not intended to belittle Resnais' and Duras' film) is in some respects a prototype: the upfront presentation of a sexual affair against a backdrop of key political events is a formula which, whether exploratory and exciting or banal and coy, has appeared over and over again in Art House hits.

Sexual mores and political struggle have been the main concerns of the so-called sixties generation and it is hardly surprising that they should be at the heart of 'alternative', 'intelligent' cinema (for example, almost all of Godard's productions). But it is not so much the themes themselves as their patterns of interweaving which characterize a very particular kind of work. In the world of books, John Berger's *G* is a perfect example: there is a lot of sex with a lot of women and enough history and 'politics' for left-wing intellectuals to feel it's significant. This mixture is what in chemical terms is called a suspension rather than a solution.

It is no coincidence that Berger has a history of film collaboration with Alain Tanner. Tanner's films have always managed to locate sex in women and politics in men. A typical scenario (from his JONAH WHO WILL BE 25 IN THE YEAR 2000): right-on, not specially attractive Thinking Man angst-ridden about the future of socialism meets very, very cute young blonde check-out attendant in the supermarket and they get it together. There is a clear dimension to this which is simply the authors' own fantasies: middle-aged socialist intellectuals meet sexy chicks.

But nowadays, smart male directors have figured that it merely exposes your sexism if you try and make this sort of film on your own as a man: Godard, for example, has shared script credits with his partner, Anne-Marie Miéville, on his more recent films, which has probably helped prevent them being torn apart by feminists. And now Tanner emerges with a new film, FLAME IN MY HEART, whose script is co-credited to Myriam Mézières — also the leading player.

Critic Raymond Durgnat falls for this device, calling the film 'androgynous, in the sense of being a collaboration between members of the opposite sex'. But what is so depressing about the film is precisely the boring and predictable way it is about as un-androgynous as it could be, allocating, as always, sex to Woman (Mézières is very keen on being Woman) and politics to Man. Tanner seems eager in this film to let us know that he knows all about cunnilingus but even doling out *oral* sex to women and politics to men isn't particularly interesting. All that 'happens' in the film is that Mézières has a lot of sex with a working-class Arab lover, leaves him, picks up a — yes, you've guessed it — middle-class socialist intellectual on the métro, has a lot of sex with him, and flips out when he goes away, i.e. stops brushing her hair, eats a lot and masturbates in front of the TV.

It's easy to laugh at the whole thing, as with any work which lacks the wit to recognize its own clichés. But it isn't, in a way, as stupid as it sounds, or rather, it isn't a silly film so much as a bad film. Intellectually it latches on to a complex set of contemporary ideas about speech and sexuality, in which signification is seen as male and femininity is identified with pre-linguistic physicality. The script is full of stuff about Woman being the 'interior' and the intellectual writes her long letters about her 'dumb mouth' (geddit?). In practice what this means is that He reads newspapers and She has orgasms. Finally she leaves him, in Cairo, for no reason, and smiles at a little Egyptian girl. Who knows the secret of the black magic box? That's about how profound this investigation of 'femininity' is.

For some viewers, profundity, or 'Art Movie'-ness is achieved in a film merely by its having subtitles. THE UNBEARABLE LIGHTNESS OF BEING, directed by Philip Kaufman, is in fact an *American* Art Movie, but with the requisite foreignness produced not only by its setting (an adaptation of Kundera's novel, it takes place in Czechoslovakia and Switzerland around '68) but by the intriguing phenomenon of a non-Czech cast all speaking English with assumed Czech accents. Daniel Day Lewis plays Tomas, the young, brilliant doctor and inveterate womanizer whom we follow through the revolutionary years in Prague in his relationships with his liberated artist lover Sabina (Lena Olin) and the country girl who becomes his wife, Tereza (Juliette Binoche).

The film's craving for authenticity goes beyond the bizarre 'Czech' accents of Day Lewis and co.; there is some virtuoso mingling of newsreel with the film's own footage to show Tomas and Tereza appearing in 'historical' shots of Prague '68. Here, while the political history is still a backdrop to the 'lovers' story' (as the film is subtitled) it is not a removable backdrop: the movements of the central figures in the erotic triangle are determined as much by political as by emotional events. The atmosphere of fear when Tomas and Tereza return to Russian-occupied Prague is vividly invoked (and may endear the film to US audiences), though the idyllic rustic life they finally create is almost impossibly romantic.

The film's picaresque quality — shifting locations as Tomas, like a Czech Tom Jones, follows his lovers across a historical landscape — in part expresses its philosophy, or rather, the philosophy of the book: Tomas comments that life allows no opportunity for rehearsals and he plunges into its many different experiences. Yet Day Lewis, who makes a face throughout which is like the male equivalent of Meryl Streep's (i.e. rigidly enigmatic), doesn't bring a sense either of great depth or great exuberance to the role.

But another spin-off effect of the episodic narrative is that it offers us a range of choices between beautifully Art Movie mises-en-scène. And this is where the expectations of the genre are really a liability. Besides being compellingly beautiful, Juliette Binoche acts admirably, but there is also a level on which one really gets into her adorable sixties skirts and ankle socks, cunningly contrasted with the fresh, flowery frocks that appear out of nowhere when they go to the country. Then there is the sophisticated fondue scene in Geneva to roll around the tongue and compare with the soup and beer on the wooden table on the farm and so on. Nice *stuff* is becoming an important component of contemporary Art Movies: and whatever other deprivations this US film shows us in pre- and post-invasion Prague, it always manages to find, among the sex and politics, enough of that stuff to satisfy an audience familiar with the Next Catalogue.

N.S. 27 April 1988

Die Young, Stay Pretty

Boy Meets Girl

When I was little, I remember my brother telling me that a film director called Godard had put a camera in a wheelchair to do a moving shot along a street. It conjured up an image of film-making that was enormous fun; pushing the baby's pram to the shops was never the same again. When I became old enough to go to New Wave films myself, I felt an excitement about how casual, in a sense, film could be: as if a bunch of people just hung out in cafés in Paris having fun with a movie camera. I could never quite understand why the women had to be so much more beautiful than the men, but even that, in its way, had a certain pre-women's movement naïveté; bung in Anna Karina, you could almost hear the boys saying, and then you'll have something really nice to look at.

I recalled all this when I saw BOY MEETS GIRL, the first film by Léos Carax, a young French film-maker who completed it in 1984 at the age of 22. It brings us: an angst-ridden, deliberately uncute boy and an angst-ridden, desperately cute girl in sparse apartments furnished with single beds and milk bottles; the lights of pinball machines in neon bars; bridges at night and the blackness of water below; the glass panes of city streets after dusk: in other words, the surface of Paris, so familiar from those sixties films, referred back to in sharp black and white by this one. And yet, and yet — the making of this is less playful, more sophisticated: even its innocence is somehow more knowing than its antecedents'.

For though BOY MEETS GIRL sounds like an adolescent fantasy, the very title is a complicated reference to a joke told by Hitchcock to Truffaut, about a director who kept a notepad by his bed for ideas and woke one morning to find that his brilliant plot was 'boy meets girl'. Age is a constant preoccupation of the film: its opening line, 'Soon I will be old and it will finally be over', sets the theme which is repeated endlessly in a script that sends words wafting through the perpetual night with what I can only describe, oxymoronically, as a *fresh weariness*: from 'desire is hard to come by these days' to 'now I'm old enough to be tortured in a war'.

All this 'hope I die before I get old' stuff recalls the sixties again — which is exactly where the film is pushing me at the same time as pulling everything back into its own sealed self. All its visual references take me back to Godard, Bresson, Truffaut, Resnais: and then leave me there, trapped in perfect imagery. For the New Wave films of the early sixties to which BOY MEETS GIRL overtly begs comparison were extremely close to the *cinéma vérité* of that period; something of its lightness and social purpose came across even in the more stylized artwork. But BOY MEETS GIRL gives a sense of being heavy, without substance; an intensely accomplished film, with some breathtaking images, its polish, even its humour, are almost too good, too beautiful, as if the energy which counterbalanced the pretentiousness of so much New Wave had here become hardened into the smartness of the image itself. Deep blacks, thick shadows, designer haircuts — *The Face* would kill for style like this.

That's not a put-down, more an attempt to contextualize: for the context of a film like this *is* what is loosely known as 'style culture'. Beineix's DIVA, Besson's SUBWAY have also brought us those city surfaces, that technical sophistication, those displaced young men and post-feministly Beautiful Women. The range both of reference and of technical ability in these new surface/romantic/tragic movies is truly impressive. Why then do I find it profoundly depressing? Because, I suppose, these films, even if they don't speak *about* something, do speak *from* and *to* something I recognize, which is precisely the enclosed world of signification Baudrillard refers to as the hyper-real.

In Carax's film, communication is blocked: lovers argue through the intercom system, conversations are drowned by kettles, thunder, the Dead Kennedys; a man spelling his name out over the phone in a bar can refer only to the name itself (B as in Bariana, A as in Ariana, etc.); an old grip describes his work on silent films in sign language and is ignored. The hero himself, however, talks a lot: when he finally Meets Girl it reminds me of the Biff cartoon, 'I'd like to go on about myself at great length if that's OK'. Of course, the Biff cartoons are themselves further postmodern references to the same period — 'Must be that piss-artist I met in Marienbad' also came to mind.

BOY MEETS GIRL has its own self-commentary, as when Boy says 'If only I could escape monologues' (if only he could), and it deals very much in self-consciousness: the hero xeroxes his letters to his girl-friend, writes out his script before phoning Girl, keeps a map of Paris above his bed on which he marks his first kiss, first theft, first fight, etc. If the film was a little lighter, this would be funny; but its closeness to its own material means that you can never quite feel whether it's a film about a romantic postmodern self-consciousness, or a film *of* it.

Evidently it's both; another sign of its postmodernity. Clichés are reproduced, yet without any tongue-in-cheek; rather they are given a new weightiness. The most obvious example is the use of the Iconic Woman, whose main function is to be staggeringly pretty enough to cut off all her hair in an apparently random way, and *still* appear staggeringly pretty. This is exactly like Godard's use of women in the sixties (and look where *that* led); the Anna Karina analogy is even more striking in Carax's second film (released next autumn) which is almost a remake of ALPHAVILLE.

It's as if nothing had changed — and everything: here's the same old stuff, and yet the sensibility is entirely different. Part of 'postmodernity' is supposed to be the decline of great narratives, ways of thinking that have some definite aim. The most depressing thing about BOY MEETS GIRL for me was its sense of pointlessness. Even when people got shot in those early Godards you had the sense that the city was *fun*. That it *isn't*, if you're young today, is hardly Carax's fault, but he captures it all too well. Everything is awful except Romance, and even that is doomed. In this world of the hyper-real there's nothing left for the subject to do but DIE — looking good, of course.

As I left the cinema I thought of Rodgers and Hart's immortal line, 'The city's glamour can never spoil/ the dreams of a boy and goil'. For me, it was the glamour of the boy and goil, or rather, BOY MEETS GOIL, that spoilt the dreams of the city fostered in me since my pram-pushing days in what now seem like much sunnier streets.

N.S. 17 July 1987

Out of Step

Ginger and Fred

Where does authenticity lie in a world infinitely replicated by video, computer, and representations which are as much about other representations as about a real world? This is the question which preoccupies theorists of postmodernism (whose answer, incidentally, is 'nowhere'); and in a sense it preoccupies everyone in a world increasingly experienced through electronic media at a time of breakdown in social and political consensus. If our identity no longer fits snugly into place in an ordered world, how indeed can we have an authentic sense of ourselves? While theorists have diagnosed a loss of depth, of sincerity, of *affect* in this 'postmodern' world, movies have taken it to the logical conclusion of videodrome addiction, computer warfare, and have turned 'replicant' into an everyday word.

GINGER AND FRED confronts the problem of sincerity in a world of spectacle — but neither by theorizing nor by projecting it into the future: Fellini the showman, who so often looks backward (or inward) for his circus material, has no need in this enterprise to search beyond the surface of modern life itself. Fellini has always *produced* a good spectacle; yet here, in perhaps his most finely controlled film, he lets go the role of ringmaster which instead is dispersed through the anonymous forms of advertising and TV. His film as it were *consumes* the repetitions of sausages, slogans, sex on hoardings; the enormous promotional pig's trotter bedecked with fairy lights hanging in the station: the fragments of food and bodies which endlessly re-form the same patterns across the chaotic and decaying landscape of the city.

This kaleidoscopic diffusion of subjectivity finds a straightforward analogy in the deregulation of Italian TV, the backdrop for Ginger and Fred's story. Ginger and Fred are, in fact, Amelia (Giulietta Masina) and Pippo (Marcello Mastroianni), elderly tap-dancers whose Rogers/Astaire act broke up after its popularity in the forties and fifties and who are brought together again to appear on a special TV show. Deregulated television is a multi-channelled stream of aerobics and sci-fi, recipes and romance, interspersed with endless salamis, roasts, sauce-tasting competitions; and the variety show itself is a bizarre collection of lookalikes ('Woody Allen over here please', 'Kafka and Clark Gable come to the lobby'), weirdos (a woman in love with an extra-terrestrial, a dog that's been whimpering since the Pope died) and celebrities (a famous admiral, a transvestite in a highly publicized court case). This may sound like a typical wacky Fellini scenario — but it is much more. Not only is TV deregulated, so are emotions and values in society at large: which is why this film brings so clearly to mind the idea of the 'postmodern condition'. Meaning itself is dispersed and spread — in a sort of parody of democracy — with equal lack of emphasis across every facet of contemporary life, from the street to the screen; and this equality extends to the surface of the film itself, which will cut from a 'narrative' shot (e.g. Amelia in her hotel room) to a group of tiny people dancing round a giant plate of pasta, with no frame, no lines, nothing to mark the TV commercial as different from any other reality.

But instead of just revelling in his meat-market of imagery, Fellini explores it both through and against the sensibility of his central characters — who are both, in a sense, past their 'time' or at least the time when their values meshed with the society around them. Tenderly but without nostalgia, in the affect-less present where edible panties come in eleven fruit flavours plus tuna-and-onion, Fellini traces the complex and contradictory emotions of their reunion: Amelia, a respectable bourgeois grandmother with a small business, and Pippo, drifter and drinker, whose unrest conceals wasted warmth and intelligence. Both Masina and Mastroianni are superb, moving one to the most utterly un-postmodern feelings — which is part of the film's extraordinary finesse. For, however real their emotions, 'Ginger' and 'Fred' don't represent a simple reality posed against the artificiality of TV, rather they themselves stand for a different kind of showmanship.

Their act is an imitation, and yet contains the truth of their relationship: in it, they perform the emotions which they cannot repeat when, in an echo of their stage setting, they part at the station. Their most intimate exchange comes when a power cut suddenly stops the whole show, bringing home the fragility of that surface whose lack of depth contrasts with the profound emotions aroused by the occasion in Amelia and Pippo. As they sit in the dark, there is a moment of openness, caught in the folds of the TV glitz and glamour — both separate from it and, in a way, produced by it, a high pitch of intensity which cannot be matched in the light of day.

It is because Fellini is such a master of spectacular cinema that the ambivalence he brings to this image-world is so poignant. There is something reminiscent of Yeats — another great wielder of imagery — moving from 'it was the dream itself enchanted me' to the 'foul rag and

bone shop of the heart' in 'The Circus Animals' Desertion'. Even the
film's music suggests ambivalence, partly composed of the Astaire/
Rogers dance music, elegant and familiar, but partly composed of the
looped theme music of the TV show itself: GINGER AND FRED is at once
being the show, *bringing* us the show, and at the same time *showing* us
how much it *can't* show. Fellini is as flamboyant as ever, but unusually
gentle and serious too: it seems relevant that the dance at the centre of
the film is the '*hesitation*'.

For in many ways his world, where trendy young producers in
leather jackets show no interest in or respect for the people they direct,
is a bleak one; yet it has its share of softness and joy. There is a
beautiful scene where, after Amelia has been disillusioned to find that
her new friend is a transvestite, she watches 'her' and her friends
dancing on the waste ground in front of a night club, a neon no-man's
land without judgment or gender — and she almost joins in, watching
a little wistfully from the shadows. And here is Fellini the ringmaster,
watching the surface circus of modern media. The 'flying priest' on the
TV show says, 'Everything in life is a miracle, it is up to us to find it in
all that we survey.' However trite it sounds, the film does just that;
surveying the modern world with a simultaneous sense of richness and
loss.

N.S. 14 November 1986

The Circus Comes to Town

La Dolce Vita

An enormous figure of Christ swoops across the Roman sky, its
shadow climbing the side of a modern housing block. Centuries of
meaning detached, suspended; and this floating signifier — a statue on
its way to the Vatican by helicopter — flies fast enough to produce a
buzz, the speedy thrill of transport combining with the heady disloca-
tion of fixed values.

This is the opening sequence of LA DOLCE VITA: itself described as
the film which opened the 1960s. Fellini's first big-budget film was

seen on its release both as shocking and as a savage indictment of the 'good life' as led by Marcello Mastroianni's roving journalist and his sophisticated Roman friends. Yet seeing it again today, particularly after GINGER AND FRED, its concerns seem to prefigure that postmodern sense that now accompanies the sixties revival.

From the very first shot the film deals in both spectacle and the exposure of meaning: the statue with its empty blessing is echoed later in the 'miracle' sequence where people eager to be photographed are left stuck in ridiculously devout poses unaware that the cameras have moved on. This is a world — our world — where the film star Sylvia (Anita Ekberg) goes back into her plane to re-emerge for better effect, her smile a series of publicity stills. Long before the word hyper-real was being bandied about Camden Lock — in fact before many of its users were born — Fellini had pounced on that phenomenon of larger-than-lifeness it refers to: Sylvia is welcomed to Rome with a giant pizza.

LA DOLCE VITA is also known for having 'no plot', instead following a series of incidents in the journalist Marcello's life. But these function in a very precise montage. Fellini cuts from the flying Christ of the opening to a masked Egyptian dancer, opening the next, night-club scene, giving them a kind of equality: everything is a façade, Marcello hides behind his shades and, as the masked dancers slide off on a moving floor — the kind of effect Fellini loves — a woman with a mad hat starts jiving. All these phenomena from Jesus to jive are somehow levelled by the equivalence of presentation. Again and again Fellini uses cabaret acts to empty out historical meanings; in one club, where the waiters wear Roman togas, Sylvia, Marcello and a motley group of friends go into one of Fellini's typically Chaucerian parades, and their shadows surge up on the Roman 'tents' in an odd overlaying of histories. When Marcello's father takes him to an old-fashioned night spot, the show includes 1920s numbers and circus-style acts whose rustiness seems quaintly 'authentic' — but they are still performance.

As in GINGER AND FRED, the ultimate circus is that of the media and this is shown most clearly in the scenes at the site of a supposed miracle. Huge spotlights surround the 'holy tree' where two school-children claim to have seen the Virgin, giving the feel of a football ground at night; villagers cluster round it praying (Oh Lord, make me win the Lottery) and then suddenly it starts to rain. The lights have to be cut, and chaos ensues when the children decide to 'see' the Virgin in all directions at once and the holy tree is torn to shreds.

This moment is like a forerunner of the power cut in GINGER AND FRED which plunges the TV show into darkness; in both cases the media 'hyper-reality' is paralyzed and the disorder it masks is briefly apparent. But LA DOLCE VITA differs from contemporary 'postmodern' analyses of the media in its sense of a *desire* for meaning — or, at least, for there to be more than just surfaces.

And Fellini's phenomenal achievement as a film-maker is to make you feel, simultaneously, that thrill of the play of surfaces and the desire for more which fuels its movement. I find it very hard to give a sense of LA DOLCE VITA without reference to music, for its stunning black and white imagery wheels before your eyes to repeated themes that go round and round like the music they play at the circus when the performers march into the ring: 'there's more, there's more, there's more' it seems to say, with a mixture of yearning and resignation.

Fellini is able to make film produce that same effect; music and movement create 'highs' that are not just the kicks of an idle society but, in a way, the expression of a wish for something more. That wish surges up again and again in LA DOLCE VITA, in its peak moments — at the top of a cathedral, in the middle of a dance — and is repeatedly let down, most drastically in the famous scene where Marcello and Sylvia are frolicking in the Trevi Fountain at night. Dawn comes and the water is abruptly switched off: nights of intensity give way to mornings of banality.

The episode with Marcello's father is a much deeper let-down; this encounter also fails to deliver the depth wanted from it, for not only does the old man's *bon viveur* act end in a heart tremor but Marcello's attempt to talk sincerely to him fails. The façade doesn't hold — then neither does the authenticity sought beneath it. And it is in its sense of the *poignancy* of these failed-authentic moments that LA DOLCE VITA differs from the postmodern position that doesn't seek authenticity at all. Given how fashionable the sixties have become, it will be interesting to see how this film is received, with its stylish summer nights, open-topped cars, café awnings and beautiful people. But LA DOLCE VITA pursues the sweet surface of city life right to its edges: both the waste lands that surround it and the 'abyss' that Steiner — the calmest character — feels within it. The richness of this brilliant film is that it reproduces the thrill of urban existence precisely while mourning its lack of substance.

At the end of the last wild party, the cast spin out of the frame to the circussy theme tune, Marcello like a ringmaster throwing feathers over them across the screen: Fellini's virtuoso ability to combine a moving frame and movements within it creates the film's last brief moment of giddy excitement. In daylight the revellers stumble onto the seashore, drained of their glamour, to find a beached whale — its great eye still staring, like us at this washed-out spectacle.

Yet the film ends with a quite different image, that of the innocent, angel-faced girl from Perugia who recognizes Marcello from across the shore and shouts out to him. He neither recognizes nor hears her; but the camera finally rests on her face, completely devoid of cynicism. If anything distinguishes the film from the sensibility it portrays, it is this final, touching image of openness and sincerity; and if anything stands between the retro-chic present and the past it purports to revive, it is probably that same image, unthinkable in a film of style today.

N.S. 2 October 1987

Being and Nothingness

8½

8½ opens among the frozen movement of a traffic jam, everyone caught in the glass bubble of their own car. Then like Fellini's own drive from neo-realism to fantasy, the film cruises between urban angst and free-floating imagination as Marcello Mastroianni literally takes flight: up, up and away, tethered to his double on the ground, until the string to his balloon-self is cut and he falls to wake in a troubled bed of reality.

Pursuing the quasi-autobiographical mode of I VITELLONI or LA DOLCE VITA, Fellini makes Mastroianni a film director — Guido — in the middle of a creative block. Endlessly fantasizing, he can't shape his latest production, a futuristic extravaganza for which a giant rocket pad has already been half built. The image of this rigid construction, scaffolded and unlaunchable in an empty meadow, punctuates the film's more loping, horizontal field of vision like a sputnicky echo of Guido's earlier effort to get off the ground. A different and more interior image of possibility recurs, bathed in the white light of the spa town where the production team are staying: Guido's fantasy of a beautiful young woman holding out a glass of water, an elixir of liquid regeneration.

The spa, with its connotations of sickness and renewal, affords
Fellini the double opportunity for À PROPOS DE NICE-like social
comment and at the same time an almost expressionist arena round
which the shadows of Guido's dilemmas can be thrown. But it is the
absence of any aesthetic distinction between the two which gives the
film its particular style: fantasy is every bit as crisp as reality. Like LA
DOLCE VITA, 8½ plays with the pointlessness of the modern chic it
both parodies ('She was Miss Nylon *twice!*') and partakes of (elegant
night life, hotel interiors, café piazzas). But where DOLCE VITA focuses
on the busy surface of a social world driven by its own emptiness, 8½,
without a visual flicker, repeatedly turns into the crowded inner world
of its empty-handed creator.

Guido's inability to make decisions on his film (he can't cast, script
or schedule it) is part of his personal impasse with a hysterical but sexy
mistress and an elegant but angry wife, neither of whom he wants to
relinquish. It is the incapacity to choose that propels him into fantasy:
the place where he can Have It All is the harem of his imagination in
which he is at once father (arrives bearing Christmas gifts for all),
ringmaster (cracking his impatient whip) and baby (his wife as den
mother feeds and bathes him and organizes his mistresses). No one
understands masculinity as passivity so well as Fellini; the harem is
topographically built on the intensely beautiful childhood memory
sequence in which the infant Guido is bathed by the women of his
family and put to bed. The spa/bath theme is repeated when Guido
seeks an audience with a Cardinal in a steam-bath; while what is
repressed by religion features a larger expanse of water as young
Guido and other boys pay the enormous madwoman Saraghina to do
her sexy dance on the shore of the sea.

In all this Fellini seems to feed off himself in a way that is both
rambling and specific. Emotional confusion is acted out through
images of extraordinary clarity and the vagueness of the film's
protagonist is excavated with cinematic precision. The gliding camera
and perfect shading combine with Nino Rota's music which manages
to be simultaneously elegant and fairgroundy, actually *sounding* like the
circular parade the film ends with, or which, in a sense, the film *is*.

The circus has always been central to Fellini's work and much has
been written about its allegory of performance and spectacle. Yet the
issues it corrals in 8½ are, more than anything else, existential: the
problem of choice, of making a move when everything *is* spectacle.
8½'s greatest affection is reserved for the fairground artists, old friends
whom Guido meets after an intellectual café-table debate, and who
perform the trick of reading his mind without knowing the meaning of

what they find there — the magical words Asa Nisi Masa from the walls of his childhood. They have no meaning, yet are filled with meaning; by memory, for Guido, by the film, for us. Just saying them is enough. And the film's ending seems to suggest that shared movement is enough, even if it is circular. As the cancellation of Guido's production is announced, all the figures from his past and present form a ring beneath the abandoned spaceship, while his child-self moves round with them. Neither triumph nor defeat, the circle is both emptiness and shape, something made in the face of nothing.

8½ lies on the cusp of humanism and postmodernism. It presents both inner and outer worlds as an endless interplay of equivalent images, yet is shot through with the yearning to find something warm and directed among them. Existentially enough, it finds it by being it.

C.L. 25 January 1990

Head in the Clouds

The Green Ray

I have been gearing up to write about Rohmer as something of a challenge. Not because his films are so heavy, but because they're so light; and perhaps because of my own ambivalent relation to his heroines (so aptly described by John Pym as 'silly girls') who know no deadlines but those of the heart.

The lightness of Rohmer's cinematic touch is in part the product of his way of working: alone of all the original 'New Wave' directors he still works with very low budgets, small and familiar crews and largely unknown performers, and he has retained that skill of almost casual directing in real locations — streets, shops, beaches — which made Godard's early films so exciting and so close to the everyday. But where other ex-*Cahiers du Cinéma* directors have gone on to bigger and 'better' things, Rohmer has become, if anything, lighter and looser: his latest, THE GREEN RAY, contains no scripted dialogue and its conversations were improvised along the broad themes of the film.

This is in itself an interesting departure, because talk has always been one of the key components of Rohmer's fables. His earlier collection of films, the six 'Moral Tales', concerned men either committed to or on the verge of commitment to relationships, faced with a sexual or romantic temptation; however, the moral note in these stemmed less from the narrative outcomes of the plots than from the gaps between the characters' words and actions — something which the viewer is left to observe with no clear conclusions drawn. One effect of this is to place the audience on the same footing as the characters in the story, with no privileged knowledge and no special access to the truth of emotions other than through this muddle of speech and half-obscured desires.

But another effect, which is central to Rohmer's work (and again, to others of the early New Wave) is to turn language into an independent component of the films. Speech becomes, as it were, a *thing*, an element in its own right: the novelty of this is only apparent if you consider its ususal function in films, which is either to further the narrative, pushing the action in particular directions, or to provide 'clues' to the characters, transparent explanations of their motives and inner selves. In Rohmer's films much time and, in a sense, freedom, is given to speech but it means neither more nor less than what it says, being almost functionless in terms of the plot and offering no hotline to characters' 'true selves'. So we are never presented with finished characters, but people in flux, whose shifting desires and half-formed wishes are hardly known even to themselves.

And we are presented with them in a world apparently devoid of material considerations, with none of the harsher determinants that affect so much of our lives. But what Rohmer does, in essence, is precisely to *give space* to this elusive life of the heart, expanding the arena for those subtle and yet important personal choices which most of the time, for most of us, are squeezed below the surface made up of work and more conscious or pressing demands. In his second series of films, the 'Comedies and Proverbs', Rohmer follows a succession of young women through the twists and turns of their romantic whims at those points where their lives are still unsettled. Often the choices they are faced with are not as important as they think, as with the young heroine of A GOOD MARRIAGE, whose almost random decision to get married comes to nothing; but, Rohmer seems to be saying, everything is still open. And yet, more disturbingly, where one heroine does make a bid for independence by taking a room of her own in FULL MOON IN PARIS, her discovery that it's not what she wants after all comes too late for her to keep her boyfriend. So these moments of whimsy are not entirely without consequence; and perhaps this is what gives an edge to the otherwise rather airy tales. Chance, too, is an important element in Rohmer films: the snowstorm in MY NIGHT WITH MAUD, or the rain in CLAIRE'S KNEE, offer unpredicted situations which can easily change the course of events.

THE GREEN RAY takes Rohmer's expansion of uncertain moments further than ever before, giving a remarkable amount of space to one of the most infinitely irritating of heroines, Delphine (Marie Rivière), who cannot make up her mind what to do with her summer, taking up and dropping friends' suggestions of holidays, dreaming of love but resisting unwanted advances, in a state of permanent waiting like a displaced fairy-tale heroine expecting Mr Right. And, such is Rohmer's indulgence, he offers him to her.

The 'green ray' refers to a Jules Verne story which claims that someone who sees this elusive last ray of sunset will be able to read their own heart. (This information comes in an overheard conversation, again a chance occurrence, but one which, typically, plays a central role.) Delphine herself is an infuriating young woman, picky, restless and fey, drifting in a sort of nebulous feminine limbo, searching for 'signs' — and Rohmer even gives her these, laying Tarot cards across her path in the street. Finally, when least expecting it, she both meets a 'special' boy and sees the green ray.

Maddening as Delphine is, Rohmer's indulgence is not so much for her as a character but for that space in which she floats, where dreams, fears and lack of self-knowledge lap together, where directions are not always known. Despite one's impatience with these 'silly girls', what is so striking is the film's own patience: the sense that it might allow you more than you allow yourself. This is, perhaps, Rohmer's lightness: for all their 'everyday' quality, these films offer spaces rarely found in everyday life. And, returning to Rohmer's style, with its deceptive ease and lack of ponderousness, it is itself like the last, clear ray of the New Wave, still making room for the apparently trivial in a film-making world that imagines it has moved on to grander or more urgent things.

N.S. 13 March 1987

Not New-Waving but Drowning

King Lear
4 Adventures of Reinette & Mirabelle

'We live in a time in which movies and art do not exist . . . They have to be re-invented.' So speaks the narrator in Godard's KING LEAR, of the world 'after Chernobyl'. And the film itself, product of a strange conception (the legendary deal signed on a table-napkin by Godard and Cannon chairman Menahem Golan at Cannes), is concerned with the possibility of some kind of resurrection for imagery, a stripping of meaning back to things themselves, the impenetrable materiality of the real world.

Yet -- to pursue the metaphor of the Christian calendar which Godard rather coyly invokes with his church bells and spring flowers -- KING LEAR leaves you with the feeling that this is the Good Friday rather than the Easter Sunday of film-making.

For one thing, its style and structure are, for Godard, far from fresh. While part of the political strength of his early films was the way they forced you to think about their production, there is a kind of easy cynicism about Godard's relation to Cannon which pervades this whole film: whose self-referential comments on its immediate context consist merely of a repetitive harping about the constraints of working on 'bankable projects' for 'philistines', and have none of the wit and simplicity of, for example, the cheque-signing sequence which makes up the credits for TOUT VA BIEN. Rather, they strike a churlish (not to say snobbish) note since, after all, no one forced Godard to make the deal.

Like so many elements in the film, this device has all the hallmarks of Godard's 'difficult' or 'political' works, but gone sour. LEAR's mythic figures of The Great Writer (Norman Mailer), the gangster Don Learo with his daughter Cordelia, and William Shakespeare the Fifth, trying to rewrite his ancestor's works in the modern world, are reminiscent of Godard's bold use of fictional characters in WEEKEND or VENT D'EST where Saint-Just and Emily Brontë, a Cavalryman and an Indian can wander on screen and sound forth; but here there is something more perfunctory about them and, while Godard simply can't help being *clever* ('are you trying to make a play for my girl?' barks Learo at Shakespeare V), he constantly implies that he is performing under duress and his jaded tone, whatever its social justification (Chernobyl, Cannon Inc.), leaves one with the sense of a cantankerous Artist rather than a passionate critic. The audience is more likely to end up disillusioned with the film than with the world around it.

The other feature of LEAR which is reminiscent of Godard's successfully didactic films is his use of wordplay on the screen: so that LEAR becomes a cLEARing, the word 'Nothing', Cordelia's famous reply when Lear demands proof of her love, becomes NO THING. And it is in dealing with things — literally with nature — that the film raises its key issues.

But even these are not new; Godard seems to be going through that disaffection with language that hits particularly hard those who are most adept at using it. 'Show — not tell' is a dictum of the film; which also tells us, 'What is great is not the image but the emotion it evokes.' It is as if, fed up with both society and language, Godard is straining towards some more direct, primal relationship between image and feeling: 'Never know, always see.' A copy of *The Waves* lies on the shore, lapped by real waves: the referent takes over. A film can floats downstream; film stock lies coiled in a field.

These surreal images, juxtaposing nature with language, have a strange bearing on the rest of the film whose tortuousness is the very opposite of clear, and which relies heavily on cultural knowledge to make sense of it (in a montage of 'Art' images and photos of film-makers the voice-over talks familiarly of 'Luchino' — meaning the director Visconti — and so on). Ultimately, though he invokes a re-birth of imagery, Godard does not produce it, and this is all the more disappointing since his consummate skill with his medium ends up in apparently effortless yet tedious convolutions.

The images were there as new — innocent and shy and strong. The line is Godard's from LEAR: but it applies almost perfectly to the latest release from another old-New-Wave director, Rohmer, whose 4 ADVENTURES OF REINETTE & MIRABELLE recently opened. It is fascinating to compare the work of these two old colleagues, both exponents of a kind of film-making that fits badly with the present climate: Godard goes on going on about what he does, Rohmer goes on doing what he does, until you feel that his constant refining of his particular style is itself a kind of resistance. There are other comparisons to be made, not least in the relation of these now middle-aged male directors to young women: Godard's increasing, infuriating voyeurism contrasts strongly with Rohmer's evident, and most unusual, liking and respect for them. He seems able to grasp physicality — a crumpled nightdress, sleep — without sexualizing it, in the same way that he produces a heightened sense of light and colour, movement and sound, the rhythms of speech and the nuances of expression. Sometimes, as in 'The Blue Hour'(the first story) the grain of the film itself, pushed to the limit in night light, seems part of that magnifying glass Rohmer holds against the daily world to show the texture of life as one experiences it when young, at once expanded and intensified.

If Rohmer's imagery here is as luminous and tactile as ever — sunlight on fabrics, thunder in the sky seem almost tangible in a way that makes his use of film far from transparent — his social eye and moral questioning are also at their funniest and most forgiving. This 'light' and incredibly low-budget film takes in issues like begging, stealing, lying, art dealing — and, as so often, indulgently lets one of its excellent heroines talk for ages and ages about silence. All this has its own gentle bearing on film-making: but Rohmer does, as Godard says, 'show, not tell'.

N.S. 5 February 1988

The Scissor-Men

Club de Femmes

If this column didn't seem to make a lot of sense last week, that's because (for a variety of production reasons) it was cut.[1] Between writing and printing it lost not only. paragraphs and sentences, but parts of sentences — leaving strange elisions, non sequiturs and abrupt turns.

Questions of cutting have been on my mind this week for a variety of reasons. The British Film Institute has just re-released a new, uncut print of Jacques Deval's 1936 French farce CLUB DE FEMMES: a jolly, feminist-humanist comedy about a girls' boarding house which,

---

1   The column was 'Man for Our Season' (p. 84); the cuts have been reinstated.

because it featured a lesbian character and an extra-marital pregnancy, was heavily censored for its brief run in New York in 1937.

Whole scenes and chunks of the plot were removed; nudity (not that there *is* any of the full-frontal sort) was suppressed entirely and the subtitles were carefully manipulated to alter the implied nature of the central relationships. But what is interesting about the complete version of the film is that its strongest quality isn't naughtiness but *robustness* — which is, in an important sense, exactly the opposite.

Thus an account of the film's key events — a young dancer smuggles her boyfriend into the house and becomes pregnant, a foreign student gets pulled into a prostitution ring organized by the switchboard operator and a beautiful young lesbian, whose beloved friend is raped by one of the ring's 'clients', commits murder — gives absolutely no sense of the film's tone, precisely because we are accustomed to thinking of these as risqué or seamy subjects. The tone of CLUB DE FEMMES is consistently *wholesome*: in this its philosophy is in line with that of the eponymous establishment.

For the Club de Femmes is a sort of hotel started by the well-meaning Mme Fargeton (Eve Francis) in order to protect young single women in Paris: it aims to provide 'modest material comforts and moral security'. The events of the film show that Mme Fargeton's ideals are less easily realized than she thought; yet they are, in the end, re-validated rather than undermined by the incorporation of the less-than-ideal occurrences.

I have suggested before that liberalism must be constantly stumbling on its own boundaries if it is to continue seeming liberal; the warm-hearted humanism of CLUB DE FEMMES is revitalized in a structurally similar way. Its component qualities of kindly innocence and worldly experience are divided between Mme Fargeton and her friend Dr Aubrey (Valentine Tessler) whose medical knowledge and professional ethics result in her knowing a great deal more about the girls' real lives than the *directrice*. Yet at the end of the film the two outlooks dovetail again when Danielle Darrieux's illegitimate baby is born at the club: 'Everything's in order — it's a girl', says the doctor — and even Mme Fargeton cannot disapprove. We are returned to a more complete (feminist!) humanity that transcends strict social codes.

But this is not to say it is *im*moral — far from it: the whole point about humanist morality is that it has to set itself up as *more* moral than the narrow and often cruel conventions of its time. There is a long tradition of this kind of humanism in cinema (think of Griffith's WAY DOWN EAST, for example, where Lillian Gish is punished by small-town moralists for her pregnancy) and this is, in a way, linked with film's capacity for realism, the sense of showing things 'as they really are'. CLUB DE FEMMES seems to say: 'Girls will be girls; this is how life *is*; incorporate it into your morality or that morality will be worthless.' And this message, hardly revolutionary in itself, is linked with the physically robust quality which makes the film such fun.

Girls in shorts leap around the gym; girls in their lingerie giggle in their bedrooms; girls are allowed to look at one another, touch one another, not because this is a 'lesbian film', though the one lesbian character is portrayed sympathetically, but because it is, in every sense, a 'full-bodied' film. Its physicality is not voyeuristic but energetic, not seamy but positively bounding (in that peculiarly thirties way) with health. It is only from the censor's viewpoint that everything suddenly becomes sordid. The only real nakedness in CLUB DE FEMMES is when the raped girl, returning to her room desperate and tearful, is shown tearing off her clothes and frantically showering in an effort to get *rid* of that sordidness from the (entirely off-screen) rape. This scene was, of course, cut: thus does censorship turn values entirely in reverse.

After its brief run, this film never took off in the America of the Hayes code. Recently, however, a New York cinema ran a 'Hollywood before the Code' season which, like the uncut CLUB DE FEMMES, gave a fascinating opportunity to consider what the code changed. I went to see Barbara Stanwyck in William Wellman's NIGHT NURSE (1931); such is our 'Danish Dentist' film culture that I had imagined it would be about a brothel. Instead, it is a highly moral tale in which Stanwyck saves two sick children who are being poisoned by their mother's drug-pushing lover. There is no 'sex' in the film at all. But there *is* sensuality, physicality, people dressing, undressing — and, when a medical student puts a skeleton in Barbara Stanwyck's bed for a prank, she hops into the next one with her friend and snuggles up for the night.

The Hayes code didn't even allow married couples in the same bed, let alone two women. But seeing pre-code films *en masse* leaves one most strongly with the sense, not of risqué subjects or underwear scenes, but of general exuberance, physical freedom, a kind of toughness. Films of the code era look stilted by comparison and, more to the point, they become insinuating and coy. (They also become more heavily symbolic, so that sex becomes lighting someone's cigarette.)

Though I started with a personal complaint, I'll finish with the real reason for thinking about cutting and codes: Section 28.[1] The point about the Hayes code was not that it tried to 'clean up' everything, but that it made everything seem dirty. It appears that we are entering another era of disgust; the time to fight that emotion is now.

N.S. 13 May 1988

Lean Cuts

The Big Heat
In a Lonely Place

Despite what feels like an onslaught of new releases I am taking time out to celebrate the re-release of two Hollywood classics: Fritz Lang's THE BIG HEAT (1953) and Nicholas Ray's IN A LONELY PLACE (1950). In collaboration with Columbia, the BFI have produced new 35mm prints, which will soon be playing throughout the country.

New black-and-white prints are particularly welcome at a time when the ridiculous trend of 'colourization' grows apace in the USA. But besides enjoying the quality of the image, there are other reasons why this is an interesting moment to see the films again. In the middle of all the fuss about FATAL ATTRACTION and SAMMY AND ROSIE, here are two movies — one about sexual mistrust, one about social corruption — made on the brink of another era of return to family values, after the upheaval immediately following the war.

Much has been written about the figure of Woman in film noir. Both THE BIG HEAT and IN A LONELY PLACE can be placed in this category, and both star Gloria Grahame as a single woman who is sexually active. While the films differ in many ways, in both she gets good lines and a strong visual presence, giving her a kind of filmic dignity which contrasts with what one might call the 'sillification' of independent women in recent movies.

---

1   See footnote on p. 68.

But it is impossible to talk about the films' sexual meanings without also looking at their construction. Unlike many films today they have an economy and lack of naturalism which add to, rather than detract from, their emotional intensity. (Economy is a greatly underrated quality in contemporary film-making: how many times do you *need* to cut between a rabbit hutch and a saucepan?)

THE BIG HEAT opens with a shot which at once provides a logo for the whole movie and launches its action: the image of a gun about to be used by a cop to commit suicide. Skilfully jumping locations through a series of phone calls, Lang introduces in a single sequence the network of key figures whose chain of corruption Glenn Ford, as Detective Bannion, unravels during the film. Grahame is the gangster's moll, while Ford figures as husband and father in an excessively idyllic family whose domestic scenes are, as in FATAL ATTRACTION, disrupted first by the phone and then by physical violence. However, it is not an Other Woman who is the source of evil here but the mob, or, more generally, the fear and cowardice that allow it to operate.

While on one level Lang sets up an opposition between the world of the Good Marriage — which takes place in interiors so brightly lit as to appear almost heavenly — and the underworld of streets and hotel rooms, on another he brings them together. At a pivotal moment, roughly halfway through, the film cuts from Ford's look around the now empty family house to Grahame behind a bar; and from this moment she starts to redeem herself by helping him crack the crime ring, so that by the time she dies she can be linked with his wife: 'You two would have got along fine,' are his last words to her.

Conversely, marriage is no guarantee of goodness. The cop whose suicide opens the film has a 'respectable' wife living off the mob: Grahame tells her, 'We're sisters under the mink.' And this, broadly speaking, is one of the film's key themes: the spectrum of good and bad along which people can easily slide in different situations. Its most topical relevance is perhaps, sadly, its theme of fear: 'I do what I'm told,' says one of the cops minding the gangster, and as Ford says bitterly, 'That's what we're all supposed to do, aren't we?'

What is disturbing about the women in THE BIG HEAT is not how they're characterized — all are strong figures — but what the plot itself does to them. The only one to come out alive is an already crippled old lady, and the film is famous for the scene where Lee Marvin throws coffee across Grahame's face. Schematically, this gives her a good side and a bad side — half beautiful, half scarred — an image which perfectly encapsulates the meanings she carries within the plot as the good Bad Girl.

Grahame herself seemed to carry this persona from film to film. In 1955 she appeared in OKLAHOMA! as a bad Good Girl with the number 'I'm just a girl who can't say no'. Often remembered as a frilly romp in the corn, this film is actually very much about both the good and bad sides of sexuality, with the disturbing figure of porn-loving farmhand Judd (Rod Steiger) who is finally burned alive.

Fear and suspicion in sexual relations is also the theme of much of Ray's work and IN A LONELY PLACE — set, interestingly, in Hollywood — is no exception. Grahame plays a girl who *chooses* to say yes, and this is the film where her stature is perhaps greatest: Bogart plays a prototype *homme fatal* and much of the plot is experienced from the female point of view. With a structure whose almost architectural organization is akin to Lang's, Ray switches our identification halfway through, from sharing Bogart's experience of being accused of murder to sharing Grahame's suspicion that he really has committed it. The fact that we end up at some distance from the character with whom we are at first led to identify suggests that the lonely place is the self; the distance between the lovers taking the graphic form of the kind of no-person's-land between their neighbouring apartments.

The analogy with architecture isn't random: Ray studied with Frank Lloyd Wright before he started directing. Both he and Lang use cinematic space not as something to be filled with props but as a precise means for placing characters in terms of their relative power and significance. Their 90-minute screen time is tightly structured and never wasted. Much contemporary movie-making seems full of clutter, both in shots and *of* shots; these two films offer the chance to see Hollywood at its leanest, and richest.

N.S. 22 January 1988

Love or Money

The Colour of Money

Someone asked Martin Scorsese at the NFT recently what advice he would give to a young film school graduate. His reply was, 'try to make films'.

The simplicity of this answer covers a range of problems facing Scorsese and others trying to produce personal projects in the Hollywood context. Scorsese has a passion for *cinema*, the institution and its history, yet the mainstream cinema industry is based on a professionalism which demands a degree of detachment: where, if a director wants to work, he must take on scripts he has had no part in devising (Scorsese was offered WITNESS but turned it down as he had no personal knowledge of the Amish). Those in Hollywood who think of themselves as involved film-makers rather than professional directors — for example, Francis Ford Coppola — have come to grief with many productions. (Coppola's PEGGY SUE GOT MARRIED tacitly admits the financial failure of some of his more personal ventures, geared as it is to the BACK TO THE FUTURE audience in a depressingly formulaic way.) Scorsese's own major project THE LAST TEMPTATION OF CHRIST, which he has been deeply involved with for years, was axed by Paramount and all his preparations for it have had to be put aside if he is to work at all.[1]

This context is important, for Scorsese's best films (which I would argue are some of the best made by anyone, anywhere, in the last decade or so) have been intensely personal, made with the kind of wild energy that could hardly exist on tap. And the tension between spontaneous enthusiasm and professional calculation is the key to the morality tale at the heart of THE COLOUR OF MONEY.

The film takes up the story of Fast Eddie Felson from THE HUSTLER — still played by Paul Newman, who initiated the project (and, with Scorsese, staked a third of his salary on its completion within budget). Twenty-five years on Eddie no longer shoots pool himself but makes money on younger players he bank-rolls in the bar he now owns. When he comes across the brilliant and 'natural' young Vincent Laurie (Tom Cruise) offering to play without stakes he is stunned,

---

1   It was completed in 1988.

recognizing exactly the raw keenness that can't be produced through mere effort: 'some guys spend half their lives trying to create something like that'. With the help of Vincent's hard-headed girlfriend Carmen (who quickly grasps the point of losing on purpose in order to up the stakes) he persuades the boy to accept his partnership and hit the road hustling.

The taming of Vincent, which is rather like breaking in a colt, takes much of the film; at first he is either too soft-hearted to win or too proud to lose, and the constraints of professional hustling fall hard on him. But as he learns the game, the roles are reversed. Eddie loses one night to a hustler and the blow to his pride drives him to break with Vincent and Carmen and painstakingly re-train himself as a player. By the time they meet for the grand tournament at Atlantic City, it is Eddie who is playing for real: when the two are drawn as opponents he believes it to be a true contest but Vincent 'dumps' (just as his mentor taught him) so as to make bigger money on backroom hustles — out of which he naively offers Eddie his cut.

Atlantic City has, interestingly, figured as a site of redemption in another film where an older character (and star) regains his professional powers: Louis Malle's ATLANTIC CITY had Burt Lancaster as an ageing gunman who redeems himself by killing two baddies. And it is Fast Eddie's return to playing — the last words of the film are his 'I'm back' — that is the point of THE COLOUR OF MONEY. Its relationships are interesting (the trio on the road is like a bizarre family) but never really take off with the passion of the relationships in, for example, MEAN STREETS, NEW YORK, NEW YORK or RAGING BULL. And the overall *feel* of the film is one of professionalism. The direction is virtuoso: the opening close-up of curling cigarette smoke as we track up to the first view of Eddie, the way the camera slides past the mirrored pillars of pool halls, the cathedral-like shots of the great hall in Atlantic City, the zip pans which swivel out of simple point-of-view shots — all these are perfectly done. The script too is tight and powerful. But nowhere does all this burst open into the near out-of-control quality that makes some of Scorsese's other movies so much more than merely good films.

The point where the film-making itself seems to intersect with its themes is precisely in that conflict between clear-headed professionalism and gut drive. Early on in the film Eddie says, of Vincent, 'He's gotta learn how to be himself — but on purpose': and this is exactly what you feel Scorsese is doing in this project. It has all his thematic hallmarks — a drive to redemption, strong relations between men — and the Vincent character has, on paper, many of the characteristics of

Johnny Boy in MEAN STREETS or Jake La Motta in RAGING BULL. But
Vincent isn't really the key figure in this film: the centre of the drama
is no longer the wild boy but the man who goes back to work. The
most memorable scene in Eddie's rehabilitation is when he goes to
have his eyes tested; surging music as he is re-kitted with corrective
glasses suggests that this moment is the moral heart of the movie.

And, looking hard for that other, less definable hallmark which is
Scorsese's personal stake in his subjects, this is where it appears to lie.
He *is* back: but one longs for something to reappear in his work as
crazy and physical as Vincent's dance around a pool table, which
turns an excellent game into a uniquely personal performance. Perhaps, in the light of all this, my favourite two lines in the film have an
extra resonance. Eddie comes to the childcare store where Vincent
works to persuade him to go on the road, and Vincent protests, 'This is
my job.' 'You think so? I don't think so. I think it's your problem.'
How close, and how far apart, one's job and one's passion may be, is a
vital question both inside and outside this film.

N.S. 6 March 1987

Lights of the World

Comrades
Good Morning Babylon
Power

So often films about politics seem lacking in a passion for the medium
they're made in; or, conversely, a passion for cinema becomes divorced
from any sense of how it might function politically. Here at last are two
films which, different as they are in both style and content, deal with
the politics *of* cinema: with both its materiality and its purpose in the
real world that film is at once in and about.

For film consists of light, thrown on to the screen; and just as this
literal illumination must inevitably have a direction, so must the
politics of its content. We are used to the apparently sourceless light of
bourgeois cinema, offering us a vision of the world as if it were the only

one possible; yet these films each in their way remind us that the light can be thrown differently, and can illuminate people and events that have been hidden in the shadows of conventional history.

Bill Douglas' COMRADES, subtitled 'A Lanternist's Account of the Tolpuddle Martyrs and What Became of Them', has the clear purpose of commemoration: and at a time when trade union politics are unfashionable not only on the right but on much of the left, the Tolpuddle labourers' fight to unionize in the face of wage cuts is as relevant as ever. Their story has to be told and remembered; COMRADES not only tells it, but engages with the problems of preserving and passing on working-class stories in a culture which works to suppress them.

For there *are* problems with telling 'history from below' and one which besets COMRADES very seriously is that of style: the tale of hardship, struggle, arrest and deportation is told in the conventional realist form that we have become accustomed to in historical dramas. Maybe working people really didn't wear bright colours; nevertheless the grim greys and greens that characterize the lives of the worthy poor in movies seem so familiar that some of their impact in presenting the experience of rainy, muddy, rural poverty is blunted. Part of this style is the way the goodies all look ruggedly honest, the baddies vicious and leering; but even worse, the good men are all good and masculine, the good women all good and womanly, while the baddies contain a disproportionate number of campy, effeminate figures, from the squire's ring-laden agent to the creepy Australian landlord with his pet boy. Not only is this whole mode of representation crude, its sense of sexual politics (the very worst character has sex with his *dog*) verges on the tabloid.

Yet COMRADES differs from conventional dramas in two ways. First, it is a narrative without a single hero and instead of being drawn into the structures of imaginary identification invited by most mainstream films, we follow the characters as onlookers. Second, this position is one we are reminded of throughout the film. A harvesting sequence begins with close-ups of the heavily exhausting, repetitive labour; shot by shot, the camera pulls out and the light falls, until from a distance we see in a golden evening glow what looks like a peaceful harvest scene, familiar from countless paintings and postcards. At this moment the film cuts to a reverse shot of the squire's family driving by in a carriage, so that this image becomes *what they see*; picturesqueness is shown to be a middle-class view of labour.

The rich also have the power to preserve their image; the Australian governor has his arrogance crisply outlined for posterity by a silhouette cutter. The poor must struggle to pass on their messages; throwing poems on scrumpled paper through prison bars. And the film-maker must take sides; COMRADES casts the lanternist (a succession of different characters played by the same actor) as witness, right from the opening scene where he watches the brutal suppression of a rebellion.

We next see him by night at the door of the manor; and as the squire's maid walks the length of the house, its wealthy inhabitants loom large in the giant looping shadows thrown by her candle, reminding us at once of the fluidity of light and its capacity for changing the shapes of our perceptions. Film is illusion, Douglas insists, yet it must be used; and COMRADES ends with the solidarity committee hosting a lantern show of the Tolpuddle story where the chairman says to the presenter, 'Go then, and make a union of lanternists.'

The Taviani brothers' GOOD MORNING BABYLON virtually picks up this thread a century later, with the lives of those who worked behind the scenes in the early cinema industry. With its elegant aesthetic utterly different in style from COMRADES, their concerns nevertheless overlap. While Douglas takes cinema's actual predecessor, the magic lantern show, as his analogy with film, the Tavianis take the Church of Miracles — a metaphor for cinema if ever there was one, both a physical structure and an institution of belief. 'The work of hands and of fantasy', as the heroes' father puts it, this building is his last commission as a professional restorer, for he goes bankrupt and his youngest sons Nicola and Andrea go to the States to seek their fortunes. From restoring bas-relief elephants on the Romanesque church, they move to designing giant elephants for the Babylonian scenes in D.W. Griffith's INTOLERANCE.

Like COMRADES, BABYLON is about cinema, point of view, light; but here the joy of looking is wound into the form of the film itself, which is shot squarely and simply with each image so beautifully and yet almost detachedly composed that watching it is like being given a series of presents — it is a labour of love, like the box of verbal images the brothers give their girlfriends. We are first shown film as shafts of light in a sideways shot of the projector when Griffith watches CABIRIA in the Italian pavilion at the 1915 Expo; the theme of its connection with architecture is echoed in the next sequence as searchlights play around the building itself. The shifting relation of the world to its light explains the film's title: 'Good morning' is the father's message to his sons each evening from Italy where his dusk is their dawn. And light creates both natural and artificial environments; dusk for the birds the brothers tend is when they put a blanket on their cages. Light makes filming possible, and filming makes preservation possible. The brothers' magnificent trial elephant, built from old cinema posters in the woods, is burned down by a jealous production manager; but it is already on film and when Griffith sees it he employs the brothers as art directors.

The scene in which the elephant is filmed is the political heart of the movie. The brothers and their friends — technicians and extras, Hollywood's 'working class' — stay up all night by candlelight painting it white so they can shoot it in the morning, and one of the women makes a key speech: 'Let's never forget the way we are now, helping each other . . . that's why this Hollywood of ours is so wonderful.' Collective enterprise is the basis of film-making — and of socialist politics.

Its antithesis is war; the film ends in World War One when the dying brothers meet, with perfect structural logic, in front of the Church of Miracles and, finding a camera, film each other 'so our sons will always know what we look like.' Yet even in this final celebration of film's capacity to preserve and pass on, the disjunction between an image and the experience it represents is brought out subtly and movingly when one brother tells the other to smile for the camera and he replies, touchingly, 'I thought I was smiling.' The improbability of this whole scene is characteristic of the way BABYLON reminds us that film is an aesthetic and political structure, not a transparent window: its every image has both grace and purpose.

Sidney Lumet's POWER, which opens this week, is also about the politics of the image and the image of politics. Well made as it is, this film contrasts with COMRADES and BABYLON in its ultimately liberal belief in a neutral image that needs no wielding and can let real honesty show through. But every image is a projection: film can never be transparent. What it can be used for is to show our world in a radically different light.

N.S. 28 August 1987

Ways of Showing

It is not only film criticism that affects the way we see films. The contexts in which they are shown, in particular the grouping of films in seasons, whether on television or in the cinema — even the selection of which movies to juxtapose in a double bill, affect the way we understand the meanings of the films involved. On top of this, different places and times in and at which films are presented makes a difference, not just to *how* we view them but to *who* views them, which audiences they pull in. An all-night horror movie extravaganza is a very different context from a seminar on censorship (a situation in which I have viewed horror films on several occasions); a screening of PUMPING IRON 2 — THE WOMEN shown at a West End 'flea-pit' may draw men in dirty raincoats, but the same film has drawn ecstatic responses in the freedom of a women-only screening at the Brixton Ritzy. Certain generic or thematic elements in films may be drawn out by their grouping, as with the examples of the film noir season and the 'epidemic cinema' season discussed below. The most common way of grouping films on TV is by director, and this has also been the traditional form of programming in Arts cinemas and regional film theatres. However, these 'auteur' groupings have in recent years given way to more imaginative, thematic programming devices which can make it possible to read films 'against the grain' of their perhaps better-known elements. (How about GONE WITH THE WIND as a war movie? RED RIVER as a male romance?)

The examples of presentation scripts and programme notes given in this section are intended to bring the issue of programming into the critical arena and suggest its importance in affecting the ways films are viewed.

Presenting: Fatal Attractions

'Old' films on TV reach a much wider audience than those shown (which happens rarely, and only in repertory) at cinemas, yet there has, on the whole, been little attempt to contextualize or discuss them *through* the medium of TV. BBC 2's now defunct programme 'Film Club' attempted for a while to do just that: present and provide informed commentary on films with the intention of enhancing the audience's interest, knowledge and enjoyment of them.

In 1988 Film Club asked me to present a season of films all falling into the category 'film noir'. In contemporary cinema, a violent fascination for sexually dramatic themes had been emerging, and been widely discussed with the release of FATAL ATTRACTION at the start of that year; its title was used to focus one thematic strand of the season. At the same time, the term *film noir* was by now fairly well known outside film-buff circles, and many of its stylistic trademarks were very much in vogue. The concept of the season was already there before I was invited to be its presenter; my contribution was to research and write the scripts which I then spoke to camera in a film noir 'mise-en-scène', dressed as a heroine of the time and seated at an enormous, Chandler-esque desk in front of a venetian blind. The movies, with these short prefaces, went out in a late Friday night slot throughout the autumn and early winter; the scripts are reproduced here exactly as spoken before each film.

The season drew a wide response, and my mailbag came largely from viewers who would have been unlikely to have read, for example,

the *New Statesman* column, and many of whom clearly made few trips to
the cinema. The capacity of television to connect audiences with both
films and ideas about films they might otherwise not encounter, offers
an enormous potential for broadening the field of film criticism.

Sudden Fear

This season called Fatal Attractions comes at a time when a lot of contemporary films are trying to deal with fear and suspicion in sexual relationships. To me, they do it in an incredibly heavy-handed way compared with these far more murky and in many ways far more unsettling *films noirs* — a term which in fact wasn't used by anyone making them but was coined by French critics, and translates simply as 'black film' or, I would say, dark films.

Visually they're characterized by a darkness, literally a shadowiness, partly the result of the low budgets and fast schedules of B-movie making. At the same time they deal with shady or difficult subjects — usually a combination of crime and violent passion — and they're also like the flip-side or shadow side of Hollywood itself. Most mainstream Hollywood films, while showing characters' own emotions within the plot, settle us very clearly into an 'objective' view of the events and feelings they depict. But film noir is in some ways anti-realist, it's almost like an expressionist form, where emotions are turned inside out so that the exterior world represents an inner landscape — as in dreams.

SUDDEN FEAR was made in 1952, and its Fatal Attractions are between Joan Crawford, Jack Palance and Gloria Grahame. But the film is extremely interesting and disturbing because it doesn't just trace the struggle for control within their relationships; it's almost as if the different figures are struggling to control the script itself. The fact that Crawford is a playwright underlines this, and the fact that Palance is an actor feeds into it to the point where, a lot of the time, you're forced to ask, whose story is it? When he first declares his love for her he speaks lines *she's written*: it's almost as if on some level she's invented him, or at least, his love for her. In several scenes he features merely as a dent in her pillow. She also writes — without giving too much away — Palance's and Grahame's letters to each other and, in fact, sketches out what is essentially a plot for the second half of the movie. So in some ways it's never quite clear whose reality we're in. There's a moment in the film where the key piece of evidence on a record is shattered, and this provides a perfect image of the fragility of any objective record or account of events. There's a further destabilizing of any sort of baseline reality when Crawford experiences a nightmare in a sequence which is like a catalogue of her fears, but not only that, a catalogue of Hollywood bad endings — almost as if the film was riffling through them and saying, Well, it could be any of these.

That's just one way of looking at the movie: another tack, as with many films noirs, is about power and class difference. She has money; he's a struggling actor. At one point they're on the phone, and we cut between two shots, each is pacing the floor but they're pacing very different carpets and even the glimpses of legs of furniture that we see suggest two completely different worlds, one of the seedy boarding house, the other of the luxurious, culture-loaded mansion.

Considering the contemporary idea of the powerful single woman, SUDDEN FEAR is also disturbing because it's almost as if Crawford's emotions are too powerful and actually conjure up this nightmare world. The film constantly uses immense close-ups of Crawford's face, which to me always seems curiously mask-like even when she's crying or something; and yet the film itself takes us behind that mask, into a world of desire and fear.

The movie was an enormous success and covered its cost many times over. Crawford, a powerful working woman herself, had wisely agreed to take a 48 per cent cut of the profits and so earned far more than the flat fee she could have had. Both she and Palance, and cameraman Charles Lang, were nominated for Oscars; but I think it's especially worth noticing the role given to Gloria Grahame, who we're going to see over and over again in this season, and who in some ways represents a sort of bad but crushable femininity in a way that Crawford, with her almost masculine postures, never does. They make an interesting pair, and in some of the later films I'll come back to talk about this doubling of female roles. But for now, I hope you enjoy it.

Farewell My Lovely

FAREWELL MY LOVELY, made in 1944, was the first full screen version of Chandler's thriller and marked a turning point in the careers both of its director, Edward Dmytryk, and Dick Powell, who stars as hard-boiled detective Philip Marlowe. Dmytryk had been directing B-movies at RKO for some years, and at this point was given a bigger than usual budget to make what the studio clearly saw as a slightly up-market film noir. This bears out the idea that film noir arose as a form of prestige B-picture making, something which was itself a product of the move to double-billing in cinemas, meaning that support features had to be made, on considerably lower budgets than the pictures at the top of the bill. What we now think of as film noir style grew up partly in response to economies — for example, night shooting is indispensable on tight schedules — and at the same time, there was a distinct self-consciousness about these films' role almost as the underbelly of the A-feature.

That consciousness makes RKO's investment in this movie, under studio head Charles Koerner, all the more interesting; because if there was one type of film that RKO was particularly known for, it was its B-pictures and films noirs of this period. It's also interesting that film noir came from the same stable as the low-budget horror film, another kind of B-picture. Scenes in the film we're about to see recall the horror movie very strongly: creeping mists in forests at night, looming reflections in dark windows, the subjective, nightmare sequences when Marlowe's knocked unconscious and even, in fact, the larger-than-life, almost horrific figure of Moose Malloy, played by Mike Mazurki — all these owe something to the development of the cheap horror thriller, like for example CAT PEOPLE, that RKO was successfully churning out at this time.

Both stylistically and in its plot, FAREWELL MY LOVELY is an almost archetypal film noir. The opening, with a pool of light from an overhead lamp on a table; the first scene in Marlowe's office, lit entirely by a neon sign flashing on and off, leaving the set in almost total darkness for long moments: these immediately set the tone for a style based on extremely low key lighting. Having said that this style originally derived in part from low budgets, the twist is that with this picture more money *was* available, and that low key look was achieved at some expense. The patterns of light and darkness were produced through complicated visual manoeuvres, for example, the gigantic reflection of Mazurki on Powell's window was in fact filmed on a special pane of glass, much nearer the camera; high speed devices were used for the falling shots where Marlowe blacks out; and Dmytryk, like Murnau in SUNRISE and Orson Welles in MAGNIFICENT AMBERSONS, had slanted ceilings built for several scenes so that when Mazurki moved from the high side to the low side of the set, he became, to the camera and to us, dramatically larger. The difference in height between Powell and Mazurki, which was only a few inches, was increased by having Powell walk in the gutter, and stand in stockinged feet, for scenes where the two are filmed together.

Here's another film with two women, the good and the bad, the blonde and the brunette; at one moment the good girl lets rip, not only at her rival but, in a sense, at all film noir heroines: 'I hate them . . . The Big League Blondes, beautiful, expensive dames who know what they've got. . .' and she is, in fact, describing the femme fatale who plays opposite her, Claire Trevor. In the story too, there's something quintessentially film noir in the way everyone's activities revolve around a pointless object, what Hitchcock called the MacGuffin, in this case some jade (a necklace), and in other films equally dumb things like The Maltese Falcon itself. People rush around going on about The Jade, The Jade, The Jade — but it could be anything, we never actually see it.

Powell seems perfect as the gritty Chandler hero, but until this point he'd been a crooner, starring in a series of Warner Brothers musicals in the 1930s. He landed this role as part of a complicated deal with RKO, who also wanted him for musicals. Again, it was studio chief Koerner who took the plunge of using Powell in such an unfamiliar role. Dmytryk said later, 'The idea of the man who had sung "Tiptoe Through the Tulips" playing a tough private eye was beyond our imaginations.' And in fact, the film's very title had to be changed in America, because FAREWELL MY LOVELY, a soft and romantic phrase, sounded like yet another musical, and people stayed away in droves. Once the title was changed to MURDER MY SWEET, the film was a great success. It was also the adaptation Chandler liked best. Although he got no royalties, since RKO had bought the rights much earlier, he sent a note to writer John Paxton to say how pleased he was with the film's closeness to his own writing, particularly in the way it keeps the enormously witty dialogue. In some places the snappy script seems almost to refer to its own one-liners: 'Remarks want you to make them. They've got their tongues hanging out waiting to be said.' I just love this image of lines, hanging around waiting to be spoken, like extras waiting to be called. It also seems to sum up something about the film.

In a Lonely Place

IN A LONELY PLACE was directed in 1950 by Nicholas Ray, who's probably best known for REBEL WITHOUT A CAUSE: another film about a kind of loneliness and, like most of Ray's work, bleak and romantic at the same time.

Tonight's film stars Humphrey Bogart and Gloria Grahame; it was made for Bogart's own company, Santana Productions, so he was clearly very bound up in the project. Ray also here directs Gloria Grahame, who was then his wife, in my favourite of all her performances. It's the role where she has the most dignity, a stature lacking in the gangsters' molls she so often plays. Unusually for a film noir, much of the plot is experienced from the woman's point of view; rather than a femme fatale, you could say it's about a homme fatal for it's the man who's terrifyingly unpredictable here. Ray switches our identification roughly halfway through, from sharing Bogart's experience of being accused of murder, to sharing Grahame's experience of fearing that he really has committed the crime; this subtle shift, pulling us away from the character we first identify with, illustrates vividly that the lonely place of the title is the self, or at least, that space between two selves when trust has gone from a relationship. It here quite literally takes the form of a spatial distance in the stretch of empty ground between Bogart's and Grahame's apartments.

This setting is in fact the apartment complex where Ray first lived when he came to Hollywood. And many places in the movie are other, thinly disguised Hollywood locations, as the film moves its central characters around the actual world in which it's made. Spatial images mark very precise aspects of the characters' relations: there are the bars, blinds, and curtains with what look like prison bars on them, at Bogart's windows; and the sort of spiky wrought-iron fence he has inside his apartment behind the door. There's a similar emotional concreteness about the steps and stepping stones between his place and Grahame's. Ray studied architecture with Frank Lloyd Wright before turning to films, and his skilled handling of both space and structure always reminds me of that background.

For this is a brilliantly constructed film, with light and dark perfectly illuminating or shadowing the moments of love or violence in the central relationship. The plot hinges on the fragility of truth, or at least, of emotional truth; but the mistrust which finally overtakes the lovers only has such power because there are such extraordinarily tender moments between them within the film. No one who's seen it could forget the sequence in the bar where Hadda Brooks sings, 'I hadn't anyone — till you.' It captures that glowing sense of being alone with someone, in a crowd. The lovers whisper to each other, but no one, not even us, hears what they say. At one moment the camera pulls back, and they become just another two people in love. It's beautifully choreographed: another couple move together in the foreground and a man passes in front of the lens in a gentle movement that's like part of the music. Lyrical moments like these are set against the increasing intrusion of fear and suspicion. Perhaps a counterpart scene, of extraordinary tension, is the morning where Bogart slices a grapefruit in Grahame's kitchen; violence echoes from the familiar scene in PUBLIC ENEMY, and, although THE BIG HEAT hadn't yet been made, the pot of coffee on the dresser also feels like a scalding threat.

One of the film's strengths besides the unforgettable central relationship is the range of supporting characters: Bogart's protective, motherly agent and Grahame's equivalent figure, her loyal masseuse, who function like the people who rub down boxers as they retreat to their corners of the ring.

Besides being set in Hollywood, this film, like many in the season, doubles back over its own lines. When Bogart crosses the courtyard one last time, to *his* lonely place, he quotes a line from his own manuscript: 'I was born when you kissed me. I died when you left me. I lived a few weeks while you loved me.' Those sad sentences encapsulate the whole film. There's something particularly grown-up about it, a sense of caution bravely overcome, a sense of delicate closeness, and, finally, a devastating distance. It really is a great film. I hope you like it as much as I do.

Human Desire

This week's film is HUMAN DESIRE, directed by Fritz Lang in 1954. Lang is a director who's often seen as pivotal in the development of film noir in Hollywood. A German film-maker, he was responsible for some of the great silent expressionist movies like DR MABUSE and METROPOLIS; his first sound film was the brilliant and haunting story of a child murderer, M. Along with many others, he left Germany during the Nazi period to work in Hollywood. Film noir is often attributed to that influx of European directors who were already working in this mode where lighting, oblique angles, visual tensions, were used to create the nightmarish expression of inner passions. HUMAN DESIRE has another European connection, it's a remake of LA BÊTE HUMAINE, the Human Beast: French film-maker Jean Renoir's version of a Zola novel with the same name, a story of violent obsession set among railway workers.

You'd think that the American context would be perfect for railroad drama. In fact, the producers of HUMAN DESIRE, Columbia, had a hard time finding any American rail company who'd let them film on their tracks once they'd seen the script. As Lang said, it was *not* good publicity for the Santa Fe to show a sex maniac who kills people in their sleeping cars. Finally a small railroad company was found, in which a Columbia stockholder had some shares, but even so, the film had to be toned down in various ways.

The railway is the heart of the film. But its use of trains goes beyond the symbolic; the film's opening, as you'll see, is a long sequence of rushing movement which gives the actual *sensation* of something unstoppable, like desire hurtling towards its goal. The railway also provides a perfect opportunity for smoke and shadows, characteristic of all film noir. But much of this film takes place in almost total darkness; there are scenes where you can barely see the characters. It's brilliantly photographed by Burnett Guffey, who was also cinematographer on IN A LONELY PLACE; he pushes low-light shooting to an extreme which heightens the sense of a sort of inner hell the film drags us through.

The film starts and ends with two men; in between, we move yet again through the contrast between good girl and bad girl, standing for different kinds of loving. Lang said sarcastically of the title, HUMAN DESIRE, 'Have you ever seen any *other* kind of desire?' The object of everyone's desire in the film is, yet again, Gloria Grahame. Here, perhaps more than anywhere else, she seems to represent a sort of acted-upon femininity, both unfathomable and ungraspable. She slips through the film like a drop of loose mercury. Neither we nor the other characters know whether to believe what she says; elusive as a cat, she is the focus of terrible actions, but unknowable herself. I do find disturbing her quality of what I always think of as 'hittability'; she must be one of the most beaten-up women in film noir, and that's saying something. There's a line in the film, 'All women are alike, they've just got different faces so that men can tell them apart', and on this note Lang tells an interesting if yukky anecdote about producer Jerry Wald. Only Lang and scriptwriter Alfred Hayes had actually read the Zola novel; Wald called them over and said, 'Look, this is called the human beast but *everybody's* bad in your picture.' Lang replied, 'Yes, because Zola wanted to show that in every human being is a beast.' Wald said, 'You don't understand it, the *woman* is the human beast.'

But I reckon you can, if you choose, see the film differently. Grahame trailing a history of abuse . . . a completely lost and anchorless being. In the centre of the film, she and Glenn Ford, who plays her lover, have an almost philosophical conversation about death, which seems to push the thriller into the realms of a kind of bleak nihilism. But at the same time, this bleakness, the sense of things closing in, can be seen in terms not only of sex and death, but *jobs*. All the action is set in a poor community dependent on one employer, and it starts when Grahame's boorish husband, Broderick Crawford, has been sacked and persuades her to suck up to a railway official to get his job back. When people catalogue the things they want, or the things they've lost, in the film, a job is always on the list.

One of its great achievements, to me, is placing this grimness in a world that can simultaneously be seen as the dark world of obsessive desires, but also — as was Zola's intention — the harsh world of the struggle simply for survival. Bleak as it is, I hope you find it powerful.

Angel Face

This week's Fatal Attraction brings together Robert Mitchum and
Jean Simmons in Otto Preminger's ANGEL FACE, made in 1952. One of
Preminger's most famous films noirs was LAURA, which features a
woman as a picture, and ANGEL FACE — a deeply sarcastic title —
brings us, while not a picture, a woman who is precisely what it says,
very much a face. The film's most lasting image is simply that
mask-like surface of Simmons' almost satanically innocent stare, the
pale face with its high fringe and blank, girlish look giving her an
impenetrability shared with many film noir women. But while still
filling the film noir role of the femme fatale, her gamine, wide-eyed
demeanor anticipates the look of Preminger's later fifties heroines like
Jean Seberg.

Simmons herself came to the film from playing classic British roles
like Ophelia and Estella, and brings a connotation of classy English-
ness to the part. Mitchum maintains his usual reticent, sleepy-eyed
style throughout. Between the two, and their respective lifestyles in the
film, it's like the meeting of two modes — grandiose Gothic, and urban
thriller — a meeting found in many films noirs. Mitchum first crosses
from one world to the other when he's called out in his job as
ambulance driver to the mansion where the young Simmons lives with
her novelist father and wealthy stepmother. Simmons' hatred of her
stepmother is accounted for in classic Oedipal terms: her real mother
is dead; she wants her father all to herself.

Yet despite the psychologizing, Simmons remains a perfectly
opaque character. Her glazed expression gives no entry to an inner
world, and what you're left with is a sense of evil, something almost
demonic. In the scene where she first seduces Mitchum, following him
to a downtown bar, he asks how she got there and she, in a kind of
reference to her own characterization, replies, 'I parked my broomstick outside.' The broomstick is, of course, a car: if you wanted to you
could even in microcosm chart the film's central conflict in terms of
what a car is. To Mitchum, a skilled mechanic, it's a thing in itself, a
means of gainful employment; to her, it's a vehicle of her own drives,
the wings on which her wicked schemes fly.

The film's suspense derives from our realization that her world is
something we can't see — we only discover where she's at from what
happens, since the plot itself is motored by her obsessions. And in this
respect, the other characters are, like us, merely passengers.

But if Mitchum can't see *behind* the Angel Face, he can grapple with
her at the level of her lines, the hero of the Thriller challenging the
heroine of Melodrama. 'How can you say that to me?' she asks at one
point, and he replies laconically, 'Oh, you mean "After all we've been
to each other"?' It's as if they're fighting over the terms of the drama
itself. Yet sceptical as he is, Mitchum, like other film noir men, is
drawn into events beyond his control. There's a lot of suitcase packing
on his part (something people are always doing in films) but this
neither puts the lid on his desires nor helps him escape from the plot.
This becomes increasingly elaborate as Simmons' clever lawyer, Leon
Ames, steers the couple through courtroom machinations which owe a
lot to THE POSTMAN ALWAYS RINGS TWICE — where Ames plays a
similar role. But unlike that film, this one has little passion in its
central relationship: Simmons isn't the smouldering woman whose
destructiveness arises from her sexuality, she's almost the opposite, an
impassive, frozen girl, an ice-maiden. This ties into the way the film
plays off a cool British 'high' culture — the Great Novelist, and
daughter Simmons playing the piano while people die — against a
warmer, American 'low' culture — the pragmatic stepmother on
whose money they live, and, of course, the hunky Mitchum with his
wholesome girlfriend, who earns her own living and whose heart *doesn't*
belong to Daddy.

The real Big Daddy behind the film was Howard Hughes, under
whose reign at RKO the picture was made. Preminger, who was
borrowed from 20th Century-Fox to direct it, said that Hughes came
to him in a frenzy because Simmons had cut her hair off and they'd
had a violent fight over the scissors. Referring to her as 'the little
bitch', Hughes went on and on about how he hated short hair and then
told Preminger to do anything he wanted. The result's what you're
about to see.

Shockproof

Tonight's film, SHOCKPROOF, was made in 1949 and directed by
Douglas Sirk, who's best known for his melodramas of the 1950s.
Interestingly it's scripted, or co-scripted, by Samuel Fuller, who also
went on to direct the powerful films that made *his* name. Fuller once
said, 'Film is like a battleground — love, hate, action, violence, death,
in one word, EMOTION' — and a few at least of this catalogue of
emotions can be found in his contribution to the script. SHOCKPROOF
almost moves between what we can retrospectively see as a kind of
Fuller world, tough, urban, uncompromising, where glamorous
women walk into dingy offices out of the street, a classic beginning of
so many crime thrillers; and what again, looking back, seems a
familiar Sirk world, of domestic interiors, woodwork and stairs,
ceilings and curtains, chock full of different angles for different family
members to be placed at — the blind mother, the ambitious son, the
noisy child.

Both these worlds are inhabited by Parole Officer Cornel Wilde,
and the woman who walks into the office is his parolee, Patricia
Knight. Knight seems to glide through different roles and situations in
this film: Sirk himself said that there's an attitude of sameness about
her, against the changing backgrounds and melodramatic action, and
in many ways the film is *about* placing emotions in different settings.
The way Knight occupies these different places is brilliantly suggested
in the film's very opening, where, with an economy seldom found in
movies today, we see first her legs, on Hollywood Boulevard — placing
the film in its own location — then within a matter of seconds, items
seen in shops, a dress in a window, a hat on a counter, appear on her
body as she walks, backview, down the street. During the film this
theme continues as her hair colour switches back and forth, and her
wardrobe changes from the lowcut gowns of the femme fatale to the
cosy check dress of the poor but devoted housewife.

Many films noirs use two women to suggest different sides of a man,
or at least, two sides of his emotions. This movie presents us with two
men: the urbane gangster played by John Baragrey, and Cornel
Wilde, who at the start of the story represents law, and order. Yet the
film's richness lies partly in the way it sets out to show how close the
worlds of crime and the police are. Crime, on the one hand, is highly
organized and does involve a degree of loyalty; the police, on the other,
are brutally tough and also, in one very specific scene, dishonest in

their methods. At one point in the film somebody asks, 'What is a criminal?' and the answer comes back, 'Someone who commits a crime.' There's something very existential about this. Nowhere does SHOCKPROOF posit an inherent good or bad, an inherent criminality.

That is exactly what Sirk liked about Fuller's script when he took it to Columbia. However, Helen Deutsch was brought in to change it — making a crucial alteration to the ending as you'll see. The fact that Deutsch was also made co-producer left Sirk and Fuller with little say in the matter. The original title was 'The Lovers' and the idea was to push what Sirk called 'the sparse freedom of human existence' to its limits. Despite the ending, the existential sense remains, of how easily people can be different things; while at the same time, there's a claustrophobia, characteristic of so many later Sirk films, which suggests the difficulty of pursuing the world of emotions within the laws of society.

The Lady from Shanghai

LADY FROM SHANGHAI is a wonderful film. It's a film noir; it's *about* film noir; it's about cinema; it *is* cinema, in fact I wish you were seeing it on a big screen. All Orson Welles' films — CITIZEN KANE is probably the most famous — seem to have this quality of being Big-Time Cinema; he directed this one in 1948, and although it was commissioned, rather than being one of his pet projects like CITIZEN KANE or MAGNIFICENT AMBERSONS, he was as deeply bound up in it as he was in all his productions.

Welles had always wanted to work with Bertolt Brecht, the German dramatist whose anti-illusionist theories had an enormous influence on radical theatre, and in this film some sense of distancing, one of Brecht's key ideas, can be found in the way both the storytelling and the image seem to comment on themselves throughout. Welles' voice-over, speaking an incredibly beautiful script, gives us not only a first person account of the plot, but does so with retrospective irony, and, while the voice *of* the film's hero, it also talks a lot about *being* the hero. When Welles — as young seaman Michael O'Hara — fights off a gang of attackers, he comments that only because they were amateurs did *he seem* to be heroic; and there's a long debate a little later about what makes a tough guy. Many films noirs have an innocent male lured into crime by an evil woman, but Welles finally remarks, 'Innocent? that's a big word, innocent . . . stupid's more like it' — again, gently undercutting himself in a way that ultimately makes it more, not less, moving.

LADY FROM SHANGHAI also brings us an absolutely quintessential femme fatale in the form of Rita Hayworth, whose long red hair had been cut blond for the part — perhaps as an echo of Marlene Dietrich in SHANGHAI EXPRESS. I say quintessential because, whatever her role in the *plot*, which I'm not going to give away, the camera just worships her through the film, in ways that have almost nothing to do with the story itself. In the yacht scenes, especially, we're offered overhead shots, diagonal shots, which bear no relation to what's going on narrative-wise; they're like free pin-ups interspersed with the action (which itself is pretty hard to follow) — they seem to jump out of it as if at those moments the film is just saying, See, isn't she gorgeous. This is what all Hollywood bathing shots of women do, but this film just *does* it: totally deliberate.

Then there's a brilliant scene on the boat where a four-way conversation between Hayworth, her husband, his partner, and Welles, is intercut in a series of jumps that give us no sense of where the characters are in relation to each other. For, of course, we're completely dependent on the camera to give us that sense that we *are* in a coherent space. Nowhere in the film are we reminded of this more vividly than in the famous hall-of-mirrors shoot-out at the end. We can see, but we can't see; we see everyone, but have no sense of their relation to one another. The multiplied, fragmented figures in this sequence also remind me of Edward Muybridge's photographic strips whose slivers of movement were the forerunners of cinema itself.

The hall of mirrors comes at the end of a fantastic, surreal fairground sequence where Welles tumbles down an enormous helter-skelter — epitomizing O'Hara's relation to the plot. The camera operator also slid the 125 feet down the chute behind him; it's an amazing moment of cinema, and one that Fellini lovingly copied in CITY OF WOMEN. Other settings that also speak about Welles' vision of cinema are the brilliant aquarium scene — where the glass tanks loom like projections of submerged emotions — and the Chinese theatre where the lovers meet at the end: a theatre that, again, was perhaps a little homage to Brecht, who drew many of his ideas from the oriental stage. But this setting also, importantly, brings us the

closest to Shanghai we ever get in the film: San Fransisco's China-
town. The exotic and unknowable are right there at home.

LADY FROM SHANGHAI is surrounded with personal stories about
the participants. My favourite detail is that the yacht belonged to
Errol Flynn, who was at the helm during the whole shoot — Welles
knew he could do with the money from its rental. But, while I don't
think you *need* to know these things surrounding a film, it does give an
added poignancy to watching LADY FROM SHANGHAI if you know that
Welles and Hayworth were married but estranged at the time the film
was started, and got back together briefly while it was made.
Hayworth apparently told Welles that the only happiness she'd ever
had was with him. His comment was characteristically acute: if that
was happiness, he said, imagine what the rest of her life had been.
Anyway, here they are.

Build My Gallows High

BUILD MY GALLOWS HIGH is an absolutely classic film noir. It was an
RKO B-Movie, made in 1947 and directed by Jacques Tourneur, who
had been making horror pictures in their B programme for several
years — his best known are CAT PEOPLE and I WALKED WITH A
ZOMBIE. This is also the film that made Robert Mitchum a star; he
was an RKO contract player brought in simply to save the cost of
hiring an outside actor, but his laconic, droopy-eyed persona in this
film was to make him famous, and carried into all his later roles.

The film's called OUT OF THE PAST in America; the British title is
taken from the original thriller by Daniel Mainwaring, who also wrote
the screenplay. Mainwaring went on in the 1950s to script films like
THE HITCH-HIKER and INVASION OF THE BODY SNATCHERS: films
which find fear and paranoia in the heart of respectable small-town
communities. He's a bold and interesting writer, who was dropped by
RKO during the McCarthy witch-hunts for refusing to work on
right-wing drivel like I MARRIED A COMMUNIST; his later comment,
'Small towns are miserable places' was a political, as well as personal
remark.

This film starts and ends in the sleepy mountain setting of a small town, and in between takes us through everything suppressed or excluded by that world — desire, danger, deceit. These are personified by the film's all-time-great femme fatale, Jane Greer, who's set against the more wholesome good girl from the township, Virginia Huston. The picture was shot in real locations — Tourneur took his crew up to the hills and down to Acapulco — and they're used very effectively to place the two women in the different worlds they offer Mitchum. Or rather, one offers, the other insists; for a key part of the femme fatale is that she leaves you with no choice. Huston, the good girl, is able to say of her rival, 'She can't be all bad, no one is', but of course in these films bad girls *aren't* rounded characters, they're the walking, talking, glistening projections of male fears and desires. Huston is always seen in the natural surroundings of woods, lake and country paths; but Greer 'Walked in out of the sun', as Mitchum says of his first meeting with her, and it's a dark world, of the city, or the exotic, that she inhabits. She has her natural settings, certainly, but they're in the sweaty climate of Southern Mexico: she seduces him among the clinging nets on a dark beach, and they make love during a tropical rainstorm.

The story, as in many films noirs, is told almost entirely in flashback; what's particularly brilliant is the way it's structured so that the trail of passion and violence comes, literally, out of the past — and into the present. Mitchum is called back from the new life he's made for himself, running a garage, by his old boss, Kirk Douglas. (Interestingly, there's an intense, almost romantic relationship between these two men in the film.) On the way to see Douglas in Nevada, Mitchum actually tells the story about the bad girl to the hyper-understanding good girl, in the car. After this point the action becomes increasingly complicated, technically, to follow — but the emotional journey it takes us on is completely compulsive.

The difficulty in following the twists of plot, full of double-crossing, triple-crossing even, links with one of the film's main themes, which is the difficulty of trusting perceptions at all. It's full of references to hearing and seeing: 'Did you miss me?' Greer asks Mitchum at one point, and he answers, 'No more than I would my eyes' — an ambiguous reply since it's his *vision* of her that gets him into trouble. In the opening scene Kirk Douglas' henchman says to the town gossip, 'Are you sure you don't see what you *hear*?' And at the heart of the film is the deaf and dumb boy, Mitchum's assistant, whose ability to *see* what's happening makes him crucial in so many places yet who, ultimately, conceals the truth in order to release Huston for a 'normal' life. But the Mr Normal boyfriend is peculiarly creepy, and the closing shot of the little community, returned to order by a lie, has a spooky quality — as if the body snatchers have got there already.

The end takes us back to the beginning. This is a perfectly compact film; everything in it seems at once casual and important, which to me is how a film should be.

The Dark Mirror

THE DARK MIRROR was directed in 1946 by Robert Siodmak, whose speciality was film noir: he made SPIRAL STAIRCASE in the same year and THE KILLERS immediately after. But DARK MIRROR also belongs to another group of films, what you could loosely call the good sister/bad sister movie, a type of film Bette Davis often stars in. Here, Olivia de Havilland — who later figured opposite Davis in HUSH HUSH, SWEET CHARLOTTE — plays both sisters, identical twins, in what was, quite apart from anything else, a feat of photographic ingenuity.

The good sister/bad sister theme always finds Hollywood at its most psychological, and DARK MIRROR is a thriller which unravels through detective work of the mind. We never actually see a crime being committed, which makes the search for guilt or innocence not so much a task of finding external clues to who's *done* something, but instead a search for clues to personality, or, as the film's psychiatrist puts it, for the 'secret patterns of the mind'. These secret patterns are what initially flummox the homey police detective, Thomas Mitchell, when he can't tell the twins apart. Mitchell is presented as a reassuringly low-brow figure, standing for solid common sense: he doesn't like people with college educations and he doesn't like posh classical music. What he *does* like — along with the audience in most thrillers — is to feel that a problem is solvable, that no one can beat a 'square rap'. So when his ordinary detective work reaches a dead end, Mitchell calls in psychiatrist Lew Ayres to investigate the twins in a different way, through a series of ink-blot tests, lie-ometer sessions and so on which are absolutely certain, it seems, to reveal 'the secret patterns of their minds and personalities' — and of course, in the film, they do. The ordered world of the square rap has initially been defeated, only to rally on another level with the aid of a psychological map; reassuring us that, in fact, those patterns of the mind are equally ordered and predictable. So innocence and guilt cease to be about crime and become, instead, fixed character traits to be discovered through a series of pseudo-Freudian parlour games.

But if one drive of the film's detective work is to pin down personality, the film itself, visually, suggests something more complex. At the beginning the two women wear identical outfits; but the moment they start to visit the psychiatrist, we have one wearing a black, the other a light dress — black, of course, for the one who adjusts her lipstick in the mirror before her session, and sees violent images in the ink blots. It's not hard to see the two sisters as twin sides of one person, or, more broadly, as two aspects of femininity. The bad sister, needless to say, is the more sexual *and* the more emotionally needy of the two: the good sister is cheery and undemanding. In the central love relationship, for example, you could see the bad twin as a kind of dumping ground for everything that must be repressed if women *are* to be 'good': anger, desire, hatred, jealousy, and, in particular, neediness, the wish to be loved. All are off-loaded onto *her*, leaving the good sister an Ideal Woman. For it's the sister who doesn't *want* too much who is chosen for love: the bad one is too eager. And, too clever; something which is particularly stressed.

In most films noirs women are a mystery; this one offers a literal dissection of the female character. But its male figures are also interestingly paired: the streetwise cop and the slightly effete psychiatrist are, on their side, like two aspects of the male system which seeks to pin femininity down. Only when they work together do they solve their puzzle, and the point when they establish definitively which twin is guilty is the climax of the film. Yet this is the exact moment when, in the shattering of a mirror, the twins are visually identified as one; and the men's efforts to keep the two sides apart, to separate the good from the bad woman, are defeated in the image, just when they succeed in the plot.

I don't think my interpretation would have appealed to de Havilland, who later said, 'The technical problems involved in playing a dual role were extremely difficult to solve, and that horrible Terry I had to play in that picture haunts me to this day.'

Figure it out for yourself!

Programming: Epidemic Cinema

For the past decade, our society has been faced by a crisis too serious to find its way directly into mainstream cinema: the Aids epidemic has had so little effect on Hollywood films, by and large, that even 'naturalistic' romances happily present sex scenes with no mention of condoms, and you would never know, from watching the big screen, that this was a means of infection with potentially lethal results.

At the same time, fears about both sex and death have surfaced in almost every other guise, a powerful example being the film FATAL ATTRACTION. This film became, in many ways, a landmark of reactionary cinema in the late 1980s; after my review of it appeared in the *New Statesman* Mark Finch, a film programmer with the British Film Institute's Distribution Division, suggested that we jointly programme, at the National Film Theatre, a season that would bring together films dealing both directly and obliquely with disease and infection — a project designed to bear on the cultural, as well as social and medical, dimensions of Aids.

We took as our title film Elia Kazan's PANIC IN THE STREETS, a movie about a TB epidemic made in the 1950s. Looking at pre-Aids films about infection made it possible for us to trace certain threads which are woven into the complex reactions we find to Aids today. Broadly speaking, the films dealing with the social impact of disease tend to the horror/thriller format (the zombie film included draws on a strand of body-infection-anxiety that goes right back to early vampire movies) while those telling individual, domestic stories use the format of melodrama (NO SAD SONGS FOR ME is a clear forerunner of the more explicit and 'sympathetic' Aids dramas on British and American TV). Besides researching and choosing the films themselves, we produced programme notes to be handed out at screenings, and the season — which took place in August 1988 — finished with an open discussion of the issues raised throughout.

Reprinted below is the programme outline (the blurb written for the NFT catalogue) followed by the notes for each film (in some cases, double or triple bills), in the order of their screening. I have initialled the pieces JW or MF; it would have been inappropriate only to include my own since the venture was a joint one from the outset. Some of the notes contain quotes from other reviewers too; the publications are given here and full details are in the bibliography.[1]

Our aim with this piece of programming was to investigate the narrative forms through which our culture is addressing a specific social crisis. Films don't just reflect social reactions, in many ways they help shape them, offering patterns of understanding or denial, dramatizations of sympathy or fear. Grouping film narratives in such a way as to draw these patterns out can play an important part in helping to *change* our reactions, as well as contributing to debate about the films themselves.

---

1   Where the programme notes include reprints from the *New Statesman* I have let them stand, despite the repetition it creates within this book; the season was intended to suggest new contexts both for films and critical writing, and cannot be represented here without including all the original material.

Panic in the Streets Season

This season aims to investigate and discuss the symptoms of an 'epidemic' cinema. Just how have film and TV responded to Aids? Here we present a range of contemporary narrative films which deal, either directly or indirectly, with the repercussions and effects of this new social crisis.

Alongside them we place pre-existing dramas of disease, from Nicholas Ray's BIGGER THAN LIFE (1956) to Terry Nation's mid-seventies sci-fi soap, *Survivors*.

While TV drama puts fragile family relationships under the microscope, Hollywood reaches for its seductive repertoire of vampire and body-horror metaphors. What is interesting about recent fictions is the way they feed off and adapt earlier images and conventions of genres like horror and melodrama. Themes of criminality, contagion and medical policing can already be found in Elia Kazan's hardboiled PANIC IN THE STREETS (1950) — a benchmark against which the present day cinema of fear and loathing can be judged. (MF, JW)

Panic in the Streets

PANIC IN THE STREETS gives its title to this season because its story incorporates the multiple themes of criminality, contagion, medical policing and a search for origins, all of which characterize contemporary discourses surrounding Aids. The film is an interesting thriller in its own right: shot almost entirely on location in semi-documentary style, its gritty, *Naked City* brand of urban realism underlines the sense of urgency with which its hero, a young Public Health Department doctor (Richard Widmark) investigates an underworld of deceit and disease.

The medical detective story is kicked off by the discovery that a bullet-ridden body found on the New Orleans waterfront has bubonic plague. The hunt for the murderer becomes not only a police affair but a matter of public hygiene because the killer is also the carrier of the disease. However, while the criminal and the contagious are thus elided, one of the film's most powerful dramatic devices is the way the legal and the medical pull in different directions, as doctor Widmark fights against Police Chief Paul Douglas's 'round-up the usual suspects' attitude; and one of its major resolutions is their eventual capacity to work in harmony, bringing the legal and the medical back into alignment in time to prevent disaster. This device of separating the police/military response from the medical response to disease (a third position is in this film embodied in the attempts of a journalist to break the story) recurs frequently in 'epidemic cinema' — see, for example, DAY OF THE DEAD.

Another point of interest from the perspective of 'epidemic cinema' is the location of the 'Patient Zero' figure — the original carrier — among, not merely an underworld, but one which is ethnically 'other'. From the film's opening, when the camera cruises the waterfront strip and moves into a bar room where a black singer croons and the soon-to-be-murder-victim mops his brow, disease is identified with difference — to the extent that the Patient Zero turns out to be an *illegal immigrant*. It is no coincidence that the ship to which Widmark traces the source is called the Nile Queen, and is crewed by black and oriental sailors. The crime network that blocks his progress on the quayside is mostly Greek. While Kazan's social realism offers fairly sympathetic portrayals of some of these characters individually, it is nevertheless stereotypical that disease is located among 'foreigners' whose criminal ways and greedy or deceitful wives encourage its spread.

With its carefully shaded style, PANIC IN THE STREETS is a film of contrasts and perhaps the strongest counter image to the low-life amongst which he plays detective is the image of Widmark's young family. As in THE BIG HEAT, it provides an important counterbalance to a world of corruption, and we are gently shown the stresses on his pretty, home-making wife, Barbara Bel Geddes (now indelibly fixed in modern minds as Miss Ellie). When she turns out to be pregnant, the sense of imminent contamination becomes a key component of the film's moral drive, with Widmark's social responsibility at its highest precisely when his own family are in the greatest danger from his crusade. Again, this sketch of the young family and its vulnerability is one that is repeated endlessly in films of the 'epidemic' genre.

There is plenty more to be said about PANIC IN THE STREETS as a film; the cast is excellent, the locations are richly used (a break with Hollywood tradition at the time) and Kazan's tendency to heaviness is not in evidence. There are some impressive scenes: such as Widmark's appeal to the massed seamen, a night-time scene between husband and wife on their porch, or the final chase where the diseased man resembles a rat on the rigging of the ship. Overall, however, its drive for the discovery and control of a disease which is presented among society's outcasts shows — as this season is intended to — that the language and narrative patterns associated with Aids reportage and fictions were developed long before the illness itself existed. (JW)

The Andromeda Strain

Michael Crichton's original novel is quite sure of its message — technological progress has been marked by increased dehumanization — and his ambition is marred only by the kind of enthusiasm for technology that he wants to condemn. Robert Wise's film isn't so clearly focused, and seems interested in pursuing a number of themes both new and familiar to epidemic cinema.

Typical markers of the genre's concerns are the primal plague scene, blood imagery, and narrative intimations of government indifference, conspiracy or disbelief. Two technicians die when retrieving a returned space satellite — Project Scoop — from a small New Mexico town. A state of emergency is declared and the Wildfire team of scientists, programmed for such a crisis, is assembled. Robert Wise uses the scene of space-suited scientists coming upon the corpse-strewn town for a grim split-screen body count. In not so much a parody of small-town life as a metaphor for the unspecified disease's anticipated effects on urban civilization, bodies lie as if struck down in the midst of everyday motions — shopping, bathing, eating, sleeping.

A clue to the infection is the victims' dessicated blood. As in many other disease dramas — LAST MAN ON EARTH, DAY OF THE DEAD, RABID — blood is the site of infection; explained, in part, by its easy associations with vampirism and horror movie disgust. ANDROMEDA STRAIN is quite obsessed with the stuff: blood is something uncontrollable, unpredictable in the sterilized scientific environment; it's a scalpel slice away from contamination. For dealing with the two survivors (whose blood abnormalities finally point the way to dealing with the disease) scientist James Olson has to don a man-size sheath which, he is warned, can easily be accidentally breached — and indeed is, in order to save the day.

In PANIC IN THE STREETS bureaucratic dismissal is pictured as the epidemic's main ally. Health expert Richard Widmark is called to account for exceeding his powers in Elia Kazan's film; conversely, in Robert Wise's world the government have — incredibly — prepared for this event with the Wildfire underground base, guaranteed scientific autonomy and military non-intervention. The unseen President takes too long to agree to wipe out the plague-struck town, but this potential catastrophe is bizarrely transformed into a blessing when the scientists discover that an atomic explosion would only help the infection multiply on a massive scale. Partly because THE ANDROMEDA STRAIN is working within a genre of science fiction-fact, like DESTINATION MOON or 2001, it's overwhelmed by a patriotism that prevents it from fingering the White House. Communication systems and human error, however, are blamed for the delay in diagnosis, and in an intriguing, confused moment there is a suggestion that Scoop and Wildfire were actually set up to provide biological/viral material for germ warfare — pre-dating the sci-fi fashion for similar conspiracies in ALIEN, OUTLAND and others.

The wish-to-detail lands the film in some trouble from the beginning: a pre-credit disclaimer assures viewers that no national secrets have really been disclosed; but text before the credits then claims (within another cinematic convention) that the following is all 'true'. Of course, the whole thing is fiction, but the makers are so worried by their own persuasiveness that they tear a hole in the text from the start. This is the kind of inconsistency that characterizes epidemic cinema. (MF)

Bigger Than Life

It is common in epidemic cinema for the family to be presented as vulnerable to disease: the young doctor's family in PANIC IN THE STREETS, the yuppie family in FATAL ATTRACTION, are counterposed to the horror of infection. Here, however, in one of Nicholas Ray's most striking films, the family itself becomes the site of sickness, with the father — usually presented as the protector (cf. DR EHRLICH, PANIC) — providing the threat (as do the HIV–infected fathers in SWEET AS YOU ARE and *Intimate Contact*). Ray shows how frighteningly fine the boundary is between 'normal' patriarchy and criminal pathology, as James Mason's football practice with his son, or shopping for clothes — one of the most memorable scenes — with his wife, become terrifying nightmares, the more so since they mimic the supposedly idyllic imagery of family life in fifties America. In fact the pressure of consumerism is one of the film's strongest themes: Mason finds he has an incurable disease after he has been working evenings on a taxicab switchboard to supplement his teacher's income (a detail which makes the film all the more topical today). Both dialogue and mise-en-scène throughout emphasize the high level of domestic consumption the family is expected to maintain.

Besides its brilliant use of CinemaScope — paradoxically, Ray manages to produce a sense of claustrophobia on a wide screen — and of colour, the film is notable from the point of view of this season for its use of overlapping genres. The 'Panic in the Streets' season sets out to trace the forms of melodrama and horror as they have developed to provide a language for talking about disease and, today, for talking about Aids. BIGGER THAN LIFE is unusual amongst other reasons in that it actually pushes family melodrama *into* the realm of horror (a

device used again, though much less thoughtfully, in the notorious
FATAL ATTRACTION). The very title BIGGER THAN LIFE highlights the
way it blows up family life until the cracks in it become chasms; the
screen itself takes on the feel of a magnifying glass, filled to bursting
point with the Inside of the Home. The intimate relation of camera to
domestic interior found in all melodrama reaches a point where the
distortion — both visual and emotional — moves the film into another
register, of horror and suspense culminating in the actual breaking up
of the interior as Mason and Walter Matthau, fighting, tear through
the banisters that we have already seen from every possible angle. This
climax, with Mason armed with scissors and a Bible trying to kill his
wife, son and friend, takes place while a band literally plays on:
blaring from the TV screen where a macabrely inane fairground scene
is shown.

It is interesting that this film, terrifying on so many levels, could
present such danger within a family at the peak of the post-war
ideology of family life. Today, such danger has, in public imagery,
been split off and externalized in the bogey figures of, for example, gay
and lesbian teachers — or the likes of Single Working Woman Glenn
Close. In such a context BIGGER THAN LIFE is as fresh and as
frightening as ever. (JW)

Survivors

Survivors's title sequence anticipates Randy Shilts' Patient Zero concept, one of the controversial constructions in his epic Aids book *And
the Band Played On*. Or, rather, while Patient Zero follows in a long line
of diseased carriers (dating from before PANIC IN THE STREETS), the
mode of transport in *Survivors* is surprisingly modern. Shilts' supposed
original carrier, Gaetan Dugas, worked as an airline steward; and even
when ill used his free flight allocation to score sexual victories in gay
communities across North America and Canada. At the site of the idea
of Patient Zero is a fear of motivation (did Gaetan knowingly infect
other men?), and phobias about immigration control which have since
become one of the loci for Aids-related legislation. In *Survivors* (and

particularly in creator Terry Nation's novelization, which turns the credits sequence into an extensive premonitory prologue), the carrier is a Chinese businessman, compacting these fears into xenophobia and referencing back to Asian flu. Another aspect of the Patient Zero theory is the fatalism it allows around the question: how did it start? *Survivors'* first shot is of an Oriental scientist accidentally dropping a full test-tube, suggesting that human technology and human clumsiness both have a part to play.

But there's more to *Survivors* than its credits sequence. Like many epidemic cinema entries — DAY OF THE DEAD, the Japanese multi-star VIRUS — it is concerned with the social consequences of mass scale disease. The tendency of these narratives is, of course, to dramatize existing social relations: in DAY OF THE DEAD, between Reagan's Right and the new liberals; in VIRUS, between international enemies; in *Survivors*, between the Unions and management; and in all of them, between men and women. To do this, the fiction often stretches back to significant moments of past social crisis for its images of post-holocaust living.

The first episode of *Survivors* is untypical of the later ones. It goes to ambitious lengths to illustrate the process of society's disintegration, picking on a specific milieu, the suburban middle classes (an unsurprising choice for a mid-seventies BBC1 continuing drama). *Survivors* manufactures some telling metaphors for the breakdown: trains running late, hospitals unable to cope, traffic jams and food shortages — in fact, all images familiar to its original audience as part of the landscape of 'strike-torn Britain'. This is veiled slightly by dialogue which harks further back: 'it's a bit like war-time, isn't it?'

The other striking aspect of the first episode is the way that the disease — a viral flu, the catch-all of epidemic cinema — puts personal relationships under scrutiny. A doctor confesses his suspicions of his girlfriend's infection as if it related to infidelity; a wife looks guiltily at her sleeping husband, who has just reassured her that they in their suburban privacy can't possibly contract the disease. The emphasis of the remaining episodes is on how the middle classes have divorced themselves from the knowledge necessary for survival in a post-technological world, and the weird sexual tenor of the first instalment translates into familiar science fiction territory (the desertion of monogamy, the need to breed children). In its deliberate refusal of conventional melodrama (unlike *Intimate Contact*), *Survivors* sets the agenda for quasi-realist fiction on post-plague problems. (MF)

Lifeforce

'The content of LIFEFORCE is basically an updated ALIEN — THE
THING — ANDROMEDA STRAIN. It seems that Halley's comet next year
brings with it an alien thing that looks like a lovely naked woman. Her
kiss, however, brings doom — just like Aids, only faster.' (Nancy
Mills, *The Guardian*)

'Colin Wilson's *Space Vampires*, on which LIFEFORCE is based, is the
third of a loose trilogy of science fiction novels also comprising *The
Mind Parasites* (to which SCANNERS seemed to owe not a little) and *The
Philosopher's Stone*. First published in 1976 it has enjoyed a chequered
production career, with several scripts apparently stumbling over both
the novel's sexual content and its weighty, neo-existential
philosophizing. . .
'Special effects cannot compensate for the risibility of much of the
(finished film's) dialogue, the mugging of Steve Railsback and Peter
Firth, or the script's unfortunate habit of interjecting lengthy explanations in the unlikeliest and most awkward of places. With the
intervention of Inspector Caine, the plot frequently threatens to
descend into Agatha Christie territory, an impression heightened by
the strangely old-fashioned and clichéd views of England and especially London. Most problematic of all is the film's unrelieved
misogyny: not content with having the female alien (but *not* the males,
who soon disappear anyway) wander around naked for most of the
time, the film also treats us to lines like, "She's looking for a man —
any man — she wants to steal some energy from him", as the alien girl
forcibly seduces a surprised middle-aged man in a Volvo. Not just
female sexuality but, as in the films of David Cronenberg, fear of
bisexuality comes into play here. This becomes abundantly clear in
the scene in which the girl tells Carlsen, "I am the feminine in your
mind", and almost causes him to seduce a male colleague (under the
illusion that the colleague is in fact the alien). It is a pity that, once
again, a genre which can carry such a subversive charge should lend
itself to the most reactionary representations of sexuality.' (Julian
Petley, *Monthly Film Bulletin*)

LIFEFORCE was in production during the first spate of British TV
documentaries about Aids. Simon Watney's analysis of one of these
serves to illustrate the construction of Aids at that time: 'In a diagram
shown on *Weekend World* . . . gay men had been pictured as a line of

boogying disco dancers at the bottom of the image, above whom was positioned the familiar figure of the family — mum and dad and two small children. In between these two distinct groups two single figures were posed, a prostitute and a bisexual, the former female, the latter male. The ideological significance of such diagrams is important to grasp. In the first place we are invited to imagine some absolute divide between the two domains of "gay life" and "the family". . . Second, we are to think of the bisexual as an "active" penetrative male, who can carry the HIV virus up from the infernal domain of Discoland and into the very bosom of the nuclear family. Third, the prostitute appears in her familiar ideological apparel as Fallen Eve, the contaminated vessel, literally a *femme fatale*.'[1]

LIFEFORCE's alien girl carries all the connotations of the plague-ridden prostitute and bisexual. With her ability to switch gender, she appears on the one hand as a character from a particular British tradition of sexual explanation, the CONFESSIONS OF A WINDOW CLEANER series (her 'bored sexy young hitch-hiker' seduction of the middle-aged happily married man); on the other, as the effete male head of a 19th-century mental hospital, a character who is also coded as gay through his act of concealment. Indeed, the ideological (and dramatic) heart of the film is, as Julian Petley notes, when the heterosexual hero finds himself compelled to kiss the doctor; around them swirl levitating objects, a vacuum of terror — all special effects stops pulled out for the worst thing imaginable: same-sex contact, the threat of contamination. (MF)

---

1   *Policing Desire: Pornography, AIDS and the Media*

Shivers
The Fly

David Cronenberg's career charts the changes in epidemic cinema's most graphic genre, the horror movie. George Romero's filmography is perhaps also as notable (THE CRAZIES and the LIVING DEAD trilogy), but only Cronenberg has earned the title 'King of Venereal Horror' — for films such as RABID, THE BROOD and tonight's first frightener, SHIVERS. In RABID and SHIVERS the contagion is transmitted individually, with discrete and bloody results. Cronenberg can't claim to be in original territory, but SHIVERS marked the introduction of a specific sexual element. The residents of Toronto's newest self-sufficient apartment block are *penetrated* by fecal parasites, and the symptom of this disease seems to be polymorphous perversity. Cronenberg's question is: to what extent does the disease liberate and realize pre-existing desires? The pursuit of an answer takes the film into some very dark shadows. Roundly decried by critics like Robin Wood for its seemingly reactionary ideology (necrophilia, incest and lesbianism are amongst the 'monstrous' acts in this plague-struck Sodom), SHIVERS nevertheless demonstrates an intelligence and — difficult to admit — a playfulness not found in later disease dramas, like Graham Baker's IMPULSE (1984) and Ed Hunt's PLAGUE (1978). By the time of THE FLY, Cronenberg's enthusiasms take on a startling and studied tenor. (MF)

'. . . The Gothic and Horror genres function very much through that frisson between the inner and the outer which characterized the Romantic modes; I say modes because the Gothic was extremely close to its less currently fashionable sibling, the Sentimental, which evoked pity where the former evoked fear (linking it in film terms perhaps most closely with melodrama). The tenacity of Romantic discourses in our present culture can be seen in our responses to disease (and specifically Aids) where pity and terror are two sides of the same coin. THE FLY is a curiously graphic film, most interesting for its suggestion of a different response to bodily sickness; though in its preoccupation with a range of disjunctions between inner and outer — with particular reference to sexuality — it is placed firmly on Gothic territory. Its hero, Seth Brundle, is a scientist whose single-minded involvement in his work makes him appear "pure", almost non-sexual at the start of the film, when he invites a science journalist up to see his

extraordinary invention, a computerized teletransporter, and overcomes her scepticism by transporting one of her black lacy stockings (a
kind of scientific/sexual initiation).

'These transporting chambers bear an intriguing resemblance to
Reich's orgone machines; and indeed a Reichian sense of the energizing properties of sex echoes throughout the film. In his "virginal" state
Brundle is at an impasse with his project, being unable to understand
"flesh" — as the script carefully tells us, several times. However, after
sleeping with his new woman friend he finds he can transport living
matter: sex has (at first) an enabling function. At the same time it is
the darker side of sexual entanglement that transforms him more
radically; in a rage of (unnecessary) sexual jealousy he transports
himself when drunk — out of control — and fails to notice a fly in the
machine, with the result that he becomes genetically merged with it.
The immediate effects of this are, again, strangely Reichian: Brundle
finds enormous reserves of libidinal energy and becomes very self-
assertive, ultimately aggressive, stomping around bare-chested in a
leather jacket instead of the shirts and ties that made him so
charmingly "straight" at the beginning. He has swapped science for
sex: knowledge has been the gateway to his sexual relationship and sex
the gateway to completing his scientific invention. The final outcome
of the two together is his hideous transformation into a giant fly.

'Of course, what this fable most resembles is the Frankenstein story
— but with a twist. For Brundle is both inventor and monster; the two
roles are elided, neatly bringing back together the two sides of "human
nature" that Gothic literature split. Mary Shelley thought that the
inventor would recoil in horror from his presumptious creations.
Brundle, however, after initial despondency, becomes remarkably
exhilarated: "I'll become something that never existed before" he
enthuses, flinging himself into his disease with great humour, bottling
the parts of his body that fall off, video-ing his eating habits for future
science lessons. There is something not Gothic, but existential, in his
excitement at becoming his own creation; and even if the film's simpler
level of horror brings us back to pity and terror in the end, this
momentary glimpse beyond Romantic self-loathing is, in the current
climate of disgust, both timely and refreshing.' (JW, *New Statesman*)

Parting Glances
The Ads Epidemic

Made at the same time and in the same city as Arthur Bressan's
BUDDIES, Bill Sherwood's film opts for one of epidemic cinema's most
familiar strains: melodrama. But whereas BUDDIES transcends its
social setting, PARTING GLANCES revels in it; Robert and Michael's
yuppie bric-à-brac is there not to signal the claustrophobia of their
culture (as in BIGGER THAN LIFE), nor to provide poignant similes (as
in *Intimate Contact*), but to naturalize the film's ferocious (and affecting)
emotionalism. John Greyson's THE ADS EPIDEMIC is a witty, alternative riposte to earlier constructions of homosexuality (DEATH IN
VENICE, pop video, tabloid newspapers), and shares the same sense of
irony and humour that marks PARTING GLANCES as 'uniquely' gay.
(MF)

'In the past few years, gay films have persistently tried to contest the
way homosexuality has usually been seen as a "problem" in heterosexual films dealing with gay themes. Some, such as A COMEDY IN SIX
UNNATURAL ACTS and THE TIMES OF HARVEY MILK, did so by
raising the issue of homophobia. Others stressed the moment of
"coming out": a device which made the acceptance of homosexuality
into a narrative problem. Much of the first part of DESERT HEARTS, for
example, is pivoted around the question of "will she/won't she?",
followed by "will she be brave enough to see it through?".

'PARTING GLANCES tries a very different strategy. Set in an almost
entirely gay milieu, it doesn't present homosexuality as a problem.
Robert and Michael have been together for years: the choice for them
is other lovers, not heterosexuality. Even the long-married gay roué
Cecil seems happy to keep his life divided. The process of coming out,
so tortuous as well as thrilling in DESERT HEARTS et al., is described by
Nick with a certain nostalgia.

'Having eliminated homosexuality as "the problem", PARTING
GLANCES is instead structured around the classic question of a choice
between two lovers: one dependable if cold, one unsteady, highly
strung — and dying. Gender apart, Michael's realization that he
really loves Nick is remarkably similar to female protagonists' choices
in a range of women-directed melodramas. In this context, it is telling
that Aids is dealt with not so much as a political issue as one of
personal fears. The "baddies", if there are any, are the performance

artists with their repugnant desire to capitalize on death. Most of all, however, the film is concerned to dissect different reactions to Aids within the gay community: responses which vary from terror to embarrassment and humour.' (Jane Root, *Monthly Film Bulletin*)

Intimate Contact
Fatal Attraction
Bob Geldof on AIDS

Holding up a condom, Bob Geldof speaks plainly: 'Some people say that these things will kill your sex life. But what choice do you have if your sex life is killing you?' This is the question which, in very different ways, both *Intimate Contact* and FATAL ATTRACTION try to address.

Intimate Contact was one of the first attempts by British TV to deal with Aids in the form of a drama series, and it shares certain narrative patterns with, for example, SWEET AS YOU ARE (and indeed, FATAL ATTRACTION). Infection is shown as resulting from a husband's infidelity (in this case, a business trip 'orgy' in New York) and, as with the other TV Aids format of 'coming out' movies (cf. AN EARLY FROST) the melodrama hinges initially not on the discovery that a character has Aids but on the revelation of how he got it. I say 'he' because there have as yet been no dramatizations of female Aids cases, and this suggests that the drama stories are as much about hierarchies of family morality as about the illness itself. In both SWEET AS YOU ARE and *Intimate Contact* the husband contracts HIV *from* a woman (a prostitute, a junkie student) but in neither case does he pass it on to his wife (although medically speaking this would be at least as easy as the former). This tends to make Aids into a marker, a boundary between the Good (wives) and the Bad (erring husbands, loose women). And of course, the very preponderance of family dramas in this area represents an idea of 'innocent' — i.e. heterosexual — 'victims' and an inability to speak about the tragedies befalling gay relationships (the 'guilty') in far greater numbers.

Intimate Contact's opening logo suggests a genealogy of contagion, its honeycombed, cell-like pattern enclosing a kind of family tree. As in so much epidemic cinema, foreign travel is the culprit: the series starts with an aeroplane landing (cf. *Survivors*).

However, *Intimate Contact* ultimately goes further than other TV dramas in its forthright presentation of death and its charting of new social bonds as the devastated wife (Claire Bloom) finds allies in a gay couple and the father of a haemophiliac child. Sharp points are also made about the shortcomings of private medicine. Starting as an upper-middle-class family melodrama, *Intimate Contact* ends by roundly criticizing the hypocrisy of this milieu — a milieu of which FATAL ATTRACTION is, conversely, a glossy celebration. (JW)

'If on one level FATAL ATTRACTION fits into that genre of films about yuppie lives in Manhattan, on a second level it is quite clearly a horror film, with both structural and thematic links to the whole genre of Body Horror, explored most interestingly in a film like THE FLY. Yet while Cronenberg uses the conventions of Horror to push our sympathies beyond their usual bounds, FATAL ATTRACTION employs Horror in order to rein them back sharply within the tight corral of the nuclear family. . . FATAL ATTRACTION is fundamentally a horror film set in yuppie-melodrama-land: its whole structure becomes blindingly clear once you realize that the part usually played by the Thing/the Blob/the Bug (the Virus) is played by the Single Working Woman, Alex.

'. . . The threat of invasion which Alex represents is conveyed cinematically by classic Horror conventions, for example, the hand-held camera circling the family house, giving us the point of view of the monster roaming menacingly outside. While the image of the single woman pressing her nose against the window of family life might evoke poignancy at her exclusion (as in the famous ending of STELLA DALLAS), here, the use of the horror film's point-of-view convention evokes something far more monstrous than the mere sight of a distraught woman with frizzy hair. In fact, it evokes no person or character at all, but rather the lurking-ness of threat itself, structured, conversely, as an intrusion.

'The horror film can eschew the logic whereby a sexual encounter may *result* in disease. Images, as Freud said, can collapse linear reasoning — the person sexually encountered *becomes* the disease. And Horror, as a popular genre structure, functions as a discourse way beyond the world of film. . .' (JW, *New Statesman*)

'BUDDIES demonstrates that drama can "tell a good story while teaching a number of facts" (Darrell Yates Rist, *Film Comment*). The titles go up over an ominous and seemingly interminable computer print-out of names, names which we assume to be of people with Aids. Here the story concerns Robert, a young gay man from San Francisco who is in hospital in New York, and David, his "buddy" from a gay centre, who befriends him. Robert is constructed as a fairly typical gay man of the Gay Liberation period, intensely aware of the politics of his sexuality, while David is shown as a rather complacent yuppie. In fact it is almost inconceivable (one hopes) that someone as ignorant about Aids should ever have been allowed near Robert or, for that matter, that he would ever have been aware of the mere existence of a gay centre, let alone have got involved in such a project. Robert had been thrown out of his home by his parents when he told them he was gay. David, on the contrary, has an impossibly supportive mother, whose phone calls punctuate the entire narrative. At the outset David judges Robert's life as wasted by his commitment to gay politics and a seven year "open" relationship which he reads as a total failure. Asked what he'd do if he could have a single day out of hospital and be "well", Robert replies he'd fly to Washington and march up and down in front of the White House with a banner protesting against the under-funding of hospital and support care for people with Aids, and then fly back to his old boyfriend Edward and fuck his brains out. Gradually David comes to understand the culture which Robert is coming from, a culture which he, in his luxurious apartment with a monogamous relationship and a "designer-everything" mentality, has never come across. He realizes slowly that the privacy which he so jealously cherishes only came about as a result of the struggles of people like Robert and Edward. His new understanding is signified in a beautiful scene where he holds Robert in his arms while he jerks off, looking at a photograph of Edward. David is finally persuaded to give a newspaper interview about his work as a buddy since, as Robert says, it might help someone somewhere to come to a better attitude towards the epidemic. . . The film ends with a shot of David, walking up and down outside the White House amongst the crowds of indifferent tourists, holding up a banner with Robert's words on it. The film thus addresses precisely the issue of the re-homosexualization of gay culture which Aids has opened up. It suggests a level of personal integrity, and the sheer complexity of the situation in which people with Aids find themselves, that has not been touched upon in any of the documentaries shown on British television to date.' (Simon Watney, *Policing Desire: Pornography, AIDS and the Media*)

BUDDIES may not have been the first feature film to narrativize the catastrophe of Aids, but it does pull off something of a coup by being so forthright and clearly focused on the issue. PARTING GLANCES details a day in the lives of New York couple Michael and Robert, whose best friend is dying from the disease; the TV movie AN EARLY FROST dwells on how Aids affects heterosexual family life, in the same way that it might deal with drug abuse or teenage runaways. 'If you can't weep for these people, you can't party with them', Arthur Bressan has said, and this is as much an instruction to BUDDIES' audience as it is a comparison with Sherwood's inconsistent yuppie comedy.

Behind the clarity of Bressan's film is a successful cross-fertilization of genres. On the one hand, like many of the entries in epidemic cinema, BUDDIES works as a low-budget Hollywood weepie, within familiar narrative conventions. The love of 'a good activist' brings David from naïveté to political understanding; in another era, Robert might have been played by the Margaret Sullavan of NO SAD SONGS FOR ME, or the Jane Wyman of MAGNIFICENT OBSESSION. The dominant colours are amber and gold, and the dialogue is hued with a similar nostalgia; regrets are for past lovers, accusations are aimed at society's lack of understanding. As Robert relates his biography, each bedside revelation is punctuated by close-ups and an aching piano theme. On the other hand, BUDDIES' intensity is also served by a different sort of cinema. In the 1970s, Bressan made a handful of gay porn movies (one of which, PASSING STRANGERS, is briefly seen in BUDDIES), and worked until his death last year as a freelance editor on other people's porn, gay or straight. Porn's budget-led short-hand shows in the inspired use of only two performers and three locations. The resemblance to the 'feel' of pornography is not discomfiting; indeed, it happily points to another Aids-related movie genre, which runs in parallel with these modern instances of epidemic cinema: the safe sex porn movie. (MF)

The Last Man on Earth
Dr Ehrlich's Magic Bullet

DR EHRLICH and THE LAST MAN ON EARTH make for interesting
stop-overs on the route to epidemic cinema. While these films may not
obviously encompass the images and themes of later melodramas, they
do demonstrate the central tendency of all the films here — to talk
about present anxieties in the guise of imagining or recalling future or
past plagues. Terry Nation's *Survivors*, for example, imagines a near-
future Britain ravaged by a deadly flu epidemic, but the images used
are those of a class-ridden and strike-torn country — the BBC vision of
Britain under Labour government. Similarly, William Dieterle's medical bio-pic says more about 1940s sexual anxieties than about the
achievements of Dr Ehrlich, historical figure, while LAST MAN ON
EARTH doggedly pursues its contemporary chauvinism: what would
happen if the world were left to flapper girls?

THE LAST MAN ON EARTH announces its anchoring point-of-view
from a prematurely-revealed punchline: 'There hasn't been so much
interest in a man since the Prince of Wales visited New York in 1924'.
In fact, for a science fiction movie, LAST MAN ON EARTH is curiously
unimaginative. By 1950 all grown men have died from an unexplained
disease, 'Masculitis', save for one — Elmer, who for the last ten years
has been living in isolation amongst the Redwoods, spurned by Gertie,
the woman he loves. When he is found and returned to Washington,
he learns that the influence of women has been less than civilizing.
Fashions have become more extreme, and the White House has
become over-run by plant life (a familiar science fiction image). There
are one or two more inspired moments: in the main streets, men's
furnishings and barbers' shops are barren and boarded up (although a
men's tailors — 'by appointment to the Man' — soon opens when
Elmer returns), and there's also an intriguing lesbian tone, not so
much in the scenes of young women holding hands and embracing
(which merely casts them as adolescent), but in the dockside bar,
where the meanest, roughest women in town gather. Frisco Kate and
her gals are a 'baccy-chewing bunch' (the inter-title tells us Kate's so
tough she rouges her lips with iodine) who see Elmer as a saleable
asset, not a sex object.

Elsewhere in THE LAST MAN ON EARTH there's a messing about
with science, as Dr Lulu Prodwell races against time to find a
man-saving serum. DR EHRLICH's entire narrative is derived from a

similar race, although Otto Kruger has test-tube-cluttered montage fast-forwards on his side; unlike John Blystone, director William Dieterle seems to put all his faith into the Great March of Medicine. Kruger's Ehrlich is an impassioned man who discovers acquired immunity while resting up in Morocco, and who sees a home-town diphtheria epidemic as a make-or-break chance to test his serum. This is the Hollywood laboratory in top gear: one of Ehrlich's admiring colleagues heroically injects himself with the diphtheria serum (to prove its safety) on a thunder-torn night, and almost every scene reiterates the movie's final legend, 'Diseases of the soul must be overcome — we are threatened by epidemics of greed, hate and ignorance'.

And yet DR EHRLICH seems to show symptoms akin to its syphilis-suffering neurotics. Does the movie know its own mind? The first sign of tension is when the film puts Ehrlich on trial for his impetuous methods — although capitalists (mass production of drugs without adequate safety tests) and politicians (eager for vote-scoring serums) are fairly fingered for the blame. In fact, the film sets up the by-now familiar confrontation between bureaucrats and scientists/doctors, where the former unconsciously aid the spread of disease through their insistence on 'proper channels' and red tape. In a striking parallel with contemporary accounts of the fight to secure funds for Aids research, Dr Ehrlich's announcement that he intends to cure syphilis is treated with derision. Problematically, the film can't steer a clear line through this contempt for the sexual, because censorship forbids a 1940s film from delving too deeply. This gives a terrible resonance to the dinner party scene where Ehrlich appalls everyone by *drawing* the disease on the table linen.

A suggestive second narrative to DR EHRLICH sets up a good blood/bad blood dichotomy. The film goes to some trouble to suggest that Ehrlich beat a number of other scientists to the analysis of natural immunity ('immunity is not a quality of the blood, but a special substance'). Pride of place goes to the distinction between 'good' and 'bad' blood, which he proves through colour-staining. (The film's microscope point-of-view shots were originally shot and screened in colour!) But this distinction takes on a contemporary tenor in the Aryan bureaucrats and government representatives who emphasize the need for 'pure German race' — for instance, when they declare their distaste for Ehrlich's Oriental sidekick. Sadly, this intriguing development is sidetracked — it runs too close to upsetting the 'purity' of the film's own project — and only picked up in the 1960s and later epidemic horror movies like NIGHT OF THE LIVING DEAD, SHIVERS and RABID. (MF)

Sweet as You Are
No Sad Songs for Me

TV dramas about Aids have tended so far to run along the well-worn tracks of family melodrama. Unable to contemplate gay relationships (except under the rubric of 'coming out' movies), mainstream TV seems only able to dramatize Aids as a threat, not to the lives of those who have it, but to the stability of the 'normal' family. But in a culture whose ideologies of masculinity, femininity and the nuclear family are riddled with contradictions, this focus on heterosexual domestic relationships merely highlights some of the conflicting emotions surrounding the disease, as this passage from a typical review of TV movie SWEET AS YOU ARE shows:

'Martin (Liam Neeson), a college lecturer, has to tell his wife Julia (Miranda Richardson) that after a brief dalliance with a student who he did not realize was a drug addict, he has contracted Aids. *He is a perfectly decent husband in a good marriage who succumbed to a banal temptation.*

'Aids has reintroduced a ready-made doom to drama that has been missing since the abolition of the death penalty. . . No matter that Martin's peccadillo was insignificant in itself, he is doomed. Aids, like a crime, can carry venomous undertows of guilt and betrayal. Martin has *mindlessly destroyed his family for a sordid gratification*. It is all the more inconceivable to the victims at first because professionally and domestically *they were a flawless family*.' (Peter Lennon, *The Listener* — my emphases.)

This summary could be a description of FATAL ATTRACTION, a film equally ambivalent about the seriousness or otherwise of a husband's affair. At one moment Martin is a 'decent husband' in a 'good marriage' with a 'flawless family', and yet his 'insignificant peccadillo' suddenly becomes a 'sordid gratification' for which he has, as this same reviewer later described it, 'soiled the home'. This insistence both on the perfection of the family, and, simultaneously, its contamination, is a familiar component of epidemic cinema, but here it is visually expressed through a very particular lifestyle: young intellectual/professional Martin has (like the Michael Douglas figure in FATAL ATTRACTION) a gorgeous wife, cute daughter (why do these films rarely feature sons?) and delightful home with venetian blinds everywhere. The endless focus on their charming domestic interior, combined with the extremely telling title song '*Stay* as sweet as you are. . .' suggests a wish to *keep* things, and the underlying implication is somehow, 'If you have everything, nice home, lovely family — why ask for more?' (A film like BIGGER THAN LIFE, on the other hand, puts the whole question in reverse, showing how oppressive an acquisitive lifestyle can be.)

The fly in the ointment of the Home is, of course, the Man; SWEET AS YOU ARE has Miranda Richardson being a goody-goody masquerading as a feminist because she starts keeping cuttings of male sex crimes — the implication being that men are somehow 'out of control' of their sexuality. The wife's purity, along with the idea that men 'just can't help it' gives SWEET AS YOU ARE a Victorian moral framework which is unfortunately topical today. And as in so much Aids drama, we are kept locked in the confession/revelation of the sexual act (in this case, infidelity; in coming-out movies, homosexuality) rather than the fact that someone is going to die.

The exact reverse is true of NO SAD SONGS FOR ME. This fascinating 1950 melodrama also combines the subjects of death and a triangular relationship but in a way that is, within its generic framework, far more complex than the moralistic TV tales of today. The 'other woman' in this story is not a conveniently dismissable floozie but is in every way the equal of the wife (Margaret Sullavan), who, knowing she is dying of cancer, actually befriends the woman she hopes will become her successor. More than a simple tear-jerker, this movie contains some fine examples of Hollywood's more dynamic domestic scenes: fast, 'naturalistic' dialogue, a home-town community quickly and deftly sketched in around the central characters. Howard Koch's script (he was later blacklisted) — unlike that of any Aids drama to date — pulls us from time to time out of the particular and into the politics of, for example, research funding: '*We could know more but we spend our money on useless things*', says Sullavan's doctor. Finally, within its melodramatic conventions, this film does attempt to examine what is left behind after death: there can hardly be a dry eye in the house when Sullavan tries to explain to her daughter how the Cheshire Cat can vanish and leave its grin behind, hoping that the child will remember her smile. It is loss and death that are conspicuously missing as real issues in most TV Aids films — where they are replaced by sex, something which for all its prudery our culture finds much easier to confront. (JW)

Invasion of the Body Snatchers

This 1978 remake of the fifties sci-fi classic brings epidemic cinema to the threshold of the Aids era; and its transposition from a small town in Marin County to the city of San Francisco involves more than a mere crossing of the Golden Gate — a crossing which we actually make at the start of the film, as our point of view travels with the strangely corpuscle-like spores through space, into the earth's atmosphere and, finally, across the famous suspension bridge to one of the most liberal municipalities of the United States.

It is this setting which gives the film its particular edge. As the take-over of humans by strangely replicated bodies spreads through the city, the authorities who should be working to halt the epidemic provide precisely the channels through which it spreads. One of the earliest sequences shows the space-spores forming exotic flowers on bushes throughout the city's parks. It is from these flowers that the body-snatching pods sprout at night: thus a civic amenity becomes, at the very outset, a source of threat. A teacher, who, we understand retrospectively, is already 'podded', urges a class of school children to pick the flowers and take them home to their parents; this is not random, but organized, contamination.

Other city facilities enlisted on the side of the body snatchers are the refuse collection service — gradually throughout the film the everyday sight of a garbage truck becomes filled with menace — and the police, for they too facilitate the 'invasion' (though infiltration would be a more accurate word), refusing to help humans attacked by pods.

Against this corrupt city bureaucracy are pitted the efforts of Elizabeth (Brooke Adams) and Matthew (Donald Sutherland) — who, significantly, work in the Public Health Department — and their friends Jack and Nancy Bellicec (Jeff Goldblum and Veronica Cartwright), whose wackiness ensures that they are about as un-podlike as possible. A more ambiguous figure is Matthew's trusted friend, psychiatrist David Kibner (Leonard Nimoy), to whom many distraught citizens turn when their loved ones seem to be 'not themselves'. By providing 'psychological' explanations for what, in the film's terms, is a real phenomenon, Kibner aids the pods; a central question mark hangs over his status for much of the film.

The successful body-snatching of city authorities, public services, possibly a prominent shrink — all this produces, in a rather eerie way, an assault on urban liberalism, on what we might now recognize in Mrs Thatcher's terms as the 'Nanny State'. The characters have indeed become heavily reliant on it; at a poignant moment (because it is already clear that the city is taken over) Matthew outlines a plan of action through the 'proper channels': 'If I could get official support I'd instigate the same kind of emergency procedures we'd use for a cholera epidemic or legionnaire's disease. I can handle the Health Department, but if panic breaks out we're gonna need the police, that kind of thing — and that means the Mayor'.

All of these 'public bodies' are, of course, hopelessly corrupted; the structure here of public health official in conflict with police, Mayor, etc. echoes PANIC IN THE STREETS, where public health doctor Richard Widmark initially finds himself in a position very like Matthew's. However, while Kazan's social drama ultimately seeks to resolve the conflict between public health and the 'authorities', there is no such satisfaction in Kaufman's horror fantasy. The authorities and the disease become creepily aligned: like the 'Nanny State', the pods know what is 'best for you' — their propaganda spiel offers an end to misery and pain, as well as of the capacity to love. And in a wider sense the whole film is a parodic attack on the alienation of modern urban life: 'Nothing changes, you can have the same life, the same clothes, the same car', says a pod in attempting to recruit one of the humans. Kibner diagnoses the root problem of modern existence as the fact that 'people are stepping in and out of relationships too fast'.

It is impossible today not to view the film through the hindsight of the real crisis that was to hit San Francisco in the 1980s — the social crisis of Aids (or even, indeed, not to see Jeff Goldblum as already part of the way to fly-dom). But of course, the film can't really be seen as prescient in any way; which makes its epidemic language all the more interesting, focused as it is on a city whose largely liberal population has been particularly health obsessed (the film's hero cooks veggies in a wok, the other hero runs a health-bath, his wife talks endlessly about pollution, etc.). Kaufman manages to turn this clean, organized city into a nightmare; his heavy use of gratuitous point-of-view shots, at times mildly irritating, at its best unsettles our perceptions, making us uncertain who to identify with. The ending, in particular, is as chilling as any in epidemic cinema. (JW)

Day of the Dead

The conflict between medical and military solutions to a plague — which PANIC IN THE STREETS presents in realist terms through its health officer and police chief — erupts spectacularly into eighties epidemic cinema with Romero's DAY OF THE DEAD. In his third zombie film (following NIGHT OF THE LIVING DEAD and ZOMBIES — DAWN OF THE DEAD) we have moved past the early stages of contamination to a world almost entirely inhabited by zombies. The film starts with research scientist Sarah leading an expedition to find any remaining humans; when it proves fruitless she and helicopter pilot John fly back to an underground base which, although peopled by survivors, is rapidly shown to be every bit as creepy as the zombie world against which it is barricaded.

The base is run by the crazed militarist Rhodes: after successfully avoiding death by zombiedom Sarah returns to the 'safety' of Rhodes threatening to shoot her for refusing to sit down during his lecture. This power-mad relic of the 'normal' world functions throughout as an acid critique of that 'normality' and its *in*human methods of dealing with anything or anyone different from it. For the central battle raging inside the claustrophobic base is between Rhodes' insistence on a shoot-to-kill policy for all zombies — despite the fact that they far outnumber humans — and the doctors' attempts to find a more constructive way through the crisis.

But they too are split in their approach. While Sarah — who is the moral centre of the film — is busy researching a cure for the zombie plague, her boss Dr Logan is trying to adapt and harness the zombies to perform useful activities. Logan's show-patient is the zombie 'Bub', who shows traces of memory, can be calmed by Beethoven on headphones, and even has the rudiments of speech. Bub is a somewhat infantilized figure towards whom Logan is like a schoolmaster; he

attempts to train 'his' zombies, in true Pavlovian style, through a
system of rewards and punishments. Logan occupies a sort of 'mad
psychiatrist' role — part of that triad Health Worker/Police/
Psychiatrist found so often in epidemic narratives — where the Goody
is always the doctor or health officer seeking a *cure*, rather than the
police, who seek *control*, or the shrink who, in a kind of compromise,
seeks ways to *adapt*.

Logan's experiments show that zombies have retained the 'primitive
core' of the brain, which is supposedly responsible for a 'neanderthal'
kind of behaviour. What Romero never ceases to bring home to us,
however, is how much *more* neanderthal many of the non-zombie men
are — or at least, the white, military men; for DAY OF THE DEAD
follows the pattern of Romero's earlier films in casting those who are
'normally' marginalized by mainstream society — in particular,
blacks and women — as the Goodies. Sarah teams up with John (who
is black) and the drunken Scottish radio operator McDermott; an
alliance of 'Others', they carry the positive values of the film,
underscoring the central point which is that the white, male chauvinist
culture zombies attack is *already* corrupt (this film was in an earlier
version to have been called 'Zombies in the White House').

Thus the Epidemic genre's themes of conflict among survivors, the
corruption of bureaucracy, an ambivalence towards those 'infected',
and a concern with the boundaries of the body (which are broken by
biting, the zombie mode of infection) are all present and developed
further in this graphic and well-paced film. Among the trails of gore
(this is not a film for the squeamish) there are some key emotional
moments; perhaps the most central is the confrontation between the
vicious Rhodes and the far less obnoxious Bub, whose beloved 'master'
Rhodes has just killed. As they stand facing each other Bub provides
an almost exact mirror image of the soldier, saluting when he salutes,
imitating his gestures — and such is the empathy set up for Bub in his
bewildered mourning that we can actually enjoy the gross-out meal he
eventually makes of his enemy. At this point we are very close to
sharing a zombie perspective, or at least our position in the battle
between humans and living dead becomes highly ambiguous. It is
Romero's supreme achievement that, even while zombies function as
the external threat to his human characters, he can simultaneously
make us feel that they are not entirely Other to them, either. (JW)

Programme Round-Ups

These are notes written to accompany three film seasons not programmed by me, but for which I was asked, in each case, to provide an overview. The aim of the pieces was to corral the different films within the overall concept of their season, to make connections, both thematic and cinematic, between movies which might in other respects be disparate.

'The Prison Film' was a season programmed at the National Film Theatre by Chris Hale in 1982. 'Business Before Pleasure' was the title of a film season about prostitution held at the Bristol Arts Centre in 1981. 'Take a Letter Darling' was written for a season of movies about working women at the Chapter Arts Centre, Cardiff, in 1989.

The Prison Film

The prison film is one of cinema's most clearly recognizable types, yet
has rarely been discussed or exhibited as a 'genre'. The NFT's Prison
Film season, organized in conjunction with Radical Alternatives to
Prison (RAP), is unique in both its scope and its approach to the
subject. There are many well-known films — I AM A FUGITIVE FROM A
CHAIN GANG, COOL HAND LUKE — alongside some less familiar
examples: ANN VICKERS and CAGED, both about women's prisons and
directed by John Cromwell (who was blacklisted in the fifties); THE
BIG HOUSE, an early 1930s film alleged to have inspired a mutiny in
Dartmoor; and Raphael Silver's recent ON THE YARD, based on the
novel by a former San Quentin inmate.

Despite these tenuous connections with actual prisoners and prisons, the prison film, however 'nitty gritty', reveals more about the
contradictions in society's *view* of punishment, than about real conditions as a social document. It has a compulsively repeated repertoire of
events and characters — the escape, the riot, the liberal governor, the
sadistic warder — which lend a particular rigidity to its structure. But
what is repetitive about the prison *film* is not what is repetitive about
prison life — working, exercising, slopping out, etc. Boredom hardly
makes for interesting movies: so the prison film must spin straw into
gold, dullness into excitement. A striking exception to this is A MAN
ESCAPED, in which Bresson's characteristic economy of sound and
image, centred on one cell and its occupant, produces a real sense of
confinement.

All the films share what might seem a strange political perspective:
the viewer is without exception invited to identify with prisoners, not

with warders. A flow of sympathy between a 'law-abiding' audience and the punished criminal is set up. A particularly powerful device for this is the 'wrongly accused' plot; but even with the 'rightly' accused, the viewer is still drawn into the experience of punishment, with fascination and repulsion — simply by watching.

Visibility is a traditionally vital part of punishment: stocks and hangings used to provide public thrills, and 18th-century prison architects designed the 'Panopticon', which made all inmates instantly viewable from one point, providing 'a great and constant fund of entertainment' (as Jeremy Bentham put it) for the public, as well as warders. Today, when the compulsion to watch remains but prisons have become closed to our view, such entertainment is provided by the prison film, in which fear and excitement still charge the uneasy relationship between audience and spectacle.

Business Before Pleasure

The image of the prostitute has always been one of the most clichéd images of women, having less to do with actual women who are prostitutes than with the 'Mother/Whore' contrast which traditionally divides 'good' women from 'bad' women (for 'bad' read 'sexual'). This division is rooted in male fantasy, but at its core is not so much a desire to divide, but to have cake and eat it too: the wife and mistress syndrome. The cinema screen has peculiar capacities for allowing people to have their cake and eat it, since it can show women in a way that provides pleasure (at its simplest, scantily clothed women's bodies), while at the same time suggesting from the moral point of view that the women whose images provide that pleasure are 'bad'. This makes it possible to be morally correct, and sexually pleased, in a most economical way.

A recent spate of films, represented in this season, has sprung up at a time when traditional ways of viewing women are being questioned; and today prostitution seems a fashionable subject not just among 'pornographers', but within 'progressive' film-making which often aims directly to attack stereotyped images of women. What is interesting, however, is the extent to which there is still a tendency in these films for the image of prostitution to fulfil male fantasies, rather than to investigate women's lives.

SLOW MOTION, Godard's latest film, uses prostitution as a metaphor for capitalism: this is a favourite view on the left, that we all 'sell ourselves' in bourgeois society one way or another. In this analogy the body of a woman again becomes a symbol, something with a meaning outside itself. Yet despite the insistent metaphor, SLOW MOTION also makes it possible to get pleasure from the prostitute herself — from Isabelle Huppert's naked body: the clash between the film's 'meaning' and the simple pleasure of viewing is still there.

Tony Garnett's PROSTITUTE starts from a totally different point of view: prostitution not as a metaphor but as 'a job like any other'. The film is strongest as a campaigning work, protesting against the imprisonment of prostitutes and made in close contact with the group 'PROs'. But what is interesting here is that in aiming to demystify the 'exotic', 'wicked' stereotype of the prostitute, Garnett has come up with another one: the earthy, warm-hearted woman who's just trying to earn a living.

The notion that prostitution is 'just a job' has become central to the new way of overtly making a moral, or at least a social point, while covertly showing sexually pleasing images. The public advertising for MAÎTRESSE reads: 'To you, these will be the most incredible things ever to appear on the screen. To the Maîtresse, it's a job'. The 'documentary' approach, 'just showing someone doing their job', is suspiciously innocent: watching the masseuse masturbate a client in PROSTITUTE is very different from watching someone clean a floor.

The film which makes the connection between precisely such mundane tasks as this, and prostitution, is JEANNE DIELMAN. Rather than showing just the 'exciting' bits of Jeanne Dielman's profession, this film deliberately shows every action of her day, and the monotonous control which she must maintain to survive. The idea of control is central to many of the attitudes to prostitution, including the apparently feminist one that women are controlling their own bodies, since they choose what they do, and are thereby exploiting men. JEANNE DIELMAN is perhaps the only film where we are shown the price of this control — which finally breaks down. Prostitution is neither glorified nor reviled: and there are no 'good' or 'bad' women, just one woman performing endless household tasks.

Given that prostitution means so much to men, perhaps it's the complicated question of what prostitution means to *women* which could provide the most useful starting point for investigating these films.

Take a Letter Darling

Women and work usually seem strangely incompatible in movies. Work is shown as a problem for women; it appears to erode femininity so that the successful woman is, conventionally, an uptight bitch. Conversely, women pose a problem for work: when feminine women enter the workplace they — equally conventionally — erode its efficiency and concentration. Just what the workplace is, varies throughout Hollywood history; if the thirties was the age of the shopgirl and the forties of the reporter, our own era is surely that of business and finance. Over half a century the focus on working girls has shifted from Lingerie and Perfumes to Stocks and Shares.

Yet certain themes are remarkably consistent. The earliest film in this season, WOMAN OF THE YEAR, stars Katharine Hepburn as a world famous political journalist whose ambition and commitment to her work are aligned with her 'unfeminine' neglect of husband Spencer Tracy and their child: a typical Hepburn role whose coldness is transcended only by the sparkiness of the actress herself. The fact that it is femininity, not parenthood, that is incompatible with work, is shown by the way Tracy, in the same film, also works on a newspaper and holds down his job while personifying the devoted father.

Over forty years later Sigourney Weaver in WORKING GIRL plays another bitchy successful woman, but, significantly, this stereotype is subordinate in the film to a newer, more positive image: the working girl whose heart and head seem, for once, able to get along together in the same body. Melanie Griffith is the smart and sassy secretary-turning-businesswoman with, as she puts it, 'a head for business and a body for sin', and who, remarkably, is not punished but actually rewarded for her efforts to succeed. Work and romance dovetail adorably as her dishy lover/business partner Harrison Ford gives her a new briefcase for a present and packs her tin lunchbox on the morning of her new career.

Part of the pleasure of this film is the way it combines a variety of Hollywood satisfactions: the rise from the bottom of the heap to the top; the triumph of the Good and Kind over the Bad and Mean; and, returning to the Woman/Work question, the way it lets the successful woman keep the love of the person she loves. For while WORKING GIRL's determination to reveal Capitalism's Heart of Gold makes it on one level hardly a 'progressive' film, on another it is surprisingly liberating since (having syphoned off 'bad' careerism onto the Weaver character) it refuses to play off its heroine's personal happiness against her professional success.

Unlike Joan Crawford in MILDRED PIERCE, the Griffith character does not have to make sacrifices; unlike Holly Hunter in BROADCAST NEWS, she isn't presented as neurotic and bossy. These two films, while giving some sense of the exhilaration of work, make their heroines pay heavily for being good at it. Crawford loses both her lover and her daughter (failing in femininity's two key arenas, the sexual and the maternal) and Hunter doesn't even get a lover or a child to lose, but cries into her wordprocessor so frequently we're left in no doubt about the pain she suffers in the conflict between her working values and her desire. The film hinges on the split between her professional standards (shared with 'best friend' reporter Albert Brooks) and her romantic love for schmaltzy anchor-man William Hurt — a schism that appears somehow inherent in her, all part of the neurosis of today's Single Working Woman.

A different schism between work and desire is at the centre of Lizzie Borden's WORKING GIRLS, with its documentary-style study of a day in the life of a New York prostitute. If work, in many films, appears as a form of prostitution, here, prostitution is shown as 'just' work, with sex merely a routine task to be performed. But perhaps most interesting of all is the way WORKING GIRLS (like 'How to Keep your Husband' manuals) presents buttering up men's egos as a job. For it's not only women wage-earners who work: Borden's prostitutes pouring out gin and tonics and asking concernedly 'How's the job going? That's Great. Let me fix you a drink' resemble nothing so much as housewives, who may well remember that 'day after day there are girls at the office'[1] and whose financial security relies every bit as much as working women's on doing their 'job' right. Femininity can be hard work indeed.

So what lies at the heart of Hollywood's obsession with women versus work? Ultimately, it isn't work itself that appears unfeminine. The key question is, what work? Contemporary films about working women don't, for the most part, feature women in shops, classrooms,

---

1

1 *'Day after day there are girls at the office*
And men will always be men
Don't send him off with your hair still in curlers
You might not see him again . . .'
— from the Burt Bacharach/Hal David song, 'Wives and Lovers'.

factories — and they certainly don't (except, significantly, in comedy) have as their heroines women in the traditionally 'feminine' service jobs like cleaning. Today's Working Woman is usually somewhere up the corporate ladder, or perhaps a successful lawyer or publisher (e.g. Glenn Close in JAGGED EDGE and FATAL ATTRACTION respectively).

And what these jobs represent is not just 'work', but power. This is what is at stake in the struggle over feminine values and it is social power, not having a job, which appears incompatible with being a 'real' woman. After all, hard work of a menial kind has always appeared supremely compatible with womanhood; so familiar, in fact, is this assumption, that its embodiments usually go unnoticed. The first person on the screen in ROLLOVER (where Jane Fonda makes it to become Chair of the Board) is a cleaning woman, wheeling her trolley through the trading floor of a large banking corporation. The last figures in MILDRED PIERCE are those of two cleaning women, scrubbing the floor on their knees.

Ways of Telling

The short review is probably the most ubiquitous type of film criticism, yet there has been little discussion about its format and function. It is the brief comments made in listings guides that most people turn to in deciding which movie to see; their influence on film culture is therefore enormous. Short length criticism usually exists to *tell* people something about a film, hence the title of this section. The tension in many short reviews is precisely between the need to provide information, and the wish to comment, to 'assess' a film which, however, the reader has most likely not yet seen: in this sense, what we call reviews are usually, in fact, previews.

While a column of a thousand words may be used to develop an argument and illustrate its points, the fifty to two hundred word review has to convey something about the film to the reader very rapidly, and there is no room to take an argument through each of its logical stages. This often results in a kind of short circuit whereby the reviewer will jump to the conclusion — as it were — of an invisible discussion, ending up with phrases like 'flawed masterpiece' — which tell you absolutely nothing. Sometimes the reviewing process sounds like a version of wine-tasting: a question of sampling and then pronouncing ('a mature little vintage') in a tone rather like someone ruminating over an after-dinner brandy. The particular style associated with this tends to suggest that the author has a vast amount of knowledge about the film/director/subject in question, but is unfortunately unable to share any of it; we have to take the flawed masterpiece on trust.

It doesn't have to be that way: short reviews can — rather paradoxically — be both more informative and more subjective. The problem with the flawed masterpiece vocabulary is that it couches a personal judgement as an objective pronouncement, while not actually offering the argument or knowledge which led to that pronouncement. Even in a short space it is possible to tell the reader something about the content of a film, plus some relevant information about its context: as well as putting forward angles that might open up debate, questions about camerawork, social issues, historical background. And part of a critic's job should be to sketch in a sentence what is meant by Realism or Expressionism, rather than merely employing terms with the assumption that everyone is familiar with them.

But it's also important for critics to let up and acknowledge that, while their (our) knowledge about film may be wider than some of our readers', our feelings about films are no more 'objective' than anyone else's. It is usually better to *say* how you feel, than to turn your response into a 'pure' reflection of the film's position on some scale of intrinsic merit. That doesn't mean that there can be no real criticism, no discussion of values, no arguments for or against aspects of a movie: but a critic must have a human voice, rather than one of divine judgement. Knowledge is power: and the more we share it the less superior we need be.

The reviews in this section are put forward as examples of film writing in the listings magazine format; but the fact that they're examples doesn't mean they're supposed to be seen as *exemplary*. They are the product of an ongoing attempt to grapple with the problems outlined here, the limitations of short space and the necessity of providing information, fast, in a constantly pressurized situation (sometimes a review has to be written in the half-hour between a screening and a deadline). I have been selective; hundreds of reviews might not have been very interesting in bulk, but I hope the sample presented here will raise further questions about film criticism in its many modes.

Short Reviews

These were written for *Time Out, Not Time Out* (which became *Not* under circumstances mentioned in the foreword) and *City Limits*, between 1980 and 1983. I have boiled the collection down to fifty, and ordered them alphabetically rather than by subject or genre because they are not intended to be — couldn't possibly be — exhaustive or inclusive in terms of the films themselves. They are, however, quite a representative sample of the film writing I churned out during that period.

All that Heaven Allows
(Douglas Sirk, 1955, US)

From the moment the opening aerial shot swoops in on ordered suburbia to Rock Hudson, the gardener, and Jane Wyman, his employer, this film starts to home in with a magnifying glass on that 'moral', social order which keeps them in place. All the sexual distaste facing an 'older' woman who loves a hunky younger man, and all the snobbery which separates a middle-class widow from a gardener, are hurled at their developing relationship with such violence as to be almost exaggeratedly painful. But the most radical twist is that it's Jane Wyman's own repulsive children (almost grown up) who stand most in the way of her happiness with a grotesque concern, not for their dead father's memory, but for his social status and for their own. Behind this brittle, youthful pride lurks not one iota of compassion for their mother, who is left at Christmas watching the reflection of flames flickering in the dead screen of the colour TV they have given her instead of their presence and affection. Linking property, class, and sexual restrictions, the drama unfalteringly blows up the great myth of Family Life, whose sentimentality is stolen by the central love affair and the battle against convention. On its release, the *Monthly Film Bulletin* called this 'as laboriously predictable as it is fatuously unreal'. Bigger than life, yes: but these fifties melodramas had to be, to turn the emotions of the weepie into a weapon to pierce the strongest institution of that era.

C.L. 1982

American Boy
(Martin Scorsese, 1978, US)

The American boy is Steven Prince: Scorsese's friend, Neil Diamond's ex-road manager, drug freak, and gun fanatic. Interestingly, he appeared as the gun dealer in TAXI DRIVER, a film which could have been made with Prince in mind in its exploration of manic energy as a source of potential destruction while still vital in itself. Red-drug-eyed, speedier than fast-forward, Prince rewinds over a life of drugs, draft, guns, death, busts and needles with incredible humour, a quality that makes no judgements. The film itself is structured with this same feeling: Prince talking in the present is intercut with home-movie reels showing him as all-American baby, the army officer's son, birthday after birthday of plenty, the image of an idyllic and innocent boyhood. The tension between these two lives takes added irony from chapter headings superimposed on the childhood clips, often consisting simply of a few key words from Prince's spoken drama. There is no comment, only the endearing energy with which the tales of violence and tragedy are told, a reflection on Scorsese's films as well as his friend.

C.L. 1982

Les Anges du Péché
(Robert Bresson, 1943, France)

Bresson's first feature is a taut spiritual drama set in the confines of a convent and prison. The closeness of the two, and the linking of crime, punishment and redemption, were to illuminate all his films: here they burn through the passionate relationship between a novice and a young woman criminal who joins the convent to hide from the police. The starkness of the film's construction produces a remarkably sustained pitch of intensity, which is somehow pure of the emotional pulls and shocks so familiar in movies, and leaves a strange sense of calm as the music runs on after the end: a screening device Bresson insisted on, making his cinema even more like church.

C.L. 1982

A Propos de Nice
(Jean Vigo, 1930, France)
Taris
(Jean Vigo, 1931, France)
Zéro de Conduite
(Jean Vigo, 1933, France)
L'Atalante
(Jean Vigo, 1934, France)

These four films make up the entire work of Jean Vigo, who died tragically young aged 29. His radical politics are combined with formal inventiveness in a way that is still unique and liberating to watch. À PROPOS DE NICE is a savagely witty sketch of the idle rich at their seaside leisure, irreverent through visual play and biting through montage; TARIS, a commissioned short about a champion swimmer, is breathtaking in its exhilaration with movement, replacing narrative with repetition and slow motion to produce sheer physical pleasure; ZÉRO DE CONDUITE is an anarchic, sometimes hilarious attack on authority through the story of boys' rebellion at a boarding school; and L'ATALANTE, with its striking imagery of gliding light and water, tells the moving tale of a bargee and his young wife, delicately raising sexual politics and conflicts. In only a few years of directing, Vigo mapped out ground that other film-makers have been building on ever since.

C.L. 1981

L'Argent (Money)
(Robert Bresson, 1983, Switzerland/France)

Loosely based on a Tolstoy story *The False Note*, Bresson's new film reinvokes his earlier PICKPOCKET, charting the circulation of a false banknote and the escalation of crimes as an innocent man (Yvon) who uses it falls into a downward spiral of court, prison and finally murder. But this is no tale of wrong-doing: it is about Evil, a line we might slip over as easily as the forged note slips from hand to hand, forming a web between strangers who glide in and out of the integrity of the frame. For the film has a kind of spiritual pacing: the camera never chases, it is calm, as lucid as a bad dream. Only Bresson makes such extraordinary films filled with both surface and soul. Surface, in the faces which do not reveal, voices whose clarity is without drama, the surface of the city, the cash dispenser at night, the shop windows and subway ceilings lit by leaving trains. Soul, through the reticent sensuality with which the frame seems to let these surfaces glide across it like a hand over skin. The money of the title does not need to be taken as metaphor: meaningless in itself, it *is* a currency for trust, mistrust and love, from the first false note set moving by a schoolboy whose cold parents are mean with pocket money, to Yvon's final, unanswered question 'Where is (the) Money?' as he kills his benefactor before giving himself up. Surfaces give away nothing, it is movement which charges emotion; and in the limbo of Bresson's surface materiality, where lives float by and between one another, both sin and redemption are always only a movement away.

C.L. 1983

Chronique d'un Eté
(Jean Rouch, 1961, France)

Using lightweight camera-with-sound equipment for the first time, Jean Rouch and sociologist Edgar Morin followed, interviewed and intervened in the lives of a group of Parisians during a long summer in the Algerian war. The resulting film inspired the revival of Vertov's concept 'Kinopravda' — cinema-truth — in the term 'cinéma vérité'. Rouch's aim was 'not to film life as it is, but life as it is provoked' by the active intervention of the film-makers, questioning the participants and letting them use the filming to present aspects of themselves which can afterwards be disowned as 'just acting'. Several of them fell out during the summer — as did Rouch and Morin over the editing — and the film bears the marks of it all, conflicts and emotions splurging out unpredictably, the camera barging into psyches and situations. (The participants' lives also bore the marks of the film; one worker was sacked after it). The effect is simultaneously messy and sharp: perhaps a failure, but one which talks about its failings. However, the example of film interacting with people's lives, rather than providing a 'window' through which to view them, produced a crucial shift in documentary whose influence can be seen in, for example, Chris

Marker's work, and whose parallel today is found in video documentaries like THE POLICE TAPES which, similarly, rely on developments in portable, high-speed equipment and which produce the same lurching immediacy and involvement.

C.L. 1982

Citizens Band
(Jonathan Demme, 1977, US)

CITIZENS BAND marked Demme's first break from Exploitation movies, three years before he made MELVIN AND HOWARD. One of the few contemporary directors to deal in small-town American lives and values, his handling of them feels uneasy, caught between a homey humanity and a cynical detachment as he wrings from his group of eccentric, mainly unhappy individuals a savagely happy ending. The popular fantasy of this film (the equivalent of 'millionaire in disguise' in MELVIN AND HOWARD) is the world of Citizens' Band radio, the transformer of identity which, in a small community, can 'rearrange their faces and give them all another name'. The town's fantasy life is finally blown into the real world as identities become known, with some pretty heavy-duty psychodramas — brother hating brother, bigamy, fucked-up relationships of jealousy and boredom — which aren't adequately dealt with simply by weaving them into life's rich tapestry. With CB legislation just going through in Britain this film is superficially timely, but its delayed release has done nothing to soften the crueller edge of its flirtation with the Down Home.

C.L. 1981

City of Women
(Federico Fellini, 1980, Italy/France)

In this rambling journey of exotic encounters on extravagant sets, Fellini turns a man's head inside out, churning feelings into images, fear and desire into the fluctuations of a plot. Snaporaz, the dapper hero, is led by his desire for a woman on a train into a string of fantastic adventures: to a feminist convention, which he flees, through an attempted rape by an enormous woman, whom he flees, to the Fortress of Masculinity, in which, among galleries of press-button talking pin-ups, its owner is celebrating his 10,000th 'conquest'. From here Snaporaz takes a rollercoaster ride through his unconscious, passing tableaux of formative sexual encounters from childhood — including The Cinema, a giant bed in which men enjoy Woman on the screen. There are many other almost feminist images, such as the inflatable 'Ideal Woman', a huge balloon who floats Snaporaz in the air until shot and deflated by her real counterpart below. This film is one of the most successful of Fellini's symbolic romps, as the coincidence of fantasy and cinema has a real bearing on the way men — including directors — invent women.

Not 1981

Coma
(Michael Crichton, 1978, US)

This gripping hospital thriller unfolds through Genevieve Bujold's perceptions of a high-level plot which she gradually uncovers in the face of great opposition from her boyfriend and superiors. In a brilliant conflation of everyday emotional realities with fast, detailed suspense devices, the patronizing tones of men take on a sinister note, as the grounds for her 'paranoia' really do exist. One of the delights of the structure is that to prevent her death, her boyfriend has to recall the discoveries which he earlier dismissed: she is proved right at exactly the moment when she is 'saved' by a man — usually a way of making women seem weak. This is the nearest thing to a feminist thriller: after three viewings I could still see it again.

C.L. 1982

Destiny
(Fritz Lang, 1921, Germany)

This very early silent film brought Lang his first critical success. Made at a point of post-war German pessimism, its original title DER MÜDE TOD translates literally as 'the tired death', and its three-part allegorical story of a girl pleading with Death for the return of her lover is haunted with the fluid and frightening shapes of darkness and light which characterize Expressionism. This style paints its fatalism as universal, but its flame-like images are also a violently depressed cry from the heart of a devastated nation.

C.L. 1981

Diary of a Chambermaid
(Luis Buñuel, 1964, France/Italy)

Buñuel's acid, subtly analytical picture of French country society, bourgeois and petty bourgeois, unfolds through the experience of an inscrutable chambermaid (Jeanne Moreau) who works for a wealthy, decaying family and must deal with a kinky old man, pestering husband and petty, repressed wife, as well as learning the pecking order below stairs. A coherent plot makes for very tightly controlled observation — of rituals, prejudice and, almost incidentally, incipient fascism. Very clear political suggestions underlie the story of a rape and murder, and inform the brutal anti-climax of the murderer's acquittal: but what the film shows best is the stagnant social order in which fascism appeared as the only momentum.

C.L. 1981

Earth
(Alexander Dovzhenko, 1930, USSR)

The story of peasants' struggle against landowners for collectivization, this film actually claims the land physically for the cause of communism, with a camera which adores the earth and those close to it. The film virtually makes love to the rolling farmland (Dovzhenko's native Ukraine) with a stark sensuality that mirrors the peasants' own relation to their country and is shown, for example, in a lyrical scene where Vasili, their leader, dances in the moonlight after breaking down the fences which divide the land. Passion and property are set as the opposites they are, as he is murdered by a kulak in the midst of his abandon; but this only reinforces the peasants' unity and closeness to the earth in which they bury him. Two other powerful scenes (Vasili's naked lover hysterically grieving, and the peasants refilling their tractor's radiator by peeing into it) were omitted until 1958: so shocking, apparently, was the combination of politics and physicality. Dovzhenko's worship of the land — constantly pointing the camera upwards as if to show its point of view — is excessive but never 'too much': the result is outstandingly beautiful, one of the rare films whose images speak passionately for the cause they embrace.

C.L. 1982

El Salvador — The People Will Win
(Diego de la Texera, 1981, El Salvador)

At a time when the war in El Salvador is making TV news, and American involvement there is a hotly debated subject, this film gives a point of view so far neither seen nor heard — that of the people's army, the Farabundo Marti Liberation Front, and of the population which supports it. Conditions under which the film was shot are revealed in an arresting postscript: a camera is delivered to a peasant woman to hide in her laundry basket by a freedom fighter who, taking up his red scarf and gun, disappears back into the guerilla war. Despite these conditions the images are powerfully framed: unlike newsreel, which is now so familiar, the colour film gives not just a picture of the war against the military regime, but of El Salvador itself, the history, the land and the people, creating a sense of the life that US and European imperialism destroys culturally as well as with arms. We are shown less of the atrocities of the American-backed Junta, than of the spirit of resistance; and Vietnam has already shown that this can be stronger than the US army.

T.O. 1981

La Fiancée du Pirate
(Nelly Kaplan, 1969, France)

Nelly Kaplan's witty story of a young girl who, after years of abuse from her 'betters' in a French village, causes havoc by setting up as a prostitute, is often regarded as a fine example of sexual politics. Mary makes a comfortable living by charging the men of the community ever-increasing prices and finally engineers a brilliant coup. Rich in social metaphors, charting Mary's rise through her steady accumulation of consumer durables which sit precariously in her wooden hut, the film is really a droll fable, saying less about sexuality itself than about provincial mores, which it caricatures with cunning skill.

C.L. 1982

The Girl Can't Help It
(Frank Tashlin, 1956, US)

Tashlin's background as animator brings a host of wonderful cartoon-gags to this bombshell of a movie: as Jayne Mansfield walks down the street, spectacle lenses crack and milk bottles shatter under the radiant force of her sex-appeal. Most of the gags revolve around her carica-tured innocence of this powerful quality, and the biggest gag of all is that the sex-pot of all time wants nothing but to be a little woman, abandon the singing career she's pushed into, and bake corn-cookies for a Man all day long. Add to this shimmering example of fifties femininity a massive dose of rock 'n' roll, a crazy plot, mix it up with

swirling style and colour, fast humour and neat timing, and you get a
bundle of joy whichever way you look at it.

C.L. 1981

Italianamerican
(Martin Scorsese, 1974, US)

A fascinating flip-side to MEAN STREETS, this documentary was made
a year after it and shows an Italian New York family from the inside:
Scorsese's own. Interesting and affectionate, the film has something
more rare: a respect and gentleness in letting the Scorsese parents tell
their own story, in their own way — often hilarious, since they are
great storytellers. Mrs Scorsese is cooking a sauce throughout, and
their narratives are punctuated with clips of period film — New York
at the turn of the century — and with their own family photographs.
The result gives a sense both that history is intimate, and that who you
are is in the way you tell it, as the Scorseses come across so vividly in
their gestures, interruptions and generosity of speech. It also gives a
sense of the life that images freeze: in one moving moment Mrs S is
framed as a future memory, an old photo. But, indomitable, her
meat-balls sauce recipe rounds off the credit sequence.

C.L. 1982

Je, Tu, Il, Elle
(Chantal Akerman, 1974, Belgium)

Chantal Akerman eats too much sugar, wanks off a lorry driver, and
goes to bed with another woman. Q.E.D.

C.L. 1982

Jonah Who Will Be 25 in the Year 2000
(Alain Tanner, 1976, Switzerland/France)

Some people love this film, especially (on the whole) middle-class, post-'68, politics-is-now-lifestyle types: personally, a couple of hours of Jonah's parents and their friends makes me very glad I'll be 46 in the year 2000.

C.L. 1982

Jules et Jim
(François Truffaut, 1961, France)

The ultimate humanist ménage-à-trois movie, this follows a German and a Frenchman, intimate friends, who share a woman (Jeanne Moreau), are separated by WW1, re-unite, and live out the complications of a three-cornered relationship with as much affection and integrity as possible. The 'warm-heartedness' which sometimes makes Truffaut seem a bit soppy feels totally appropriate here: the mood is Renoir-esque, lyrical, full of a decent understanding of human problems, luminous and sensitively shot, playful and serious at the same time. (Renoir in fact joked that he should have made it.) This general sense of exhilaration, in both film-making and acting, tends to over-ride the basically Tragic (and reactionary) nature of a story where human contradictions can only be resolved in death. The basic message is a bit off, but it's impossible not to be charmed by the whole thing.

C.L. 1982

Lady Chatterley's Lover
(Just Jaeckin, 1981, GB/France)

This film really brings out the worst in Lawrence's novel, limited as it
is by the irritating notion of women's sexuality as centred on male
anatomy. But *Lady Chatterley* the book was radical in its time for its
explicit portrayal not of 'sex' but of sexual desire across classes ('would
you let your servants read it?'), an uncompromising passion that broke
the bounds of an 'affair'. However, the film, with its soft and seamless
construction, its misty landscapes, its coy and cowardly treatment of
masturbation and fucking and its obvious delight in the production
values of stately homes and period costumes, achieves none of the
rawness of passion, only the sugariness of nice clean sex. It would have
been better to keep the interestingly cast Sylvia Kristel (Lady C.), and
make this as a porn film — for how on earth do you deal with a story of
obsessive phallus-worship in a form where you can't even show male
pubic hair, let alone Lawrence's favourite organ?

C.L. 1981

The Leopard
(Luchino Visconti, 1963, Italy)

Even with enormous cuts, appalling dubbing and Hollywood colour
printing THE LEOPARD was one of the richest films of the last twenty
years; and now Fox are releasing it as Visconti intended — subtitles,
original colour, and over three hours long. But not one second drags
on the eye as Visconti's lavish and lingering camera draws out the
heart of Lampedusa's novel, that sense of 'voluptuous immobility'
which characterizes both the heat-soaked landscape of Sicily itself, and
the over-ripe aristocratic class, decaying in the face of bourgeois
ascendancy. Burt Lancaster is the Prince Fabrizio, head of an ancient
Sicilian family which has to adapt to the upheaval of Italian unification: his nephew Tancredi (Alain Delon) fights with Garibaldi's
red-shirts and marries the daughter (Claudia Cardinale) of a wealthy
and repugnant middle-class mayor. Lampedusa could have written
especially for Visconti's operatic realism, welding as it does personal
and class fortunes through both the emotions and the materiality they

share. Each individual strand is shot with the texture of a whole fabric, each encounter riven with the fluctuations of a historical moment. Yet like the sensual billowing of fixed curtains in the hot summer breeze (in the unforgettable opening movement), sameness oozes from the social rearrangements which at first seemed so drastic. Tancredi joins the new King's army; soldiers who stay with Garibaldi are shot at dawn as Fabrizio walks home from the climactic ball: a ball where both the in-bred decadence of the old class, and the bold inevitability of the new, are choreographed through a breathtakingly elaborate and erotic sequence which remains one of the greatest pieces of sustained filming ever.

C.L. 1983

Letter to Jane
(Jean-Luc Godard, Jean-Pierre Gorin, 1972, France)

This is a detailed, perceptive analysis of a newsphoto which shows Jane Fonda in Vietnam, looking concerned in conversation with some Vietnamese. Godard/Gorin argue very soundly that this emphasis on the 'concern' of the West, through an image of a film star, rather than on the Vietnamese themselves and what they have to say, is only another form of the colonialism which dominates the Third World. The use of film to analyze the ideologies of still images is very effective: but Godard/Gorin fail to engage with the way meanings are *constructed* in news images (and other media) by naively turning what should be an investigation of the *photo* into a 'letter to Jane', *telling her off* for constructing her image in this way. The very title and form of the film imply possession, since 'Jane' instead of 'Fonda' would only be used of a 'girl' (imagine 'letter to Jean-Luc'??) and the only reason Godard/Gorin assume the right to upbraid her about her image is that she had just been in 'their' film TOUT VA BIEN, and her appearance in this photo somehow betrays 'their' revolutionary correctness. As so often happens, the film-makers' ingrained patriarchal attitudes work in direct contradiction to an otherwise sharp, radical approach to the material.

T.O. 1981

The Little Foxes
(William Wyler, 1941, US)

Bette Davis' brilliant performance as the greedy, vicious Southern woman who sacrifices human relations to grasping ambition has a peculiarly topical note. The veneer of graciousness strained thin over crude monetarism has a strangely Thatcher-esque quality, as does the exploitation of cheap labour, stressed in Hellman's carefully political script. But the emotional power of the film lies in binding this capitalist immorality into family relations, so that we follow the trauma of seeing the truth through the eyes of Davis' young daughter who combines growing up with learning not merely to 'stand by and watch' wrongs, even those of her mother. Heart-rending — and Right-On.

C.L. 1982

The Lusty Men
(Nicholas Ray, 1952, US)

All that being a man means in Westerns is thrown against the material harshness of life, in this film, and cracked like a head against a brick wall. Robert Mitchum is the injured, isolated ex-rodeo champion who, returning to his old home, meets a young couple, a ranch-hand and his wife, who hope one day to buy it. The men become friends and set up as rodeo partners, to disapproval from the woman (Susan Hayward), and all three embark on a life of travel round the dust and danger of the rodeo circuit, which begins to consume the husband (Arthur Kennedy) while Mitchum falls for his wife. But ambitions rise above romance, in this group on the fringes of society — 'I used to envy people who lived in houses' says Hayward — whose choice is between working a lifetime away as a hired hand, and chasing the rough glamour of the rodeo where 'you can earn four hundred bucks in two minutes'. In a triangular web of needs which just miss one another, each character in their different way grasps at the elusive prizes of a society whose values are being lived out to the death by precisely those it excludes from material well-being. In a world where sexuality is pushed aside by the need to survive, Mitchum's final, fatal bid for competitive masculinity is intensely moving, as is the turn of his naked shoulders towards the woman he loves, as he dies.

C.L. 1982

Mädchen in Uniform
(Leontine Sagan, 1931, Germany)

Made when the Nazis were on the verge of power, this extraordinarily radical film turns the imagery and feel of Expressionism to an anti-authoritarian end, in a story of love and resistance at an oppressive, spartan boarding school for daughters of German Officers. Manuela, a new girl, falls in love with the only teacher to treat her kindly, beautiful Fräulein von Bernburg; the film puts into its evocation of this relationship all the emotional power and strength of image normally reserved for the portrayal of women to men, in heterosexual contexts — molten close-ups, charged moments, a sense of desire lovingly produced through timing and looks. Equally important is the relation of the girls to one another: their physical closeness, and active solidarity — which in the end saves Manuela from suicide. MÄDCHEN's politics go much farther than an attack on militarism and incipient fascism: the film clears a space for women's feelings in a way that strikes not only at imposed rules, but at the fears and conventions which bind us to them.

C.L. 1981

Man of Aran
(Robert Flaherty, 1934, GB)

Like his earlier NANOOK OF THE NORTH, Flaherty's first sound documentary was produced after several years living with the inhabitants of a harsh environment, in this case Aran islanders. The film is as much a drama of natural forces as a story of human life: the constant struggle against the elements — in particular a violent storm sequence where a repeated wave breaking almost takes on the status of a character — is even more striking than in NANOOK. Flaherty made free with constructed 'documentation', such as the re-enactment of obsolete traditions like shark-hunting which the islanders perform with relish; but this hardly undermines the film's 'truthfulness', which is rather in the way of life it records than in the way it is made. Around this time Grierson was asking Flaherty to instruct his film unit, so this powerfully romantic form of realism fed directly into British documentary of the 1930s.

C.L. 1982

The Men
(Fred Zinneman, 1950, US)

Brando's first screen role as a paraplegic WW2 veteran provides a literal frame for the frustrated masculinity and pent-up passion that characterize all his later roles. Set in a hospital ward, the film deals at plot level with very real problems of war veterans' readjustment, like Wyler's THE BEST YEARS OF OUR LIVES, though with the emphasis less on social, than sexual limitations. But on the level of the image Brando's sexual persona really takes off: the tension between his heaving, muscular chest as he weight-lifts in bed, and his waist-down paralysis, creates exactly that sense of suppressed but explosive energy which became his hallmark. While the camera courts this sensuality with tight facial close-ups and long gazes at *that* body, Teresa Wright as the goody-goody girlfriend courts him in a dogged quest for marriage, which serves more as a reminder of his castration than of his smouldering sexual power. Wright has to be grovellingly weedy to prevent any inversion of sex roles (the ultimate fantasy, his sex in your hands) and on their wedding night even gets down on her knees to scrub the carpet, obsessively cleaning the stain from the flooding champagne bottle which Brando holds trembling uncontrollably. It's peculiarly fifties, this soupy marriage-as-taming business: the happy ending is when Brando consents to let his wife help him up some steps. But it's precisely the restrictions of this era which channelled sexuality into that repressed macho form so special to Dean and Brando, and which still nearly burns the screen.

C.L. 1983

The Milky Way (La Voie Lactée)
(Luis Buñuel, 1968, France/Italy)

One of Buñuel's favourite projects, this film has been out of distribution in Britain for ten years and is only now being re-released.
Superficially, its structure is loose, following the journey of two tramps
to the shrine of Santiago di Compostella. Their surreal encounters on
the way range from the rites of a 4th-century erotic-religious sect, who
manoeuvre dogmas to justify 'debasing the body' in orgies, to a
modern restaurant where the dogmas of bourgeois life are polished like
the glass and silver, and a 'religious' maître d'hôtel denies the tramps
food. As the scenes weave through eras and ideas, you're forced to
abandon a search for narrative progress: instead, a complex and
thicker structure builds laterally, not just a history of Catholic dogma
and heresies but a set of questions about belief. The liberation from
plot development made me nostalgic for 1968: Delphine Seyrig as a
prostitute in one part of the forest, Jesus healing blind men in another
— all this leaping in and out of woods and history has the same feeling
as Godard's VENT D'EST and I realized we live in less daring times.
Strange how depression reaches cinema, but it does. Despite its
weighty subject matter, this film is *fun*; its irony, its non-sequiturs and
un-naturalism produce a kind of humour that's gone out of fashion.

Not 1981

Model
(Frederick Wiseman, 1980, US)

With MODEL Wiseman continues his dead-pan investigations of
institutions: but this one, a New York modelling agency, doesn't lend
itself so easily to the kind of treatment so effective in WELFARE or
HOSPITAL. Itself very stylish, beautifully shot in black and white, the
film shows the work of the agency, interviews with would-be models,
and long photography sessions where the glossy ad images we are so
familiar with get manufactured. But once you've seen this, there are
other questions to be considered: why are these images required, how
are they seen, what do they mean? The film, though, just continues to

show more models, more photography sessions: the occasional inter-
cutting with street scenes is perhaps meant to provide a contrast, but
could equally be a glamorizing of New York life. Modelling is to do
with images; but the film takes this end-product as given, concentrat-
ing on the process by which it's reached, rather than on the conventions of glamour and sexual stereotypes. The process *is* interesting —
but more could be done in two hours.

T.O. 1981

Mother
(V.I. Pudovkin, 1926, USSR)

Pudovkin's ideology and technique were very close to Eisenstein's (his
contemporary) but he sticks far more to the stories of individuals in
depicting political issues — a more conventional and 'human'
approach which, interestingly, saved him from the official disapproval
Eisenstein faced in the 1930s. Both Eisenstein's STRIKE and
Pudovkin's MOTHER are set in the abortive 1905 revolution; but
whereas STRIKE breaks up one of the main conventions of narrative
and channels sympathies not towards an individual, but a class,
MOTHER directs our sympathies through the story of one woman,
whose personal trials are felt individually, and *represent* those of a class.
We follow the experiences which finally radicalize her: her husband's
death in a factory strike, her son's imprisonment for helping the
strikers. Montage stokes up, rather than broadens, the narrative,
creating an intensely powerful and purposeful film.

C.L. 1981

Nanook of the North
(Robert Flaherty, 1922, US)

Flaherty's first film is not only a landmark in documentary history, it's also the exciting story of a battle: the battle between Eskimo life and a fierce Nature — the North. Children (and adults) are always drawn to the igloo image of snugness in the midst of the inhospitable; and the husky dogs, the seals, the activities which make up Nanook's life and struggle for survival are intriguing as fantasy come true — a picture of an actual life, but one which tugs at our imaginations. This gives an idea of the quality of Flaherty's work; documentary fired with drama, the drama of extremes in real experience.

C.L. 1982

News From Home
(Chantal Akerman, 1976, France/Belgium)

Over long-held shots of New York streets, the wondering view of a stranger in a city, Chantal Akerman reads aloud letters from her mother in Belgium. It's a simple structure, but the feelings it produces are complex: the 'news' or non-news from home is a steady stream of trivial events, anxieties, exhortations to write, starting 'my dear little girl' — while the dead-pan camera of teeming street corners seems to cut off the mother's voice to an echo from another world. The gap between the mother's view, heard, and the daughter's, seen, is powerfully moving and familiar: and, something rare in films, it leaves space for thoughts and feelings in the viewer, while showing strong and beautiful images.

C.L. 1981

New York, New York
(Martin Scorsese 1977, US)

A dazzling modern musical, this is one of the rare films which is actually constructed with as much passion as it depicts. The central love story between Minnelli and De Niro, both talented musicians, is full of storms, desire, and music, which finally pushes them apart as they split up after the birth of their baby to pursue separate careers. It's a movingly accurate depiction of a relationship hemmed with the limitations of two very demanding people, and contains some of the most convincing rows in screen history. Scorsese uses the camera and music in a way that produces the glamorous and yearning emotions of the traditional musical, while the real love story takes place on the darker side of this excitement, where desires over-reach themselves.

Not 1981

Nightmare Alley
(Edmund Goulding, 1947, US)

With a lower budget, this might have been a B-movie classic, but Fox took the weird, rather tacky script to town, with Tyrone Power (never known to lose money) and extravagant sets which included pitching a real carnival over ten acres. This, with the eerie effects of studio lighting and mists, provides both backdrop and metaphor for the story of an ambitious fairground 'mentalist' or mindreader, whose charlatan career reaches vast possibilities when he teams up with a clever woman psychoanalyst. The film doggedly pursues its own implications, connecting religion and showmanship, fear and superstition, acting and the power of superior knowledge. But it just falls short of a more coherent bleakness: the image of the geek which haunts the plot is as disturbing for the predictable hamminess of its use as for the degradation it represents. It is this strange mixture of clumsiness and tenacity in handling heavy psychodrama which creates a morbid fascination about the whole movie.

C.L. 1981

Outland
(Peter Hyams, 1981, GB)

From the opening sequence, with shots that look as if they came from
Voyager II and the wide screen tracking through smouldering darkness down the lights of a space-age mine, OUTLAND pulls you into its
simple plot with skill and power. It channels the technical sophistication of science fiction into the emotional structure of a Western: Sean
Connery is the Marshall (with a badge) who comes to inspect a mining
base on one of Jupiter's moons, uncovers corruption, and does what a
Man's Gotta Do. The film consciously plays off its superior sci-fi detail
and gut-level morality: after a chase sequence in space involving lavish
special effects, Connery finally swings into the bar and knocks the chief
baddy on the jaw as if it was Texas. There is also an implicit politics of
work: the first event is an industrial accident on an understaffed shift,
and the central aim of the baddies' plot is 'high productivity'. Visually
stunning, emotionally exciting, politically interesting — what more
could you want, except a little less macho?

Not 1981

The Philadelphia Story
(George Cukor, 1940, US)

This fast, witty film about a wealthy divorcée (Katharine Hepburn)
who gets entangled with her ex-husband (Cary Grant) and a newspaper reporter (James Stewart) is quite extraordinary and in some ways
deeply disturbing for its handling of a 'strong' woman. Hepburn at her
sharpest and liveliest is seen as unyielding and, to men, castrating:
Cukor seems to go along with this in that she is forced to surrender her
dominance like a stolen toy, and coaxed out of her 'frigidity' in a way
that's uncomfortable to watch. In one of the most searing scenes,
Hepburn's father accuses her of coldness and lack of feeling, while
tears run down her cheeks. Such flashes of sympathy in the direction
make the overall message more complex: perhaps the strong woman's
come-uppance is less a punishment than a warning.

C.L. 1981

Pickpocket
(Robert Bresson, 1959, France)

This extraordinary film tells the simple tale of a young man whose career as a pickpocket ends in prison, where he finally recognizes his true love. The idea of the 'thinker' to whom crime becomes an obsession is derived from Dostoyevsky; as is the relation between criminal and detective, characterized by paranoia and fatalism. The spoken story unfolds as a confession or diary: what makes the film unique is the way this combines with an austere visual style to produce a detached yet passionate account of events without the usual sense of identification induced by films. The presentation is deliberately material throughout, the pickpocketing sequences in particular taking on an almost sexual quality while the film's formal technique gives it the inescapable logic of a dream. Made in 1959, PICKPOCKET is still radical cinema: Bresson's notes show that his own conception of his work is fundamentally religious, but for the viewer it produces a tension and a pleasure which are intensely filmic.

T.O. 1980

Pillars of Society
(Detlef Sierck aka Douglas Sirk, 1935, Germany)

Even in 1935, with Nazi censorship closing in, Sirk was able to sharpen Ibsen's stage tragedy into an almost Dickensian social melodrama, centred on shipyard owner Councillor Bernick whose wealth and status are founded on deceit. In his fourth film, Sirk is already developing his particular skill of making you both see the material solidity of society's pillars — the turgid statue of Bernick 'the benefactor', the objects that impede the camera's view on its travels around his room — and at the same time feel the fragility of their meaning: the statue is defaced, and scandal can destroy social position. The classical Tragedy would be Bernick's beloved son stowing away in one of his own unseaworthy ships. But the film gives as much space to the sailors' and fishermens' struggles precisely to avoid such danger, and with deadpan close-ups of their faces as Bernick is reunited with his boy, Sirk provides not a happy ending but a biting comment on the hypocritical individualism that sets caring for your own against caring about society; moreover, he shows how this ideology brings misery even to those who believe in it.

C.L. 1983

Raging Bull
(Martin Scorsese, 1980, US)

Beautifully shot, breathtakingly accurate, RAGING BULL goes still further into the territory Scorsese has mapped in all his films — men and male values; in this case through the story of 1949 middleweight champion Jake La Motta. De Niro's performance as the cocky young boxer who gradually declines into a pathetic fat slob forces you to question the rigid and sentimental codes of masculinity which he clings to even as they destroy him, like a drowning man clutching a lead weight. His blind jealousy of his wife, the pride and inability to communicate which keep him locked in a feud with his brother, are made literally unattractive as Jake himself becomes physically, as well as emotionally gross. Certain gestures are unforgettable: Jake fiddling in frustration with a TV set, the swagger round the ring after beating an opponent to pulp. The anti-realism of the fights — brilliantly shot and cut — prevents them sinking back into the narrative and instead creates a set of images which resound through Jake's personal confrontations: their smashing, story-less violence is relentlessly cut with domestic scenes until you learn to flinch in anticipation. This film does more than just make you think about how men act — it makes you *see* it.

T.O. 1981

The Reign of Naples
(Werner Schroeter, 1978, W. Germany/Italy)

Most films show people's personal lives as if they were outside history, and History as a dry document of political events. REIGN OF NAPLES breaks down this comfortable separation in its telling of history — Naples from 1944 to '69 — as everyday existence. And not, as in so many Italian art films (THE DAMNED for example) as the everyday existence of the upper middle class; Schroeter follows the lives of a few families in the poor quarter and shows us post-war Italy in the flesh. The young girl trying to keep her dignity and earn a living, her brother working for the Party, the woman whose daughter dies from lack of penicillin — all are shown with as much passion as if this were a romantic melodrama. In contrast, standard historical information is cursorily sketched in at intervals over shots of posters, documentary footage, old stills: standard images for 'History'. It is rare that politics is shown to be the substance of real life: this film achieves it.

T.O. 1981

Rocco and His Brothers
(Luchino Visconti, 1960, Italy/France)

The story of a southern family who have moved north to poverty in Milan, this seemed like Visconti's return, after SENSO and WHITE NIGHTS, to his earlier style of 'neo-realism' — that combination of social concern and natural settings which inspired many Italian films of the 1940s. But this film focuses more on the individual family, and the violent boxing-ring drama in which Rocco (Alain Delon) is caught, than on wider social conditions; and the black-and-white photography shares some of the lush visual texture of his less 'realist' work. It's a long, physical film, like THE LEOPARD, and like much of Visconti's work paints a social environment through a particular family's disintegration.

C.L. 1982

Saturday Night Fever
(John Badham, 1977, US)

With Italian-American social backdrop and fantastic soundtrack (a
sort of MEAN STREETS hits the dancefloor) what is really unusual
about this story of Brooklyn kid as disco hero is its physical portrayal
of male narcissism — one of the central features of Disco — through
visual technique. The use of camera in relation to John Travolta's
body produces the kind of fetishization (caressing pans over J.T.
reclining, near-naked; fragmentation of feet and hips in speedy disco
sequences) that is usually reserved for women — who can in this case
enjoy the position of voyeurs. I certainly did.

T.O. 1980

Sisters or The Balance of Happiness
(Margarethe von Trotta, 1979, W.Germany)

Made before THE GERMAN SISTERS, von Trotta's previous film also
centred on a sister relationship. Neither drama is just about family
relations, it is rather that the tension between sisters is used as a
charge for other conflicts: in GERMAN SISTERS between violent radicalism and reform, the sisters embodying two sides of the same choice. In
THE BALANCE OF HAPPINESS the choice is internal, since the three
women in the film can be seen as aspects of one person; and the issue
this time is the suppression of one's inner life in the name of work and
getting on in the world. Maria, the older sister, works as a super-
highpowered secretary, supporting the younger Anna, who while
dependent on Maria is also deeply resentful of her dominating
matter-of-fact values. The blatant contrast between the mechanized
efficiency of the one, and the quivering sensitivity of the other, is
sometimes rather irritating and too deliberately partitioned — but
maybe I speak as an older sister, rather than a critic. In fact, the
qualities are split three ways, as Miriam, a bouncy young typist who
befriends Maria, provides the element of fun and playfulness the other
two lack. After Anna's suicide and Miriam's rejection, Maria realizes
that she must make time to dream, and incorporate the other two into
herself. This psychological lesson is drawn so sharply that the

characters suddenly become too obviously symbolic; but the more general ambivalence between psychological allegory and realist drama creates an unease which is at once fascinating and disturbing.

C.L. 1983

Slow Motion (Sauve Qui Peut — La Vie)
(Jean-Luc Godard, 1980, Switzerland/France)

Primarily a narrative concerning a man and three women, this is the least formally experimental of Godard's films to date: the slow motion is an attractive but isolated feature. Four 'chapters' — the Imaginary, Fear, Commerce and Music — roughly correspond to different characters: Nathalie Baye's dream of leaving the city for the country (the Imaginary), Isabelle Huppert's prostitution (a tedious and exploitative metaphor for Commerce); but all the sections are pervaded by the Fear of a flailing male ego — threatened, not by women's independence, but by what it *sees* as women's independence. It would be a mistake to think that the film is in any way about *women*, whom Godard has always had difficulty in portraying other than as surfaces, reflecting male paranoia/desire. But no investigation of the male psyche can usefully begin with a nasty little smirk at homosexuality, as this does. The whole film is curiously insubstantial: an extended short. Billed as 'Godard's Latest', I would have loved to hear reactions had it been screened anonymously.

T.O. 1980

Snow White and the Seven Dwarfs
(Walt Disney, 1937, US)

One of the most fluid and graceful pieces of animation ever, Disney's first animated feature is still a real emotional puller for all ages. Its powerful good vs. evil plot combines with skilful drawing and effects to produce an almost expressionist drama, especially by use of light — the flying clouds and flashing lightning of the storm sequences — and darkness, the entry into the woods at night, where sounds have no source and disembodied eyes puncture the black. This sequence is presented subjectively, through Snow White's terror, and in the light of morning the woodland inhabitants are revealed as friendly; but the initial recognition of the fear they arouse prevents the habitual Disney view of Nature from completely sterilizing the harshness of the brothers Grimms' original. Snow White herself may be an all-American dream of a girl (very domesticated — looks after *seven* men) but she has an almost tactile charm of her own. Her animator, Grim Natwick, had previously worked on 'Betty Boop', but here initiated careful and lengthy drawing from film of a model: the result transcends the usual caricatured reduction of the human form, and produces a genuine delight in liveliness which is what makes animation like this great.

T.O. 1980

Song of Ceylon
(Basil Wright, 1934, GB)

Made by the GPO Film Unit under John Grierson, this is one of the outstanding examples of British documentary in the thirties, showing how film techniques, especially montage and use of sound, could radicalize even such a potentially unpromising project as a promotion film for the Empire Tea Marketing Board. In four parts, it sets out to depict the culture of Ceylon, and then to show the activities and effects of Western commercial enterprise. Without actually undermining the position of its producers in the tea trade, the film makes blatantly plain the relations of imperialist markets and colonial production, through striking sequences such as a series of dissolves between women tea-pickers in the fields of Ceylon, and the share price boards at the London stock exchange. This is one of the several documentaries of the period that attempted to show a world different from ours in its own right (sometimes that other world meant working-class life, as in Edgar Anstey's HOUSING PROBLEMS): the idea of bringing different experiences together through film was central to Grierson's notion of film-making as a unifying tool promoting social understanding in 'progressive democracy'.

C.L. 1981

'10'
(Blake Edwards, 1979, US)

Dudley Moore splashes out in a new role as Julie Andrews' sexually insecure partner, approaching middle age, who has a roving eye and rates girls out of ten (from a distance) — finding his dream (10) in Bo Derek. The film is an interesting update of the Hollywood Romantic Comedy: it provides all the reassurance of this genre through a classic moral plot of fantasy pursued/realized/exploded, sending Dudley back to the arms of his rightful mistress. Signs of the times, however, are found in both Julie Andrews' and Bo Derek's dialogues, which respectively employ the rhetoric of women's liberation and sexual liberation, and which, if taken seriously, would reveal Dudley's voyeuristic sexism for what it is. Instead, our hero's physical incompetence is used to represent sexual inadequacy through a string of slapstick gags, mistimings, etc. as director Blake Edwards lays on the kind of farce which is sometimes as funny as his earlier PINK PANTHER, but here serves to make sexism lovable.

T.O. 1980

Voyage to Italy
(Roberto Rossellini, 1953, Italy)

This film unfolds in the aching gap between a beautiful place laden with the past, and the tensions of the present, the faltering marriage of a couple who travel to Italy to deal with a relative's property. The details of distance in a 'close' relationship burn in black and white images and few words as intensely as the sharply sunned landscape, the parched buildings from another era, the cypresses black at mid-day. In the endless, still space between past and present the cramped partners start to move, first apart and then togther. It moves me too, to tears, every time.

C.L. 1982

The Woman in the Window
(Fritz Lang, 1944, US)

In this brilliant film noir Edward G. Robinson plays a homely, middle-aged professor who is drawn into a melodrama-mystery by meeting a woman who seems to be the living subject of a portrait he is obsessed with. Robinson's 'ordinariness', the plot's winding of fantasy into real events, and Lang's visual investment in detail, bring out most sharply the qualities of all his thrillers: a sense of danger lurking beneath the familiar surface of life, trivial fears and desires transformed into unfathomable, racing currents hemmed in by social frustrations whose fatalism appears cosmic.

C.L. 1982

Ways of Speaking

The last section of this book is made up not of 'writing' but of transcribed 'speaking' about films. Public discussion is, as I have suggested earlier, a crucial part of any lively film culture and the interviews and discussions (or parts of discussion) presented here are drawn from different media and situations which have one thing in common: they involve dialogue, they are all products of some kind of interaction. A large part of the critic's job is, in fact, talking with other people: on television, at conferences, workshops and festivals, interviewing film personnel, taking part in debates and speaking directly to audiences, often alongside movies themselves. This section is intended as a reminder of that often ephemeral, but none the less important, dimension of film criticism.

Interviews

Interviewing is in many ways a strange situation. You have to give your interviewee space to say what they want, but at the same time, interviews which are merely vehicles for a director's or actor's opinions are usually not all that fascinating without some contextualization or commentary from the writer/interviewer. It is sometimes quite hard to strike a balance between making one's own points, and letting the interviewee talk freely about their work — and then to write up the whole thing as part article, part question-and-answer. The two examples here both use an interview as part of a broader feature, without — I hope — entirely swamping the film-maker's speech.

Who Is Truth? What Is S/He?

An Interview with Frederick Wiseman

Every year at our school concert the Juniors were allowed two songs on stage and were then marched off, round the back of the building and into a musty hall to watch a film. A fiction film would have been too like pleasure, so it was always a documentary. Documentary film was obviously meant to be educational — which is why it felt like a punishment, a penance, sitting on the bare floorboards watching black and white (not even *colour*!) images, our ears automatically cutting off the solemn Home Service male voice which accompanied them.

If you don't encounter documentaries at school, you find them on TV: men with urgent voices speaking over starving children or urban violence, men with reassuring voices speaking over zebras galloping in slow motion. This may sound silly, but what is really bizarre is the category 'documentary' itself: the films it classifies range from travelogues — 'Look at Life' stuff — to heavy propaganda, like Leni Riefenstahl's Nazi OLYMPIAD. The only thing documentaries appear to have in common is that they are non-fiction. This suggests that they are somehow 'true' while fiction films are 'stories'. However, what documentaries really have in common is not so much truth, as the *idea* that they are true. Where a voice-over accompanies the images (the standard TV style), it's fairly clear that, however 'objective' the voice sounds, it does have a point of view.

It's much harder to grasp what a film is 'saying' when there's no commentary at all. This is what Frederick Wiseman's films are like.

His documentaries consist of images with the sound and dialogue from the actual event, no voice-over or added music. They all deal with institutions: HOSPITAL, HIGH SCHOOL, WELFARE, JUVENILE COURT, and so on. Wiseman himself started off as a lawyer and teacher of criminal law: he used to take his students on visits to places like law courts and prisons, so they could see where they would be sending convicted offenders, and how these institutions worked. His film-making is like a direct extension of these trips: his first film, TITICUT FOLLIES, was shot in a State Hospital for the Criminally Insane, and was banned by the US Supreme Court. The film contains no 'comment', so the authorities' anger and censorship hinged on what the film *showed*: the struggles of inmates to preserve their dignity under degrading, often brutal, conditions. The social comment implied by the material is made all the more powerful precisely *because* it stands without commentary.

Wiseman's second film, HIGH SCHOOL (1968), was the one which first brought him critical acclaim. It was shot in a large, mainly white and middle-class high school in Philadelphia. 'The only criteria within the choice of an institution is that it's thought to be a good one. In the sense that it's not a sitting duck target. I didn't make a film on so-called inner-city schools, black schools, because everybody knew they were horrible. With a middle-class high school you could see what the blacks were aspiring to — and it turns out to be straight situation comedy.'

The comedy is pretty grim. In an interview with the Dean of Discipline, a boy explains that he has been given a detention through a misunderstanding. The Dean tells him to take the detention anyway, because 'We are out to establish that you can be a man and that you can take orders'. A girl is hauled up on the day of the School Prom and told that she is being 'offensive to the whole class' by not wearing a long dress. As we see students repeatedly humiliated and harrassed, the staff clearly feel they are doing a good job: the film's presentation is therefore ironic. A gym-full of girls in baggy knickers drill in almost army fashion to the pop song 'Simon Says': a sequence which works as a metaphor for the school ethos.

The material is never too crudely subordinated to one point of view. In an English class a young teacher uses Simon and Garfunkel to discuss poetry: as she plays the music, rows of weary kids stare vacantly, and a close-up shot of the tape disc going round and round suggests how even 'innovative' teaching becomes just part of the same old boredom. It's not presented as the teachers' *fault* that the school is so repressive: what is shown is a repressive society, especially through the parents. One girl's mother, present at a telling-off, says, 'The main thing in our home has always been respect for an adult. To me, one of the worst offences is being disrespectful to an older person. Regardless of what the condition might be.'

The film ends on Graduation day with the Principal reading a letter from a graduate in Vietnam who wants to leave his GI insurance to the school if he's killed. He writes that he is 'only a body doing a job', and thanks his teachers for all they've done for him. 'Now when you get a letter like this,' says the Principal, 'to me it means that we are very successful at Northeast High School.'

BASIC TRAINING is like a sequel to HIGH SCHOOL: it charts the course of a group of boys in the Vietnam draft. Again, without overt comment, we are offered a critical view of the process whereby these kids are methodically dehumanized from the moment they lose their civilian clothes and their heads are shaved, while their ID cards punch out of a machine in lines: another example of Wiseman's use of juxtaposition to make a point.

One boy who can't keep in step properly tries to commit suicide; the chaplain comments 'that doesn't sound like somebody who's really trying to get to the top, does it?' Gradually through the film the boys 'progress' from lessons on how to clean their teeth, to how to bayonet a Vietcong. At the final graduation ceremony, the speeches ring with irony, as the boy soldiers march in perfect step before proud parents.

Although they are 'non-fiction', Wiseman's most successful films, like these two, do tell a story, as we follow kids *through* particular institutions: this is perhaps also true in JUVENILE COURT, HOSPITAL or WELFARE, where people confront institutions from the outside. The boundaries between 'fact' and 'fiction' are not so obvious as they first seem: 'From my point of view these are consciously created fictions, because they are completely arbitrary. They aren't fictional in the sense that the events are staged — but the organization is completely fictional.'

However, Wiseman also claims 'I don't start from any particular ideological premise. I know next to nothing about these places before I start . . . The shooting of the film is really the research. I think it's important that the final film reflects what you have learned as a consequence of making the film rather than simply imposing a pre-conceived ideological view of the material. Otherwise, why make a film? Why not just say high schools suck, or doctors are all bad?'

Wiseman says various conflicting things about how much he is actually 'putting across' in his films. Nobody could possibly start off without any ideological premise: when his films work, they are giving a political view, but seem not to be; the ones that don't work also seem not to be, and *aren't*. This explains why many of the later films are much less effective: they are *genuinely* ambiguous. MANOEUVRE and SINAI FIELD MISSION are both about the US army, but unlike BASIC TRAINING they don't show it doing anything to anyone.

MANOEUVRE follows an army field practice in Germany, but it could easily be a publicity film made for the army itself, since it just shows army life — soldiers chatting, arguing, tanks, helicopters. SINAI FIELD MISSION, the portrait of a US monitoring force isolated deep in the Sinai desert, also shows the army from the inside rather than in terms of what it's *doing*. Questioned about this, Wiseman says that the institutions he has filmed function partly as metaphors for American society and that this is the perfect microcosm: 'In a sense it is pure because you have 160 Americans plopped down in the middle of the desert and they are creating an American small town and that's what interested me about it. It isn't meant to be an analysis of America's role in the Sinai desert but rather what kind of life a group of Americans have established in the middle of a desert.' A statement like that shows the limits of this kind of documentary: it's like Brecht's famous comment that a photograph of the Krupp arms factory reveals nothing of the relations within and around it. For example, Wiseman's MEAT could equally be propaganda for an abattoir, or a vegetarian exposé. It simply *shows* meat production.

Wiseman suggests that documentary is more effective when a view is not just imposed, 'on top' of the footage. 'I'm trying to use film in a way that is particular to film. Frequently with the traditional TV documentary, you might as well be reading it.'

It's this quality which tends to make documentaries fit that school stereotype: it's no coincidence they slotted so easily into the atmosphere of the lecture hall. (If only they'd shown us HIGH SCHOOL!)

The problem is not that documentaries are educational, which they are, but that 'education' tends to mean not letting people think. Wiseman treats the viewer, in his best films, as though s/he *will* think about what they see: 'The assumption, correct or not, is that the audience has that capacity — because the only safe assumption to make about the audience is that they are as smart or dumb as the film-maker.'

T.O. 13 March 1981

Prisoner of Love

An interview with Martin Scorsese

RAGING BULL provoked such controversy when previewed in 1981 that Rank, the distributor, initially refused to open it. This feature, written in collaboration with my colleague Don Macpherson, was first published under the title 'A Sense of Outrage'.

RAGING BULL is hardly likely to win Martin Scorsese the Sensitive Male Film-Maker of the Year award. It has already aroused much hostility. A picture about a strutting, obsessive boxing champion whose every gesture seems to embody all that the modern liberation-seeker casts out in disgust, a picture with repeated scenes of almost unbearable violence, appears to offer little to the Caring Person, the Concerned About Relationships, those striving to avoid the nastier aspects of masculinity in themselves or others. For here they are, flung at your face, those unfashionable qualities like rage, jealousy, paranoia, and also blind desire. But do liberating films have to show liberated people?

Talking of liberated men, Jake La Motta (Robert De Niro), the boxing hero of RAGING BULL, certainly *isn't*. La Motta was 'The Bronx Bull', the 1949 middleweight champion who later fell from grace: a nightclub owner in Miami, he was sent to jail for allowing juvenile prostitutes on the premises, and wound up in the Bronx as a strip-club comic, where he recited speeches from Shakespeare to Tennessee Williams. (One of his favourites was Marlon Brando's famous confession from ON THE WATER-FRONT: 'I coulda been a contender, Charlie. . .'). As a fighter he was famed for having an unusually thick skull.

In a central scene from the film, Jake is in his living room with his brother, trying to get a picture on the TV. His wife Vikki is upstairs. As he messes with the faulty set, Jake's huge, powerful body is useless, and his pent-up frustration builds at this thing he can't make work by hitting — like his home life.

Confronted with something too complex to be bent to his will in the only way he knows, Jake goes berserk on a quite different tack. His suspicions rise to an accusation of his brother: 'You fucked my wife? You fucked my wife?' 'You ask me that, your own brother? You expect me to answer that?' Both are outraged with a sentimental concern for their own pride that's peculiarly masculine. Jake goes upstairs to his wife. His insane jealousy takes the form of both physical obsession with what he imagines to have happened — 'You sucked his cock?' — and physical revenge. In the culmination of the episode he beats up both his wife and his brother.

The success of RAGING BULL in *not* just showing more male violence lies in the fact that the TV-set build-up is inseparable from the whole sequence, and creates, not the sense of Jake's strength, but of his impotence. When, in another scene, Vikki observes idly that a young contender has a pretty face, Jake can't rest until he's knocked the boy's nose halfway to his ear, in one of the film's most brutal boxing scenes: 'He ain't pretty no more.' But again, instead of power we feel the inadequacy of using the ring to work out a paranoid personal obsession.

These connections and comparisons between feelings and images are aided by the black-and-white photography, the slow motion, and the *lack* of realism (contrary to the publicity) in the fights: a film in the more familiar colour, told like a realistic story, might perhaps glorify what the more formalistic RAGING BULL presents as contradictory.

For, although Jake sounds like one big shit so far, what should we make of the film's very tender love scenes? After Jake has beaten up Vikki and his brother in the scene described above, he enters the bedroom to apologize as she's packing to leave. When he finally stops saying sorry and touches her, she lets the pile of clothes drop from her arm and turns to him . . . This sensual scene of *mutual* physical passion prevents their relationship being reduced to one of simple oppression.

Jake himself cannot be reduced either, simply to an example of how not to be. Like so many of Scorsese's heroes, his masculinity is in crisis, riven by explosive passions and impossible desires. Jake La Motta is literally a tragic figure; for the same thing which makes him great — his body — can destroy him.

The crucial role played by his body in the meaning of RAGING BULL is shown by the fact that De Niro put on sixty pounds for the film's latter sequences, ruining his own physique in the process. With its central character fundamentally inarticulate, the film, like La Motta, has to find physical forms of expression. Jake's painful destruction through his own frustrated energies is *felt* as he hurls himself against the walls of his prison cell; the poignancy of his clumsy passion for his wife is *visible* in the love scene where his bloated, lumbering body is a parody of its former beauty (seen in slow motion in his leopard-skin dressing-gown) or its hideous destructiveness (pummelling an opponent's face to pulp).

Scorsese himself is no tough guy ('I don't punch people in the face. I'm too short, and I can't run — I've got asthma. So I talk my way out of things, I guess.') Asked about the presentation of masculinity in the film, he said, 'The film's the complete opposite of macho. The essence of it is that we *are* macho . . . but it's a matter of turning it inside out. Bobby and I never really intended to do that kind of thing, but we did it by doing this inside thing that we know. We did it as honestly as we know how. There's no point in doing anything else.

'At a certain point in your life you realize something's there that's part of your background, part of your make-up. That you *can't deny*. You have to be honest with that. You have to deal with what are called the "negative" aspects. You have to claw your way through them. Maybe, if there is a criticism to be made, it's too negative. People are always saying I'm too hard on myself. Maybe so. I feel something from making this picture that closes off a whole area, and that's that. . .

'Emotionally it's very difficult for me to go on doing things like RAGING BULL. People say, "It's only a movie". But it's not that. It happens to be a movie, because that's the way you're expressing it. It could be a painting or the way you make a sandwich. So I'm not asking anyone to go and sit through my primal situation. That's what it's about. They should know that's what they're gonna be in for.'

This may be what they're in for, but it's all too comfortable to dismiss a film like RAGING BULL, or perhaps especially films like MEAN STREETS and TAXI DRIVER, by seeing their disturbing qualities as the film-maker's hangups. Much has been written about Scorsese's background (raised in New York's Little Italy, could have been a gangster but wanted to be a priest), but the feelings and conflicts he shows in his films aren't confined to him, and must touch a raw nerve in most audiences. There has been little serious criticism of his work which confronts *what* he is dealing with — perhaps because it is something too close to home. Why has RAGING BULL aroused such indignant moral criticism? Why was NEW YORK, NEW YORK a box-office flop?

Unlike RAGING BULL, NEW YORK, NEW YORK focuses not on one man, but on the relationship between a man and a woman (De Niro and Liza Minnelli) in a way that is strikingly honest. The gradual transition from De Niro's insistent demand for the woman he wants, to his desire to escape from a relationship which he finds restrictive, his babyish attitudes, his inability to *understand* what he feels — all these are shown in relation to another person: the woman who at first resists him but becomes increasingly unhappy and dependent as he withdraws, finally regaining her own energy and ambition as their relationship collapses. It's a depressing picture, but a familiar one. And it's the accuracy of so many gestures, conflicts, phrases, that strikes below the belt. As Minnelli lies in hospital after having the baby he doesn't want, De Niro comes in, fucked up, lost (how about her?) and cries on her lap — demanding, even at this stage when he's drawing away from her, that he be the only baby, filling the centre stage.

So why are these films often criticized not as 'films' — since they're brilliantly made — but on the 'moral' grounds that Scorsese has a yen for Macho, that in nakedly showing certain attitudes he is somehow advocating them? The only film where this point may be valid is TAXI DRIVER, where the murkier side of masculinity gets way out of control. The most violent image in it is not cinematic, but verbal, and is spoken by Scorsese himself, playing the cameo role of a jealous husband in the back of a cab threatening vengeance on his unfaithful wife: 'Did you ever see what a .44 can do to a woman's pussy, cabbie? I'm going to put it right up to her, cabbie. Right in her, cabbie. . .' Reactions to the horror of that scene are so ambivalent that even years later Scorsese is still surprised: 'A lot of famous guys come over to me and say "I love it when you say that line". . . It's amazing. I'm embarrassed, because it slipped out by accident.'

It hardly needs to be said that this is horrible and deeply shocking. RAGING BULL also is packed with possessive, violent and belittling attitudes towards women. But the film makes you *see* these, and gives an insight into the central male character that could never be produced if such things were suppressed. Should films show the world as it ought to be or as it is? For what seems to be demanded more and more nowadays by those with ideals of liberation is a cinema of the superego: as if to make a 'sensitive' or 'progressive' film now, you have to show people *being* sensitive and progressive. There is a scene in Alain Tanner's JONAH WHO WILL BE 25 IN THE YEAR 2000 (a film packed with sensitive post-marxist men and terribly pretty women) in which two men have a conversation as they peel potatoes in a kitchen. An invisible arrow points from the corner of the frame: 'This is how you should be . . . This film is not chauvinist and oppressive because we show the men peeling the potatoes. . .' It's presented so smugly, so righteously, that in watching the film some of its ideological soundness actually seems to rub off on its viewers. You *feel* progressive.

But it is also *repressive*, this desire for cleaned-up images of oneself and the world. Change certainly doesn't come through denial, even though it feels comfortably non-sexist to watch two women hitch-hike

round Switzerland doing nothing, or a left-handed one sitting round
the house looking elegiacally serene for no apparent reason. Cleaning
up the screen doesn't necessarily help anyone clean up their act: it's
precisely repression, a refusal to face things, that produces violence —
as in RAGING BULL. It's no wonder that so many movies now seem to
offer one of two choices: either exploiting mindless male aggression for
easy shock value, or subduing it, neutering it, pretending it just
doesn't exist. Those things which 'slip out' in Scorsese's films may not
be fashioned by him into a deliberately moral shape, but they do force
you to confront unpleasant and awkward realities in yourself.

Pauline Kael has said that Scorsese confuses cinema with church.
But despite his Calvinist scriptwriter (Paul Schrader), Scorsese's
religious mode isn't the puritan ideal, it's the Confessional: dig deep
for it, churn it out, tell it in sinful and erotic detail. Instead of judging
what comes out, his films focus on the energy itself; and, moving out of
the realm of right and wrong, they show how that energy can either
celebrate or destroy.

'That repressed energy eventually has to come out. It may go the
wrong way (Scorsese bursts into laughter) . . . but it's not a good way
to be to yourself. Bresson in DIARY OF A COUNTRY PRIEST says God is
our torturer, but wants us to be merciful with ourselves. He's right.
But I wish I could live that way.'

Instead of drawing spiritual conclusions though, Scorsese invests
spirit into everyday events, sometimes through sex, but always
through music. Every film he's made has had the quality of a musical,
not with the trappings of chorus lines and song-and-dance routines,
but in its essence: charging the most mundane events of a hateful daily
life with motion, energy and passion. Walking down the street,
catching the subway, hanging out in a bar, take on the electric
intensity of desire. Even moments like getting up or going to sleep —
in MEAN STREETS, a man moves his head off the pillow and you hear
the crashing opening drum-beats of the Ronettes' 'Be My Baby'.
'They just say "watch out" . . . musical, mad, mad opera, crazy . . .
but that's the way it is. . .' We're a long way from the bland
withdrawal from daily rhythms in, say, a Wim Wenders movie —
which isn't so much a musical as a vacuum pack.

Maybe it's coincidence, but Travis the psycho in TAXI DRIVER just
doesn't listen to music. 'The sense of the first shots of TAXI DRIVER
(yellow cab moving through New York streets at night) came out of
listening to "T.B. Sheets" by Van Morrison. We wanted it fading in
and out of the whole picture with lines like. . . "foreign bodies" . . .
"steppin' out" . . . "turn up the radio, turn up the radio" . . . "Gotta

go" . . . just slipping in and out like a dream. That's how I got the first image. Then I realized I couldn't do it, because Travis wouldn't listen to music.'

So what's at stake in all this? Just nostalgia for adolescent frenzy? A possibility Scorsese admits when he says 'Oh god, it seems as if I'm stuck in a period of around 1961 to 1964'. Maybe MEAN STREETS really is just a punk's AMERICAN GRAFFITI, anguish and despair set in motion to those oldies but goodies, the Marvelettes, the Shirelles, the Miracles, the Chantells. But apart from wondering why Scorsese just gets music that's so much *better* into his movies, it boils down to this: his people cling on to music and dreams — anything which will save them from the imminent prospect of drowning. They move through these things, sharing a common language of emotions and problems, but it doesn't help solve them. Cut off from that dream they lose the craziness and longing that make life liveable; but with it, their every action is a mystery to them, illogical and inexplicable. As in La Motta's favourite song 'Prisoner of Love', they're trapped by the very thing that inspires them. And without figuring why they just go round in circles.

Scorsese: 'What's interesting is that a very, very famous American rock musician . . . poet, turned to Robbie Robertson when he said I was going to record THE LAST WALTZ on film, and said "What's Scorsese doing it for? All he does is make pictures about how women fuck over men." I mean the guy who said this is extremely . . . he's one of the greats (reverential stare and tone of awe of the unnamable — it could only be Dylan he had in mind). But the point is I don't do that.'

Us: 'And there we were thinking how they were about how men fuck over women.'

Scorsese: 'Yeah. I mean it's much more complicated than that.'

T.O. 20 February 1981

Discussions

Of all the many discussions I have participated in at conferences, at festivals, and on television, few have been transcribed; so the selection of material here has been determined largely by what was available. In order to keep the flavour of the original interactions, I have deliberately refrained from editing out the 'spoken' style.

Body Horror

This was a contribution to an item on contemporary horror films —
'Body Horror' — produced by Paul Kerr for Channel Four's *Media
Show* in 1988. The questions were asked by Louis Heaton, the item's
researcher. Only parts of the interview were used in the final TV
version but I was given the entire transcript and with only minor
editing it is reproduced here. It draws on ideas also found in this book
in discussions of 'Symptoms' and in the programming project on
Epidemic Cinema.

LH: How would you describe the genre known as Body Horror and when do you
think it started?

JW: Well, you can see a very particular change in horror movies round
the late seventies. A good marker of this can be found in John
Carpenter's work. HALLOWEEN, which he made in 1978, has a scene
where the main characters, the children, watch the 1951 version of
THE THING on telly on Halloween night. Now it's interesting that the
first version of THE THING is a horror movie where you barely see the
monster at all. It occasionally appears in silhouette in doorways, it's a
very exteriorized figure, there are almost no close-ups of its features.
HALLOWEEN, in which you see that glimpse of the old THING, is also a
film where you barely see the monster, you hardly even see his face
close up, there's almost no blood and gore, it's very much a suspense
thriller whose scariness is about timing and chasing.

Then only four years later, in '82, Carpenter himself has remade

THE THING and in that film the emphasis is almost entirely on the kind of gore, the blood, the entrails, the stuff that can come out of people, and even the camera functions really differently. I think it's partly a change in the content of horror films but also a shift in how they deal with showing things or looking at things.

In the 1951 THING the camera sets up spaces — usually communal spaces, men in a community playing ping pong and so on — it sets up a space into which the monster intrudes. For a few moments you see the monster in a doorway or the monster coming down a corridor, but it's always hovering around or moving *into* the space that the camera has set up, a shared space that the monster's invading. In the later THING what you have is a very different relationship between the camera, the monster and the viewer. You have things like some blood on the snow and the camera gets in really close up and tracks along the blood and you're wondering all the time how close it's going to go, when you're going to see the thing that left the blood. It's the camera itself that moves in to show you things; the camera moves in on the scene of horror rather than the thing which is horrible moving into the space of the camera.

That's one element which has changed, and I'm stressing it because the emphasis is on showing and seeing which is different from the sort of suspense horror film like HALLOWEEN, which is more about movement and surprise. In a sense with Body Horror there isn't so much a surprise; you know you're going to see something horrible and the only question is how horrible will it be, how far will it go, how many maggots can crawl out of somebody's stomach, how many horrible things can rupture out of whatever it is, you know, how much skin can come off somebody's body and they still stand up? Those kind of questions. And then going back to how you would define Body Horror or what's different about it: the phrase Body Horror, which I think was coined in *Screen* magazine, is basically used for films where you go *inside* the body, the boundaries of the body are broken. While traditional horror films do usually have a monster, it has an enclosed exterior. It may be absolutely hideous and revolting — in the original version of THE FLY there's a moment where the cloth comes off the head and you see that the guy has a fly's head and that's meant to be really horrible — but I would argue that even in those kinds of films, even in, say, a Dracula film or films with horrible figures in them, the figure has boundaries, the figure is an entity. In Body Horror you get the opening up of the figure, everything comes out, so it is quite literally breaking the bounds of the body.

I would say if you have to take a moment in film where Body Horror arrives in a big way it's the moment in ALIEN where the alien bursts through John Hurt's stomach — the ultimate rupturing of the flesh.

LH: **Why would you say there has been a shift towards this particular kind of explicit showing of the body in horror films?**

JW: Well I think this particular shift in films goes alongside an awful lot of other shifts which are happening in society. The most obvious thing you can link it to is a focus on the body in general, it's a political point really: people's sense of control has become so limited that it almost ends with the boundaries of their body. The obsession with health, health foods, jogging, looking after yourself, keeping fit, aerobics, all those trends, I'm not saying they're bad but they make it seem as if the only thing you could really *change* in life was your own body. And if it starts to seem that the only thing you can improve, the only thing you can work on, the only thing you can really deal with is just your own body, you could say that's a kind of privatization, if public interest and concern have closed in so narrowly. It's a form of individualism, if you like. At the same time you can see that commercially, the body's become the focus of a new consumerism, in terms of products an enormous growth industry in the last fifteen years has been things for the body, stuff to put on the body, stuff for inside and outside the body. Within that sort of commercialization and commodification of the body, you also have a proliferation of *imagery* — particularly advertising imagery — which fragments the body, takes it apart. That's something you can see changing across time very clearly in things like women's magazines. In the fifties you would have an ad for lipstick showing the whole figure of a woman or at least her whole face, looking glamorous, wearing the lipstick, and so forth, but by the time you get to the late sixties and seventies you're starting to see just a mouth cut off from any body and this kind of taking apart of the body publicly seems to me linked, though not directly, with the issues in Body Horror films. They've grown up alongside this relentless focus on the body, on *bits* of it, on how it's put together or how you can put it together yourself and how you can deal with it or fail to deal with it. It's all part of something much wider.

LH: **Could you explain very briefly what the main dramatic concerns were say of fifties horror movies and why they might have shifted in the last few decades towards this individualization and the concern of the body?**

JW: Yes, well, one thing about fifties horror films is that they're very concerned with the community, a lot of them take place within communities. The original BODY SNATCHERS is a very good example, it all takes place in a small town. Then again, the original THING was produced by Howard Hawks who's very much into male communities in his Westerns, or in a film like ONLY ANGELS HAVE WINGS. His production of THE THING is really, on one level, all about these guys hanging out on their own in the arctic or antarctic wherever it is, and how they relate to each other. In all those fifties films there's the sense of the community which may be invaded, very often by something from outer space, and people have, maybe rather crudely but I think with some reason, linked those kinds of horror films with cold war fears. But more specifically, there's a fear of a kind of mental invasion in a lot of those films and I think that goes with concerns about brain washing, about identity — but still within a framework of *social* identity.

Not only are the fifties horror films much more concerned with communities, they also tend to have more *global* concerns. In the original THING they talk about atomic reactions, about the bomb, they constantly go on about mankind, the future of humanity, about saving the planet and that kind of thing. In the original FLY, the backdrop of the institution the scientist works for, the Ministry of Air or whatever it's called, means there's always the sense of a social setting and of some wider, almost political concerns. In the Body Horror films you get down to individual bodies and it's as if identity is defined as *being* the body, the self *is* the body, and it's much more common in those films to be removed from any kind of social setting. ALIEN is quite interesting because it is a community, but it's like a microcosm right out of the way from everything else and in the end it really comes down to a one-to-one battle between the Sigourney Weaver figure and the alien. So these individual, one-to-one battles, as opposed to the community struggle for existence, seem to be much more current. There are other differences as well just in terms of filming which I've already mentioned. A different way of using the camera, a different way of tantalizing. I think all horror films tantalize, but I think contemporary horror films tantalize in a different way in relation to how much you can bear to look at, literally, it's like how much glug can ooze out of something, and that's different from suspense, which is like, how long can you wait?

LH: What are the social and political forces that might have helped shape that shift from the fifties community to the concern of the individual in the eighties, the concern with the body?

JW: Well it seems to me clear to anyone who looks at our culture, Western culture in general, or say British and American culture to be more precise, that there has been a general shift away from concerns about community, the public, the social, the welfare state. You now have things like Mrs Thatcher saying that the social doesn't exist, there is no such thing as society, only a collection of individuals, now she actually said that. I don't think one should necessarily look at these kinds of things as cause and effect, but if you see alongside a speech like that, — her 'There are only individuals' speech — some of the movies that we're talking about where in a sense there is only the body, only the self as incarnate in one individual body and no real sense of a social self, you *can* see those two things going together. I don't think it's cause and effect, and I don't think in terms of the films I would say this is bad, or feel a kind of nostalgia for a different kind of *movie*, but I do think that the things you can see happening — returning to issues around health and the individual body as a focus of one's aims and aspirations — all that seems to me to have a political dimension, and I do think it's a problem.

LH: **How much of a part would you think the increasing sophistication of special effects would have contributed to this Body Horror?**

JW: I think the special effects issue is quite interesting because you can take a sort of technicist argument and say, well, because special effects have developed so phenomenally these things are possible, but the more interesting question is, well, *why* have they been developed, why did the wish for them to be developed come about? And that comes back to looking at this particular trend in horror films which I think nobody can fully explain or find one simple reason for, but which does seem to go with other kinds of social shifts and other kinds of perceptions and concerns. There's a lot of talk at the moment about disintegration, people talk socially about disintegration. I mean, you can't open a serious newspaper without people talking about the breakdown of consensus which in a sense is also the breakdown of community. There's also a lot of talk on the left about a new fragmentation in politics — usually presented as a good thing politically, people have conferences about 'difference' and 'identity politics' — different groups of people are meant to pursue their own interests and so on. But whether it's seen as positive or negative, the word fragmentation does seem to come back again and again in serious political talk, and in a metaphorical or at least slightly oblique way, I'd link it with Body Horror, a falling apart of things, a sense of things coming open and disintegrating in some way.

LH: **Why would you say the body has become such a central theme of eighties movies or an eighties issue?**

JW: Well as I've said, you can certainly see that in our particular time the body is a focus of people's attention, and you see this not only in Body Horror films but in the kind of flip-side to them which is the type of FAME, SATURDAY NIGHT FEVER, FLASHDANCE perfect-body-movie where the bounds of the body are important in a different way. The whole trend in health, aerobics, the fitness boom, is quite closely linked with movies, I mean all that wearing of leg warmers and *Kids from Fame*-type gear as if you were about to leap into song in the street. Body Horror films are like the other side of it. Instead of the perfect, perfectly enclosed body — the kind of narcissistic body of a Kid from Fame — you have the sort of reverse narcissism of a horribly opened up individual body, with all the imperfect yuk and glug inside it. If you see those two things together you can see that one is like a defence against the other and that in a way they function together. I've already said that there's a trend which has taken place over a longer period when the body has been a growth area for industry — the commercial success of something like the Body Shop is a good example — but also things like dance studios and gyms have been some of the great business success stories of our time. When you look at the closing in of public health concerns and the frenetic interest in activities like jogging and then you also look at Body Horror films and you look at the films like FLASHDANCE and FAME, altogether you have a major economic and cultural configuration. I wouldn't want to say which bit of that causes another bit because I don't think it's that simple, but you can see that all those things happen together and have a range of mutual effects.

LH: In terms of what you've just said about the Fame/Flashdance type of films, what do you think is shown by the kind of images that are presented in Body Horror movies, is there a common theme between some of them?

JW: Well, the common theme at its broadest is that kind of yukky stuff about the body, but if you think about what yukky stuff about the body means for many people, it's sex. It's also to do with illness, sickness, any kind of operation upon the body by which I don't only mean what happens in hospital. It's about ageing and death which is where the body obviously quite literally becomes a material object and disintegrates back into the earth, so all those things are called up by what appears as yukkiness. It's also something very material, on quite a profound level — I mean almost a kind of philosophical materialism.

Fifties horror films are very moral. They usually have a very clear message of one kind or another, they're very much about humanity and mankind, their word not mine, and so on. Body Horror is not *im*moral, it's as if it's *a*moral. It really is just about showing. Now that isn't necessarily something I would call bad, in that there is a material dimension to one's body and to the world which is on one level, just *stuff*. These films seem to be really setting out to deal with it *as* just stuff in a neither good nor bad way, in a way that's maybe frightening but not weighted with any very clear human messages, to use a rather old-fashioned phrase. So they're partly about materiality and the fact that the body is matter, it is cells, it is a whole bunch of material stuff that you can't fully control, it does get diseases, it does ultimately die, that's one thing that happens to everybody. They seem to be dealing with those issues, but in a specifically physical way and not in a way that seeks to find some moral or purpose. I'm being careful not to weight either of those positions because I don't think it is a value judgment issue. I think the imagery itself, returning to the idea of yukky feelings about the body, is very revealing. I mean you don't have to be deeply into psychoanalysis to figure out that some of that, for most people, is to do with sex, and one of the strong features that a lot of the imagery in these Body Horror films has in common is that it is very sexual imagery. It's often a sort of strange combination of male and female imagery, like when the monster comes out of the stomach in ALIEN for example, it's a kind of phallic thing, it suddenly thrusts up in a very obviously phallic way. At the same time it's like a grotesque birth, it breaks out from the belly, you get a combination of what you could call very different kinds of sexual imagery, running right across gender.

LH: **Could you expand on the last point, the way a lot of these films have a combination of the phallic image and a birth image.**

JW: Well, there's been a lot written about the particular kind of imagery in films like, say, ALIEN and ALIENS and the way it relates to some extent to the fear of women's bodies. I'm going to say this very simply so it may sound crude, but the Freudian notion of a child's, particularly a boy's, fear or anxiety aroused by a woman's body because it does not have a phallus, doesn't have a penis, raises a whole set of ideas which I think are quite useful in looking at these films. They are very much about anxiety about women's bodies, a lot of the sense of yukkiness in them concerns things opening up. The film POLTERGEIST constantly has children being horrifically drawn down tunnels, almost as if they're being pulled back into the womb in some way, by a monstrous, reincorporating mother. The monster-full-of-tunnels-and-holes in ALIEN, its sort of globby eating up of things — even more so in ALIENS which uses eating-up imagery a *lot* — that's obviously a kind of sexual image and it can be analyzed in those psychoanalytic terms. For me though there's a broader thing which is how in a quite interesting way the imagery combines male and female, I've already mentioned the scene in ALIEN where the phallic thing leaps out as if it was a birth, but in many more of these films, genderized sexual imagery's collapsed together and I think perhaps that's what makes it particularly powerful.

The other interesting thing is that these films are focusing on a disgust about sex, in tandem with an obsessive but very antiseptic focus on sex in other public imagery. A very cleaned up but at the same time very voyeuristic stress on sex. The *idea* of sex is constantly present in our culture in a way that hasn't actually been true for all cultures and for all moments in history. And yet there are very strong fears and taboos about sex itself. The tension between a cleaned up version of the body and of sexuality and an anxiety about, fear of, what has been cleaned up or what may still be there, is expressed in lots of these films. In ALIEN you have a really interesting contrast between the yukky, messy birth image and the kind of mechanical or, well, not mechanical but scientific 'wombs' at the very beginning when all the space team are in very neat, clean, ordered pods — like a perfect, non-female, non-sexualized womb. At the end, as well, Sigourney Weaver is on her own in this sort of perfectly sealed capsule once she's ejected the alien from it, it's the last in a string of scientific, cleaned up images of bodily enclosure. Sigourney Weaver herself always seems rather squeaky-clean, and both ALIEN and ALIENS seem to need the figure of a woman who's the all-American type, nothing messy about her, you don't easily think of her in any way connected with the mucky side of sex, and she is set against this repeatedly globby, oozy sort of imagery. So you could almost see in ALIEN and ALIENS a splitting, a separating out of things that may appear frightening or unpleasant about women's bodies, hiving them off from the woman herself, Sigourney Weaver, the ultimately clean American female type, onto the endlessly pulsating, soft, slippery, gaping monster.

LH: So how — how might audiences actually perceive these films? Are they able to appreciate the subtleties you've been talking about or is the point simply to shock them and give them a cheap thrill?

JW: The question of audiences is really important, though not so much in terms of that old argument of are audiences really stupid, do they understand what the films are about on a deeper level. Of course audiences aren't stupid, but I think two issues are raised by that. One is about genre. The horror film is a very particular genre, i.e. a type of film with very specific concerns and structures which an audience that goes to it is familiar with, knows what it's getting, knows what it's expecting. This is a wider issue but what's happening in Hollywood, in mainstream cinema right now, seems to me partly to do with a very strong emphasis on particular genres with particular audiences, and the audience for many of these films is very much a young audience. That's something else about contemporary horror films that you don't get quite so strongly in the fifties — the way that these are horror films speaking to young people.

The average audience age for horror films is something like between 15 and 25, and having talked a bit about sexual imagery, the moments of horror in a very large number of these films come about through early sexual experiences or so called promiscuous sexual experiences. In NIGHTMARE ON ELM STREET, what's happening? The parents are away, kids go to bed with each other, awful things happen. Look at HALLOWEEN, what's happening? In fact who is the girl in HALLOW-EEN that actually masters the whole situation? The one who doesn't have boyfriends and does her school work, and who are the first ones to be killed? The kids whose parents are away and they're making out in their parents' bed. All those kind of teen horror movies focus on moments of incipient sexuality and those are the moments where horror seems almost to burst forth, stuff sort of literally comes up, rises out of things, bodies, floorboards and so on. So I think horror films are speaking very closely to their audience and it's a very knowing audience.

Somebody writing about Body Horror used the word 'saturated', because it's a genre which has just become so full of its own imagery that we know the imagery already, we know things are going to pop up, we know what kinds of things are going to happen. So the compact which arises with any genre between the audience and the film is a very very close one, and therefore the means for creating horror or surprise or unwatchableness are quite finely tuned, precisely because so much is already known by the audience. The questions of what will be shown, what won't be shown, how long will it be shown for, how much more can be shown and so on, become quite sophisticated ones and the bond with a genre like that and its audience is very intimate. Yet people often just dismiss that audience as stupid.

Having said all that, I think the Body Horror films we've been discussing actually do reach a slightly larger audience, more diverse than the teenagers-in-peril horror films I just mentioned. Someone like Carpenter is a big cult director and has a particular following. And films like ALIEN obviously do speak to a wider audience. There are a variety of reasons for that, they're bigger budget films, they're often made by people who aren't specifically Horror directors, Ridley Scott and so on.

LH: How would you respond to those critics who would say a film like THE FLY is irresponsible in its portrayal of the person coping with a disease?

JW: Well I think THE FLY — that's the new one we're talking about — is more interesting than it's been seen as by people just focusing on the maybe exploitative nature of showing this kind of disease. I'm perfectly aware of how that touches on the context of Aids and what could be wrong with that, but I think there's something *more* happening in THE FLY. One important aspect of it for me is that it shows somebody who doesn't ultimately become passive in relation to a horrible thing happening to them. I think that is the one point where I would disagree with people who say it's all negative, it's all bad. There is a point where Brundle starts to get into what's happening to him. He actually accepts that it's happening and instead of acting totally passively, he tries to take an active relation to it and to get involved in it, to understand it. That's only a part of the film, I know it ends in a very gruesome way, but I think this point about activity is worth giving attention to because passivity and victim status are two of the things that have often made traditional horror films really repulsive in terms of sexual politics, not only to do with Aids but to do with, for example, women being passive victims. I like Jamie Lee Curtis in HALLOWEEN fighting back, I like it that she gets it together to find a coat hanger and attack her attacker, and I like it in THE FLY that Brundle doesn't just fall back and collapse under what's happening but finds some kind of energy in what's happening. Now that isn't to say I entirely endorse either of those as being progressive films, but I do think that given how creepy passivity is, how its portrayal can even make a film like a little piece of mini-fascism, in the sense of producing oppression without resistance — in that context I do think films that show a kind of resistance and a kind of energy in the face of things which are horrible and frightening are doing something else and I think possibly for their audiences they're doing something else as well. They certainly are for me.

Two Kinds of Otherness:
Black Film and the Avant-Garde

This was a talk given at the 'Black Film, British Cinema' conference organized by Kobena Mercer with Erica Carter at the ICA in February 1988. The conference drew a wide range of black and Asian film-makers and cultural critics, and those involved in oppositional film-making generally; it was an informal and productive event, mainly because the atmosphere was easy enough to allow the raising of questions which, if they had been asked before, had certainly not been asked very publicly or loudly within this milieu. In my recollection of the day, Stuart Hall was a key figure in moving the discussion towards these hitherto undebated areas, and my contribution to it started from the point at which he had suggested that 'films are not necessarily good because black people make them. They are not necessarily "right-on" by virtue of the fact that they deal with the black experience'.

I'm going to start from where Stuart Hall finished off. When he was talking about the possibility of a criticism that would neither hold up certain independent films quite uncritically as being 'right-on', nor criticize them from a mainstream position — that's really what I've been trying to do over the last few years on the *New Statesman*. And I want to talk, not only about criticism, but about the kinds of forms available for film-makers engaging in oppositional practice, and the way our notions of those forms cross with issues of race to produce a sort of doubly Other cinema. Finally, I want to try and resuscitate the question of class, which recently seems to have been dropping right out of the race-gender-class trilogy.

I'm also starting from my own position as a critic because part of what I try to do in my work is to engage with mainstream criticism. In practice that means, for example, that in doing a critique of SAMMY AND ROSIE GET LAID, a film I really didn't like, I had to spend about a third of my column engaging with Norman Stone's reactionary attack on it and carrying on that debate with other critics while trying to criticize the film as well. I think that's the kind of thing Stuart was talking about and it's quite a difficult thing to balance.

But I'd like to make a distinction between mainstream criticism and mainstream cinema. This is really quite important. While I would say

I'm totally hostile to mainstream critics and the kinds of assumptions underlying almost all the cinema criticism in the national press today, I don't feel the same extreme opposition to all forms of mainstream cinema. And I think it's important *not* to collapse together, as the oppositional movement often has done, a cinematic — i.e. film-making — practice and a critical practice. It's become a sort of tenet of the oppositional area of cultural politics we all move in (and not only in film) that practice and criticism go hand in hand, until they're almost seen as the same. This collapsing together — which is part of that whole seventies idea of theoretical-practice-as-part-of-practice — has, I think, to some extent gone past its useful point. Because, as I said, it's important to me to be able to attack mainstream critics but not always to sweep out everything within mainstream cinema at the same time — certainly not to sweep out the mainstream cinema *audience*, which is what I mean when I talk about class in this context.

I'll come back to that point, but for now I'm setting up this slightly unfashionable dichotomy between film-making practice and criticism or theory because I want to consider the effects of their elision on the kind of oppositional area that most of us work in. I was educated as a Marxist to understand the relation between theory and practice as a dialectical relationship, where theory isn't a blueprint for action but, almost the reverse, an attempt to find translatable patterns in what *has* happened, translatable in that they can be used to help understand other situations and prevent repeating mistakes. So, as I see it, theory isn't so much a set of guidelines for what to do, but a sort of stock-taking where you try to get to grips with a situation. I'm saying this because most of us feel the pinch of certain orthodoxies that have grown up around what you could very loosely call '*Screen* theory', and people are now working in an area where oppositional cultural theory sometimes feels every bit as rigid as the orthodoxies of the dominant cinematic practice we're meant to be against.

I'm not saying I disagree with oppositional theories, in fact, I'm one of the people who are always going around saying they should be *more* oppositional, but I'm trying to diagnose something about the atmosphere in the field of independent, oppositional film-making within which the new work from black film-makers here is broadly located. I do believe our fear of criticism from one another is sometimes stronger than our engagement with those people 'out there' who we don't actually know, but who are, in fact, the readers or viewers of our work. This fear and the anxiety that goes with it have crippling results for film-makers and critics alike. And what happens when people can't make or take criticism openly on a professional level is that it goes underground and becomes far more snide, which in turn fuels people's fear of being criticized, and so on and so on.

This is probably the moment for me to say something which I think has to be said which is that, while I don't feel uncomfortable about it, there are problems with being a white critic speaking at something like this and writing about black film practice. Without wanting to make too crude an analogy or simply superimpose race and gender, I know I have spent years personally complaining about male critics edging in and intervening within feminist debates about film and I am aware that I could be in a similar position here. I'm saying this not as an apology — since I was invited to speak at this event — but because it isn't often discussed and there seems to be enormous embarrassment around this area. I've found — at a pragmatic level of noticing what people say in private and comparing it with what they will say or write in public — that there is a reluctance by white critics to make criticisms of films by black film-makers because they feel (sometimes quite rightly) not qualified to do so, or, to put it more bluntly, they are afraid of appearing racist.

On the one hand, I think it's quite right that white critics should hesitate when they are confronted with films coming out of a different experience from their own. But on the other hand, there are, to continue being blunt, problems with being a white critic in a different way because it makes criticisms which may have some substance more easily dismissable. Kobena Mercer has written in a paper on the aesthetics of black independent film in Britain that white critics' and audience's perception of the 'influence of Euro-American avant-garde cinema and film theory' on works like PASSION OF REMEMBRANCE and HANDSWORTH SONGS 'suggests an underlying anxiety to pin down and categorize a practice that upsets and disrupts fixed expectations and normative assumptions about what "black" films should look like'.[1] Nevertheless, most of the film-makers at this conference whose work we're discussing learnt their craft — frequently at Art School — within the the Euro-American independent film tradition. I'm raising this particular piece of argument because it pre-empts my main point, which deals precisely with this issue, the place of avant-garde cinema, or rather, of these films within that place. The issue of theory I've already tried to deal with a bit. Anyway, whatever the status of my perceptions are as a white critic I just think the point had to be raised

---

1   'Diaspora Culture and the Dialogic Imagination: The Aesthetics of Black Independent Film in Britain'.

and it would be a strange day if nobody said it. So I'm saying it.

Coming back to what I would call oppositional criticism, the one loosely based around *Screen* or which operates in the area of developing criticial practice that Stuart Hall was outlining — within this sphere there is another kind of good/bad dichotomy alongside the one he described. And I'm glad he was the person that said it: a film made by a black film-maker is not 'good' automatically because the director is black any more than a film made by a woman is good because it's made by a woman. Basically he's saying goodbye to the simplistic black-film-good/white-film-bad dichotomy in favour of a more complex way of understanding the politics of ethnicity. Of course, just saying it doesn't change things overnight and I think it will be some time before those black films which are especially in the limelight at the moment lose their aura of untouchability. Apart from making the critic's job more difficult, that aura must in many ways be a burden to the film-makers, who have to be constantly producing show-pieces and be on show themselves — a position which in my experience never helped anyone to develop their work, and which reflects somewhat dubiously on the film culture that makes such demands. Those demands are, in a sense, a part of that polarity Stuart described, and in the long run I think it will be the highly pressurized, young black film-makers who benefit most from his attempt to dismantle this simple equation of black film-making with 'right-on' film-making, an equation which keeps it locked in a particular kind of Otherness.

For besides that good/bad orthodoxy centred on race which Stuart described, there is another kind of orthodoxy within this critical arena, another good/bad dichotomy which, to parody it rather crudely, says, realist, narrative, mainstream cinema: bad; non-narrative, difficult, even boring, oppositional cinema: good. We must all be familiar with this, and whether or not one agrees with that formulation it has had a great influence on the kinds of positions people can take up as film-makers or critics. Pursuing my analogy with Stuart's point: there's another Other that I want to tackle from my position as film critic, which is the avant-garde as the Other of Hollywood cinema.

We've all become adept at handling this term: as women and feminists we have become skilled at understanding our position as 'Other' to male culture, and the whole black political movement has for years put forward very highly developed theories and perceptions of how the black functions as 'Other' to white culture and so on. Within film criticism I'm constantly confronted with the avant-garde or the 'difficult' as the 'Other' of Hollywood or mainstream cinema and I think this otherness is just as problematic a relationship, just as much inscribed within what it's supposed to be different from.

I'm only going to invoke one theorist in this talk, but I think the work of the French writer Pierre Bourdieu is really useful in theorizing the way that the place of the avant-garde in art or film as the oppositional or the difficult is one that's actually written into and circumscribed by the culture to which it's meant to be opposed.[1] I'm not trying to be all gloomy and suggest that one can never do anything different or oppositional or make new forms that will push people's perceptions beyond the usual — far from it; I just think that to be productively oppositional, the place occupied by the avant-garde as the structured-in-opposite of the mainstream is something we have to be aware of.

Of course, the concept of Third Cinema was developed exactly in order to avoid that mainstream/avant-garde dichotomy, in recognition of the fact that neither side of it is inherently oppositional or politicized, or, to put it differently, that the whole polarity can still be completely contained within first-world and colonialist culture. The concept of Third Cinema also presupposes a different constituency, an audience which is neither necessarily the predominantly white, mainstream cinema audience nor the (also predominantly white) avant-garde, cinématèque audience. But I don't quite know where that gets us in this context, which is, frankly, closer to the avant-garde than anything else. Looking around the room I see lots of people who were at the Third Cinema conference in Edinburgh, where battles were raging about what black cinema was and whether a straightforward narrative film could be a truly oppositional form of film-making. I'm dragging that argument back into *this* conference because the film-makers that Kobena Mercer describes in his article as drawing on a strong third-world inheritance were actually, at that event, arguing *against* various African and also black US film-makers who advocated what I would call fairly un-avant-garde but politically strident work. The key debate about the possibility or the concept of a black aesthetic or a specifically black form of film-making is one that's central here; because if there *isn't* such an aesthetic, then black film-makers are faced with precisely the problem that confronts all film-makers, in that rather inhibiting context I set out to describe — which is how to pitch your work. And related to that, although it's not always within the film-makers' control, is dealing with how your work is taken up.

And that's where my point about the avant-garde comes in. It is

---

1   See *Distinction: a Social Critique of the Judgement of Taste.*

particularly striking that the black British work that's been taken up
most widely in the world of theory, been most written about and also
picked up at festivals, on tours, and so on, is the work that fits most
obviously into that category avant-garde. This isn't a criticism of the
work and it isn't necessarily the work's 'fault', so to speak. But, again
on a level entirely to do with personal observation, the reception in
somewhere like New York of Black Audio's and Sankofa's work has as
much to do with its being formally inventive and, for lack of a better
term, avant-garde, as to do with its being black, or rather, it's to do
with the combination of the two.

What I'm saying is not a criticism but an observation; I think it's
helpful to make it because the formal properties of those films have
somehow, in most of the critical discourse surrounding them, been
subsumed into their 'blackness'. Yet, say, a Ceddo production like
THE PEOPLE'S ACCOUNT is just as 'black'. Coco Fusco has said quite
rightly that it's easier to import one's Others than to confront them at
home. And I would add that it's sometimes easier to confront the
political Other — the Other of ethnicity and, in the case, say, of
PASSION, sexuality — when it occupies the space of Other in that
cinematic dichotomy I was trying to describe. Coco's monograph on
the work of Black Audio and Sankofa (for whom she's arranged a tour
in New York) is called *Young, British and Black*.[1] But, more accurately,
it should be called 'Young, British, Black and Avant-garde', for this is
what distinguishes the work she has chosen to tour from that of other
equally young, equally British, and equally black film-makers.

Now I too, like Coco, find the work of these particular groups
especially interesting, and that's precisely because I *am* interested in
finding new forms and experimenting: with documentary (HAND-
SWORTH SONGS) and with narrative (PASSION OF REMEMBRANCE). All
I'm saying is that we should be clear that black film-making and
experimental film-making are not automatically the same thing. I'm
hardly the best person to sound off at a black cinema conference on
whether or not there *is* the possibility of a black cinema (though I've
always understood that question, in other contexts, as one of audience
rather than aesthetics — I'll come back to this). But truly, I don't see
how there can be such a thing as a homogeneous black aesthetic, as
became clear in the disagreements at Edinburgh. Or again, using an
analogy with feminist debates, where I feel better qualified to make

---

1   This was also the title of the touring exhibition itself,
        curated by Coco Fusco, produced by Ada Griffin and
    presented by Third World Newsreel, New York, May 1988.

definite pronouncements: during the seventies those of us involved in feminist discussions about cinema were endlessly having these fights about 'is there a women's cinema' (my answer is 'yes, if it's one that women watch') and 'is there a feminist or female (which I know aren't the same thing) aesthetic' — to which I would be inclined to say 'no'.

I remember a particular debate that took place at the London Film-Makers' Co-op, about whether, if a woman was behind the camera, you would avoid having the voyeuristic gaze analyzed by Laura Mulvey as the male look at the female object.[1] There were actual rows about whether or not it was wrong to have a man behind the camera even if a woman was directing. Of course it may be a hassle for quite other reasons to have a man behind the camera, but I don't think there is anything essential to gender or race about either a gaze or an aesthetic.

There *is* a *cultural* dimension to it, but then that brings us exactly back to cultural forms and how to use them. I've made this detour into feminist territory because when someone asked in the last session 'can a white person make a Third Cinema film?' my instinct was to answer 'no'. It's like 'can a man make a feminist film?'; my answer to that would be 'why the hell would a man want to *think* he was making a feminist film?'. And frankly that response seems to be contradictory, having just said there is no inherent female (or black) aesthetic. But there *is* something in between essentialism and a complete denial of people's different positions and experiences, and I think that the more concrete one's analysis of film culture, the more possibilities for it there are.

Looking at the three films at the focus of today's debate (HANDSWORTH SONGS, PLAYING AWAY and PASSION OF REMEMBRANCE) you can see very clearly that there are common issues in black politics with which all three are engaging while aesthetically they're all very different. Just from seeing these three films it's obvious that there isn't one black aesthetic. In the light of all this I would say that any kind of oppositional or any questioning cinema is going to have to engage with both mainstream and avant-garde practices, and perhaps challenge that very dichotomy — which after all rests on all those high culture/low culture ideas. Colin MacCabe talked about the outmoded counterposition between realist and avant-garde aesthetics, but I'm going into it in more detail because I think you have to find ways to engage with *both* of them. The eliding of these two 'good/bad'

---

1   See 'Visual Pleasure and Narrative Cinema'.

polarities, with the white film-reactionary-bad/black film-progressive-good dichotomy and the mainstream film-realist-bad/avant-garde film-difficult-good dichotomy just marrying each other, lets you fill the avant-gardeness with, say, a black cinema, so you have a black, avant-garde cinema and it can function as the Other to white mainstream Hollywood stuff. I'm simply trying to draw attention to that other binary structure which I think has already begun to adhere to the first one, and to pull apart all those four corners, white, black, avant-garde, mainstream.

This is where I want to come back to audiences, because I think audiences do matter. I don't see how you can talk about oppositional or political film without talking about audiences. I really don't. I never have done. Audiences *do* matter. It's not enough to say, 'Oh well, everything's fractured, everything's just diverse' — that's not adequate if you are to be political. If you're political you do want to reach people beyond your buddies; I think lots of issues arise here which aren't specific to black cinema but which are important to it. There are lots of obstacles as well. There's the kind of right-on-ness of the workshop movement, into which the black groups have come fairly late, and it is a problem that the movement as a whole has never successfully grappled with, the question of audiences. Obviously it's a complicated issue and partly it's tied up with funding, money, dependency. The problem that I'm talking about though is that the struggle to set up the workshops, which I myself was involved in, was such a big one that once they were established and funded there was a huge sigh of relief and then people forgot to talk about the products, the actual films.

Thinking about actual films and how they work — I'm glad also that Stuart brought up MY BEAUTIFUL LAUNDRETTE because outside the *Screen* circles that I to some extent move in, a lot of people I know who are not at all theoretical just love MY BEAUTIFUL LAUNDRETTE. They love it! And many of them are *not*, for example, people who have thought at all about heterosexism. I'm thinking maybe of neighbours, old school friends, not people that I know professionally. It has in some way reached out to people. As Stuart said, it's been a highly *enjoyed* film. In some ways it's an absolutely classic romance. You're just dying for those people to kiss — and they're both men. And one is black and the other is white. And you're sitting there in the role of the classic Hollywood spectator thinking 'are they going to get off with each other? Is he going to say it? Will he be late?'. The cinematic structures that it employs are completely mainstream: it is not an avant-garde film in its form at all. There's nothing that interesting about it visually, I don't want to be rude to the makers but it is not a formally exciting work. And yet it had this enthusiastic reception just about everywhere except in what you might call the *Screen* world where it was, well, to put it bluntly, kind of sneered at by all those people who are anti-mainstream. I'm afraid I'm drawing on what I actually hear people say but they don't print, and I'm sorry to do that, but otherwise these things don't get properly aired. I think these issues are too important to let them slip by in odd remarks — because, as I keep saying, audiences really are important.

So my personal bench-mark of one aspect of political film-making would be, that you would want your film — I would want my film — to reach some people, maybe not the whole of the people, maybe not a mass audience, but to reach *some* people who aren't already engaged in the kinds of debates we've been talking through, certainly to reach people outside the sometimes esoteric or privileged arena of film theory. This is a very rough and ready definition, but it brings the issue of audiences back without saying either this must speak for the whole black community or this must speak for all women, or this must speak for everybody. You simply want your work to reach *somebody* outside your own circles, or at least that's what I want.

And in coming back to audiences I think we are coming back to the question of class. I know that what I'm saying might be challenged by the kind of postmodernist analysis that sees everything as already fragmented, but when we're talking about mainstream cinema and why people enjoy a film like LAUNDRETTE we are talking about class, if not in a completely rigid sense, at least in the sense that Bourdieu addresses when he talks about 'cultural capital' — some level of education into film language and forms.

For about the first five years that I ever watched avant-garde work, I found it really difficult; it was incredibly hard to learn to expect different things from films, not to expect resolution, not to expect closure, not to expect to care about the characters and so on. *Now*, I can truthfully say that some avant-garde movies are among my absolutely favourite films. But the point is you don't just sit down one day and find 'difficult' films really enjoyable. Without confronting that fact and its connection with class I think we're deceiving ourselves. The reason that I got to be able to like avant-garde films is because I had all that time in college and if you don't want to call it class, call it education or call it cultural capital, to take up Bourdieu's useful term.

We're talking a lot nowadays about race and gender, and their relation to representation is being very highly theorized at the moment. But it's interesting that we haven't talked so much about class and representation, because it does raise major formal issues and that is where you come back to notions of difficulty which aren't just to be put aside. I mean the difficulty which is something to do with having a class or educational position different to the one where you learn to sit through WAVELENGTH without getting fidgety. Now I can do it, but it took me a long time! And these are really things we have to think about.

Having started with my position as a critic I'll end by thinking from the viewpoint of a film-maker, because I think a key issue in all this is the problem of *learning*. It's very out of date at the moment to talk about learning the skills of your medium, but nevertheless that's something that film-makers have to do, just as learning to watch rather more difficult films than ususal is something that audiences have to do. The whole oppositional movement has a lot to learn about cinematic pleasure. That isn't to say, 'let's make films in a totally conventional way', but to say, 'let's reclaim certain kinds of pleasurable cinematic experience without throwing them out with the politically unacceptable bathwater'. Any kind of progressive new cinema involves learning how to make films that can engage and be appealing without necessarily running back to precisely the same old realist modes. And part of that learning is actually listening to what people say about the films they see.

I'm not holding that up as the only factor in making a film, but I'm emphasizing it and I'm finishing on it because I think it's a thing which has been missing in many of these debates. A cavalier attitude to audiences is the very opposite of a politics that's concerned with people changing their perceptions. This may seem to have moved off the subject of black cinema, but perhaps it is a sign of the strength of black film-making practice in Britain now that we can stop asking 'what *is* black cinema' and start addressing some of the more complex questions raised by actual films and their audiences, questions which all oppositional film-makers could learn from.

Index Section

This section is intended to provide as much information and cross-reference as possible and is therefore not entirely conventional in its organization. The filmography and bibliography, besides incorporating credits (films) and publication details (books), are also each an index, with page references for every film and book. They in turn are indexed, so that authors and directors listed in them, even if not mentioned in the main text, will be found under the appropriate categorized index headings.

Everything not falling under one of the categorized index headings will be found in the general index, which is intended primarily to function as an index of subjects and themes.

I hope this turns out to be useful and accessible.

Filmography

This filmography lists in alphabetical order every film and video mentioned in the book. In two cases, where a TV drama has been discussed at length (in the Epidemic Cinema section) I have included it in order to provide directorial credits, but otherwise TV programmes will be found in the general index. Unless otherwise stated (video, TV drama) the titles below are those of films.

The information provided in brackets after each title is the director, year and country of production. Dates for movies are often hard to ascertain because the year of completion, year of registration and year of public release may not always coincide. The information here has been culled from other dictionaries so I cannot claim to have produced any original research in this area but have taken the year most generally acknowledged as that of a film's completion. Where two films of the same name are included the earlier version has been put first. I have listed foreign films under their English titles where these are commonly used, cross-referring where necessary (e.g. where several titles are in use) and giving the original title in brackets. Where a foreign title is used in the main text of the book (e.g. LA RÈGLE DU JEU) I have given credits under this but cross-referenced the accepted English version (unless it is substantially the same). In the cases of TV movies or TV dramas I have included the network of the original braodcast, and with the TV dramas I have indicated the original transmission date (tx). For the country of production I have used common abbreviations: Belg (Belgium), Can (Canada), Fr (France), GB (Great Britain), GDR (German Democratic Republic), Ger (Germany), It (Italy), Jap (Japan), Mex (Mexico), Sp (Spain), Swe (Sweden), Switz (Switzerland), US and USSR.

This filmography is also an index. After each entry, the page numbers on which the film is discussed or referred to are listed. The filmography is also itself indexed: any director named in the credits below will be found under 'Directors' in the categorized index section.

324 Deadline at Dawn

Bibliography

Reference

This part of the bibliography lists non-fiction books and articles (including newspaper articles) either mentioned, quoted or drawn on in the main text. They have been alphabetized by author, and page numbers for each reference are given after the publication details. In a few cases, where a book or article is drawn on for some theoretical terms not in general use, or mentioned in passing, without the author's name being given in the text, the relevant page numbers have been put in brackets. The idea is that anyone wanting to pursue certain approaches or ideas which are not my own can follow up their sources. However, this is in no way a comprehensive reading list on the subjects covered in the book, and it cannot possibly represent the background reading which, in a looser sense, has informed my work here. What it does do is provide an index of specific references, with the information necessary for anyone to get hold of them.

N.B.: Unless otherwise stated all periodicals are British.

ANON, 'All That Heaven Allows' review (*Monthly Film Bulletin* Vol. 22 No. 261, October 1955) 256

BAUDRILLARD, Jean, *Selected Writings* (ed. Mark Poster; Cambridge GB: Polity Press in association with Basil Blackwell, 1988; US: Stanford University Press, 1988) (68), 170, (171, 172, 175)

'BIFF' (Chris Garratt and Mick Kidd), *The Essential Biff* (London: Pavement Press, 1982; reprinted in *Best of Biff*, London: Biff Products, 1992) 127, 171

BONE, Ian, SCARGILL, Tim and PULLEN, Alan, *Class War: A Decade of Disorder* (London/New York: Verso, 1991) (50)

BOURDIEU, Pierre, *Distinction: A Social Critique of the Judgement of Taste* (tr. Richard Nice; London: Routledge & Kegan Paul, 1984) 314, 318

BRECHT, Bertolt, *Brecht on Theatre* (tr. John Willett; London: Eyre Methuen, 1964; New York: Hill and Wang, 1964) 212, 213

BROPHY, Philip, 'Horrality' (*Screen* 'Body Horror' Issue, Vol. 27 No. 1, Jan/Feb 1986) (308)

BROWN, Helen Gurley, *Having It All* (New York: Simon & Schuster, 1982; London: Sidgwick & Jackson, 1983) 53, 145

CREED, Barbara, 'Horror and the Monstrous Feminine: an Imaginary Abjection' (*Screen* 'Body Horror' Issue, Vol. 27 No. 1, Jan/Feb 1986) (306)

DOUGLAS, Mary, *Purity and Danger* (London: Routledge & Kegan Paul, 1966; Binghamton, US: Vail-Ballou Press, 1980) 33

DURGNAT, Raymond, 'A Flame in My Heart' review (*Monthly Film Bulletin* Vol. 55 No. 650, March 1988) 167

DURKHEIM, Emile, *The Rules of Sociological Method* (tr. Stephen Lukes; London: Macmillan, 1982) 57

DYER, Richard, 'Entertainment and Utopia' (*Movie* No. 24, Spring 1977; reprinted in *Genre: The Musical* ed. Rick Altman; London: Routledge & Kegan Paul/British Film Institute, 1981; New York: Routledge & Kegan Paul/Methuen Inc., 1981) 150

DYER, Richard, *Stars* (London: British Film Institute, 1979) 136

DYER, Richard, *Heavenly Bodies: Film Stars and Society* (London: British Film Institute/Macmillan Education, 1987) 136

EISENSTEIN, Sergei, *Film Form* (tr. Jay Leyda; London: Dennis Dobson, 1951; New York: Meridian, 1957) 125

FOUCAULT, Michel, *Discipline and Punish: The Birth of the Prison* (tr. Alan Sheridan; London: Peregrine Books, 1979; New York: Viking Penguin, 1979) (247)

FREUD, Sigmund, *The Interpretation of Dreams* (tr. James Strachey; London: Pelican Books, 1976; New York: Avon Books, 1971) 28, 68, 103, 234

FREUD, Sigmund, *Introductory Lectures on Psychoanalysis* (tr. James Strachey; London/New York: Pelican Books, 1973) 30, 33

FRIEDAN, Betty, *The Feminine Mystique* (New York: W.W. Norton, 1963; London: Penguin Books, 1965) 55

FUSCO, Coco, *Young, British and Black* (New York: Third World Newsreel, 1988) 315

GABRIEL, Teshome, 'Third Cinema: Guardian of Popular Memory' (Third Cinema Festival Papers, Edinburgh, 1986) 113–14

GRIERSON, John, *Grierson on Documentary* (ed. Forsyth Hardy; London: Faber and Faber, 1966) 282

GUATTARI, Félix, 'Concrete Machines' in *Molecular Revolution: Psychiatry and Politics* (tr. Rosemary Sheed; London: Penguin Books, 1984) (157)

HALE, Chris, 'Punishment and the Visible' in *The Prison Film* (London: Radical Alternatives to Prison, 1982) (246–7)

JACQUES, Martin, 'A Ritual Locking of Labour Horns in Place of Constructive Thought for the Future' ('Commentary', *The Guardian*, 31 March 1988) 64

KAPLAN, E. Ann (ed), *Women in Film Noir* (London: British Film Institute, 1980; US: University of Illinois Press, 1980) (48)

KUREISHI, Hanif, *Sammy and Rosie Get Laid* (London/Boston: Faber and Faber, 1988) 129

KUREISHI, Hanif, 'England, Bloody England' (*The Guardian*, 15 Jan 1988) 129

LAHR, John, *Prick Up Your Ears* (London: Penguin Books, 1980; New York: Viking Penguin, 1980) 88–9

LENNON, Peter, 'Good As It Is' (*The Listener*, 28 January 1988) 239

LYOTARD, Jean-François, *The Postmodern Condition: A Report on Knowledge* (tr. Geoff Bennington and Brian Massumi; Minneapolis: University of Minnesota Press, 1984; Manchester, GB: Manchester University Press, 1985) (173)

MALCOLM, Derek, 'Round Midnight' review (*London Film Festival Catalogue*, 1986) 95, 96

MARX, Karl, *Capital* Vol. 1 (tr. Ben Fowkes; London: Pelican Books, 1976) (87)

MARX, Karl, and ENGELS, Frederick, *The German Ideology* (London: Lawrence & Wishart, 1970; New York: International Publications, 1970) 19

MERCER, Kobena, 'Diaspora Culture and the Dialogic Imagination: The Aesthetics of Black Independent Film in Britain' in *Black Frames: Critical Perspectives on Black Independent Cinema* (eds. Mbye Cham and Claire Andrade-Watkins; Cambridge, Mass: MIT Press, 1988) 312

MERCK, Mandy, 'Lianna and the Lesbians of Art Cinema' in *Films for Women* (ed. Charlotte Brunsdon; London: British Film Institute, 1986) 138

MILLS, Nancy, 'In Sickness and in Wealth' (*The Guardian*, 3 October 1985) 228

MULVEY, Laura, 'Visual Pleasure and Narrative Cinema' (*Screen* Vol. 16 No. 3, Autumn 1975) 316

PETLEY, Julian, 'Lifeforce' review (*Monthly Film Bulletin* Vol. 52 No. 621, October 1985) 228

PYM, John, 'Silly Girls' (*Sight and Sound* Vol. 56 No. 1, Winter 1986/7) 179

REICH, Wilhelm, *The Cancer Biopathy* (London: Vision Press, 1974) 135, 231

RIST, Darrel Yates, 'Fear and Loving and AIDS' (*Film Comment* (US) April 1986) 235

ROBINSON, David, 'Testament to a Powerful Will' (*The Times*, 9 January 1987) 79

ROOT, Jane, 'Parting Glances' review (*Monthly Film Bulletin* Vol. 53 No. 634, November 1986) 232–3

SCREEN, 'Body Horror' Issue (Vol. 27 No. 1, Jan/Feb 1986) 301

SHILTS, Randy, *And The Band Played On* (New York: St Martin's Press, 1987; London: Penguin Books, 1988) (222), 226

STONE, Norman, 'Through a Lens Darkly' (*Sunday Times*, 10 January 1988) 128–9, 310

TRUFFAUT, François, *Hitchcock* (with Helen G. Scott; London: Paladin, 1978/Grafton 1986) 170

WALKER, Alexander, 'A Fiendish Attack on the Family' (*Evening Standard*, 13 July 1987) 34

WALRAFF, Günter, *Lowest of the Low* (tr. Martin Chalmers; London: Methuen, 1988) 99

WARSHOW, Robert, 'The Gangster as Tragic Hero' in *The Immediate Experience* (US: Atheneum Books, 1970) 82

WATNEY, Simon, *Policing Desire: Pornography, AIDS and the Media* (London: Comedia/Methuen, 1987) 228–9, 235–6

WILLIAMSON, Judith, *Consuming Passions: The Dynamics of Popular Culture* (London/New York: Marion Boyars, 1986) 14, 29

WOLLEN, Peter, *Signs and Meaning in the Cinema* (London: Secker & Warburg, 1969; Bloomington: Indiana University Press, 1973) 122

WOLLEN, Peter, 'Two Weeks on Another Planet' (an interview with Simon Field, *Monthly Film Bulletin* Vol. 54 No. 646, November 1987) 123

WOOD, Robin, 'An Introduction to the American Horror Film' in *Movies and Methods Vol. 2: An Anthology* (ed. Bill Nichols; Berkeley:

University of California Press, 1985; first printed in *The American Nightmare*, eds. Robin Wood and Richard Lippe, Toronto Festival of Festivals, 1979) 33
WOODS, Donald, *Biko* (London: Penguin Books, 1979) 156

Fiction

This part of the bibliography has been alphabeticized by title, rather than author: every author will be found in the categorized index section, but titles are used here because for the most part they have been used in the book itself (which mentions, for example, *Middlemarch* but not George Eliot. Nevertheless, George Eliot will be found under 'Writers and Critics', below — etc.).

For the sake of providing general information I have given the author and year of original publication of each book in brackets after its title. (In a couple of cases where a work was published posthumously I have indicated the year of completion as well.) Many of them are out of copyright and so publication details are not necessary (there may be dozens of different editions) but with more recent works I have given the current British, and if possible American, publisher.

As with the non-fiction section, page numbers are given for every reference to the books listed below. Here, where the book's *title* is not directly mentioned in the text, these page numbers are in brackets.

THE ADVENTURES OF DON QUIXOTE OF LA MANCHA (Miguel de Cervantes, 1605) 119
THE ANDROMEDA STRAIN (Michael Crichton, 1969; London: Pan Books, 1988) 223
LA BÊTE HUMAINE (Emile Zola, 1890) 207, 208
BUILD MY GALLOWS HIGH (Daniel Mainwaring, 1942) 214
CASTAWAY (Lucy Irvine, 1984; London: Penguin Books, 1984) 76
THE COMPANY OF WOLVES (Angela Carter, 1979; in *The Bloody Chamber*, London: Penguin Books, 1981; New York: Harper & Row, 1981) 105
CRIME AND PUNISHMENT (Fyodor Dostoyevsky, 1866) (277)

Categorized Index

Studios

These are major studios and production companies. Individual producers, as well as film workshops and companies which claim 'directorial' credits, will be found under 'Directors and other Production Personnel'.

Directors and Other Production Personnel

Unless otherwise stated, the names below are those of directors mentioned in the text of the book and/or listed in the filmography. The indexing of the filmography is intended to make it possible, via *this* index, to look up any reference to the work of any director anywhere in the book.

The roles of other production personnel are identified in brackets after their names, e.g. (cinematographer) etc. Film workshops, where they assume 'directorial' status, are also included here.

Actors and Actresses

Journals

This category includes all periodicals, whether academic or popular, mentioned or quoted from in the book. It also covers references made in the bibliography, above.

References to *Time Out, City Limits, Not* and the *New Statesman* have been restricted to actual mentions of those magazines and does not include the initialled indications of sources at the end of reviews.

Writers and Critics

This category includes all authors mentioned in the book, and/or whose writings are listed in the bibliography. It does not include *screen*writers, who will be found under 'Directors and other Production Personnel', above.

Musicians and Composers

General Index

N.B. With specific film terms, theoretical terms, or events which might not be widely known (e.g. the ACTT Workshop Declaration) I have put a 'd' after the page numbers where the item is best defined or described. Where this involves a whole section or a run of pages, I have put 'd' after the first one, e.g. Body Horror, 300d–309. In a few cases where the most apt description of a phenomenon or concept does not include the *word* it is indexed by, I have put the reference in brackets, e.g. narrative (105d).

Other Books by Judith Williamson
published by Marion Boyars

DECODING ADVERTISEMENTS
Ideology and Meaning in Advertising

'*Advertisements are selling us something else besides consumer goods: in providing us with a structure in which we, and those goods, are interchangeable, they are selling us ourselves.*'

Advertisements constitute the most 'acceptable' face of the modern capitalist economy, one that is familiar to us all and even enjoyable. This book does not simply criticize their dishonesty and exploitation but examines in detail their undoubted attractiveness and appeal. The overt economic function of this appeal is to make us buy things. Its ideological function, however, is to involve us as 'individuals' in perpetuating the ideas which endorse the very economic basis of our society and make our economic conditions *seem* necessary.

If society is to be changed, this vicious circle of 'necessity' and ideas must be broken. *Decoding Advertisements* attempts to undo one link in the chain which we ourselves help to forge, in our acceptance not only of the images and values of advertising but of the 'transparent' forms and structures in which they are embodied. It provides not an 'answer' but a set of 'tools' which we can use to alter our own perceptions of one of society's subtlest and most complex forms of propaganda.

CONSUMING PASSIONS
The Dynamics of Popular Culture

'We are consuming passions all the time — at the shops, at the movies, in the streets, in the classroom: in the old familiar ways that no longer seem passionate because they are the shared paths of our social world, the known shapes of our waking dreams. "Consuming passions" can mean many things: an all-embracing passion, a passion for consumerism; what I am concerned with is the way passions are themselves consumed, contained and channelled into the very social structures they might otherwise threaten.'

Judith Williamson explores the forces that channel our taste and structure our lives: films, books, women's magazines, television, advertisements, photography, music, political movements and even the royal family.

'Judith Williamson is the best cultural critic we've got.'
New Statesman

'Her essays examine the ways in which popular culture recycles our passions and sells them back to us in familiar but sometimes deceptive forms . . . among the clearest and most even-handed cultural criticism. . .'
New York Times Book Review

'It's enormous fun, enlightening and provocative. . . Reading Williamson is a tonic for those who have been made to believe that political analysis is a dry, emotionally alienated business.'
Guardian (U.S.)

'Judith Williamson is articulate, humorous and deals in the currency of Continental semiotics without the smallest impulse towards mystification or obscurity . . . her essays are a delight to read.'   *The Listener*

'This collection will be indispensable to anyone interested in popular culture or in feminism.'
Women's Review

'These spunky essays about how films, books, TV and advertisements delineate the limits of acceptability in society criticize the way popular culture reinforces the status quo, but never resort to doctrinaire Marxism.'
Los Angeles Times

'. . . (an) entertaining pom-pom fire at the images of women put up by films and romance and the media.'
The Guardian